Exploring What is Lost in the Online Undergraduate Experience

This book examines the significance and meaning of undergraduate online learning using a hermeneutic phenomenological study, asking what is lost when there is no face-to-face contact and exploring the essence of technology itself.

Drawing on data from undergraduate students across various higher education institutions, including both interview recordings and written reports of their lived experiences, the author seeks to uncover the essence of the phenomenon by engaging with themes around the philosophy of technology and the purpose of post-secondary education, using Heidegger's essay *The Question Concerning Technology* as a crucial interpretive lens. Rather than offering generalized conclusions, it presents a basis for further understanding of the experience of online learning and ultimately asks whether the efficiency afforded to undergraduates by online classes or degrees can ever replace what is learned in a classroom with other people.

Providing a novel approach to the topic of online learning, which centers the concept of experience, and drawing links to current conditions and pedagogy in online higher education, it will appeal to scholars working across education and philosophy with interests in higher education, technology and education, phenomenology of education and philosophy of education.

Steve Stakland is Associate Professor and Philosophy Department Chair at Northern Virginia Community College, USA.

Routledge Research in Digital Education and Educational Technology

This series provides a forum for established and emerging scholars to discuss the latest debates, research and practice in the field of digital education and educational technology globally, including distance and open learning.

Theoretical Issues of Using Simulations and Games in Educational Assessment
Applications in School and Workplace Contexts
Edited by Harold F. O'Neil, Eva L. Baker, Ray S. Perez and Stephen E. Watson

Remote Learning in Times of Pandemic
Issues, Implications and Best Practice
Edited by Linda Daniela and Anna Visvizi

Open World Learning
Research, Innovation and the Challenges of High-Quality Education
Edited by Bart Rienties, Regine Hampel, Eileen Scanlon and Denise Whitelock

Pedagogy of Tele-Proximity for eLearning
Bridging the Distance with Social Physics
Chryssa Themelis

Exploring What is Lost in the Online Undergraduate Experience
A Philosophical Inquiry into the Meaning of Remote Learning
Steve Stakland

For more information about this series please visit: https://www.routledge.com/Routledge-Research-in-Education/book-series/RRDEET

Exploring What is Lost in the Online Undergraduate Experience

A Philosophical Inquiry into the Meaning of Remote Learning

Steve Stakland

First published 2023
by Routledge
605 Third Avenue, New York, NY 10158

and by Routledge
4 Park Square, Milton Park, Abingdon, Oxon, OX14 4RN

Routledge is an imprint of the Taylor & Francis Group, an informa business

© 2023 Steve Stakland

The right of Steve Stakland to be identified as author of this work has been asserted in accordance with sections 77 and 78 of the Copyright, Designs and Patents Act 1988.

All rights reserved. No part of this book may be reprinted or reproduced or utilised in any form or by any electronic, mechanical, or other means, now known or hereafter invented, including photocopying and recording, or in any information storage or retrieval system, without permission in writing from the publishers.

Trademark notice: Product or corporate names may be trademarks or registered trademarks, and are used only for identification and explanation without intent to infringe.

Library of Congress Cataloging-in-Publication Data
Names: Stakland, Steve, author.
Title: Exploring what is lost in the online undergraduate experience: a philosophical inquiry into the meaning of remote learning / Steve Stakland.
Description: New York, NY: Routledge, 2023. | Series: Routledge research in digital education and educational technology | Includes bibliographical references and index.
Identifiers: LCCN 2022039427 (print) | LCCN 2022039428 (ebook) | ISBN 9781032391618 (hardback) | ISBN 9781032392561 (paperback) | ISBN 9781003349051 (ebook)
Subjects: LCSH: Education, Higher--Effect of technological innovations on. | Web-based instruction. | Internet in higher education. | Social distancing (Public health) and education.
Classification: LCC LB2395.7 .S7635 2023 (print) | LCC LB2395.7 (ebook) | DDC 378.1/7344678--dc23/eng/20221011
LC record available at https://lccn.loc.gov/2022039427
LC ebook record available at https://lccn.loc.gov/2022039428

ISBN: 978-1-032-39161-8 (hbk)
ISBN: 978-1-032-39256-1 (pbk)
ISBN: 978-1-003-34905-1 (ebk)

DOI: 10.4324/9781003349051

Typeset in Sabon
by SPi Technologies India Pvt Ltd (Straive)

To the teachers who face-to-face *first* set my life on a trajectory that was greater than I had imagined: Jeffrey S. Nielsen, James L. Siebach, K. Codell Carter, Daniel W. Graham and Mark A. Wrathall.

Contents

Foreword   ix
Acknowledgments   xii

1. Introduction: The Phenomenon, Methodology and Background to Participants   1
2. The Withdrawn or Lost Face of Online Undergraduate Learning   39
3. The Irksome Face of Online Undergraduate Learning   46
4. Experiencing the Synchronous but Absent Face   53
5. Writing to No Face and Everyone: The Present Absence   60
6. Solitude and Inauthenticity   67
7. Vulnerability and Community: Body and Conversation   73
8. Reciprocal Voyeurism: Hiding from Others Together   80
9. Narrowed Purpose: Text, Money and Efficiency   88
10. The Game of Facelessness   95
11. Response-Ability   102
12. Facing the Void: Body and Soul   108
13. Facing Some Parts of Learning Online Post-COVID-19   117

viii *Contents*

14	The Post-COVID-19 Lacuna in Higher Education	124
15	Interlude: Engaging Poetically with Insights and Implications	132
16	Works and Days: A Response to the Void in Higher Education after COVID-19	138
17	Face-to-Face Learning Is a Focal Practice	146
18	Death in the Desert: Finding the Soul of Undergraduate Learning	155
19	Teaching Undergraduates after COVID-19: Harder to Learn to Let Learn than to Learn	164
20	What Is the Meaning of What Is Lost in Non-Face-to-Face Teaching?	170
21	Questioning Is the Piety of Thought: The Wonder of Education	176
	Index	183

Foreword

Living (and Learning) Humanly in the Digital Age

By Holger Zaborowski, *University of Erfurt*

For quite some time now, we have been living in the digital age. Some of us are "digital natives" who do not know a non- or pre-digital world from their own experience. Their world has always been *both* the real *and* the digital world (but is this world less real?). Others were born too early and have moved or immigrated into the digital sphere where they feel more or, indeed, less at home. It is not possible to evade digitalization. It concerns almost all areas of human life. It has a deep impact on how we live. It touches, however virtually, on how we act, how we relate to others or, in more concrete terms, how we learn, how we study, how we work and how we love.

But this is not all that can be said about digitalization. When we speak of the "digital age," we refer to a phenomenon that cannot be reduced to the mere introduction of new technical gadgets. There are, to be sure, digital instruments. They are all around us. They often make our lives easier and frequently bring with them yet-unheard-of new challenges. But there is something different going on, too. What it is, is more difficult to capture, but it is truly a revolution of how we understand ourselves and reality altogether.

Digitalization is no longer a new phenomenon, but we still need time to understand the real nature of this revolution, its implications and its wider dimensions. It is a media revolution. But this does not, as has already been mentioned, limit this revolution to merely one area or aspect of human life. Media revolutions can hardly be overestimated. They start in a little corner of the world and quickly and radically transform human life on the globe. The invention of script was such a world-changing media revolution as was the invention of the printing press. The rise of modernity – in all its complexities – is intrinsically tied to the possibility of printing books, pamphlets and newspapers. Our modern or post-modern world still stands in the light of the printing press. In recent decades, another source of light has developed with the rise of digital technologies. What does it all mean? Many scholars and scientists currently deal with this simple yet utmost difficult question: in philosophy and theology, in history, political, media and cultural studies, in the social and natural sciences.

The question "What does it all mean" has in recent years become much more urgent. This is because the COVID-19 pandemic has accelerated the digitalization process in many areas, not only in administrative contexts, in the health sector and in the work world but also in the realm of higher learning. There are many students in the whole world who for two, three or even four semesters did not experience any other kind of learning than remote learning. Remote learning has become very common – and will remain common. There is no doubt that after the pandemic the educational system will have significantly changed.

Education is a deeply human act. It is not merely the transmission of information or of technological skills, but a relation between human beings that is often life changing. It is a personal encounter, something that happens from face-to-face. What happens if the face of the other person, as it is now possible, is absent or missing? What exactly is remote learning? How does it affect our souls and bodies? What is its inner sense, its meaning? How can it be understood – not just technologically or economically, but in its deeply human dimensions?

Steve Stakland deals with these and many other important questions in this beautifully written and convincingly argued book. His phenomenological approach provides him with a sound basis for his educational interests. For him, Martin Heidegger and the phenomenological tradition develop helpful interpretations of the human being and of the "essence," of the happening, of modern technology. Modern technology for Heidegger is not merely a means nor an instrument that humans have invented and can utilize. It discloses or reveals truth and thus makes beings, the world around us including ourselves, to be seen or understood in a specific way – as "standing-reserve," as things at one's disposal, i.e., resources to be optimized. For human beings this is a challenge – and, indeed, a danger as it threatens a common human way of life. We cannot, however, avoid or undo modern technology. We have to find a way of living humanly in the technological age.

Making best use of his excellent knowledge of Heidegger's thought, Stakland develops his own phenomenology of the meaning of learning in the digital age. In doing so, he provides an in-depth critique of non-face-to-face learning, that is to say, he helps his readers to understand the phenomenon itself, he shows its benefits, but he also does not overlook its problematic features and dangers. In online learning, as Stakland argues, important aspects of face-to-face learning get lost. It is, as he concludes, not a mere copy of face-to-face learning, but something different that is in need of further analysis.

Stakland's book is a timely, powerful and highly persuasive study that will prove important in our contemporary context. It shows the value of truly inter-disciplinary work and is of interest to everyone concerned with higher education, but also to everyone who wants to understand digitalization and its consequences in other areas such as medicine, religion and public administration. Who has ever been touched by the wonder of education, be it online or offline, will be touched by this educative book.

Erfurt, July 20, 2022

Acknowledgments

Gratitude is the meaning of life. There are many who have helped me to complete this work. I name only a few here. Francine Hultgren and Holger Zaborowski were the ones who encouraged me to publish this book. I am thankful for Holger's generosity toward me. Always joyful, positive and honest, he has inspired my commitment to philosophy and teaching. Francine gave me the wonderful gift of teaching me how to do phenomenology. I am immensely grateful for her patience with me and her support of my learning and goals. This book would not have been possible without Francine. I owe her an immense debt. I am extremely grateful to the three preliminary students and nine official research participants who sacrificed their time to create the phenomenological text on which this book is based. Without their willingness to share their lived experience, this book would not have been possible. I am grateful for my children, Calvin, Eve, Wesley and Zara, who may not have fully realized the sacrifice that they were making to help me finish this work. They all played a part, and their influence winks throughout. I am thankful for my wife Jesse. Besides helping me to become a better writer, reader and teacher, she has also helped with editing and formatting. Being married means that Jesse and I are one. What we do together has deep symbolic meaning. The completion of this work is as much my success and joy as it is hers. I could not have done it without her. This book is a goal that we had together. It was something we were committed to doing jointly because of its inherent worth and intrinsic value.

1 Introduction

The Phenomenon, Methodology and Background to Participants

The Phenomenon of Non-Face-to-Face Learning

The year my wife was pregnant with our second child and was a full-time graduate student while also working all day at the Pentagon, I was an adjunct at three universities teaching eight classes per semester. It was a crucible. Passion, that simultaneity of joy and pain this confluence of demands created, changed me. I taught two consecutive philosophy classes at Howard University late afternoon three days a week. At the end of one day, a student named Melchizedek gave me a warm embrace. I didn't know how obvious my need appeared.

When I am teaching, I am putting on an act. I ham it up. I gesticulate dramatically and move around. My behavior is more enlivened and exaggerated. I run my hands through my hair and stretch my arms out wide. I pace around the room, sit down next to my students and gaze intently at the board with them. We talk together, and I let them debate with each other. I tend to create a slight spectacle, a tiny tempest in a teapot that is our brief time and space together. I can smell my students. I know what they are looking at and hearing. I can see what they are eating. I can feel the temperature of the room with them. I experience the same distractions with them as they happen: spilled coffee, the weather outside the windows, hallway commotion. When I teach, I know I am not being what most people who know me would call my "normal self." It is a sort of highlighted or intense expression of myself. I understand my teaching is not what many of my students are used to, and I can see that it is not to everyone's taste, but it is just how it always happens.

When I teach, I feel like I am being my truest self, my most real self. I fall into the experience of teaching and experience the timelessness of flow. It is an eternal life. If I'm sick, my symptoms fade. A pounding headache recedes as I try to open up my joy to my students. At the end, I feel energized and completely exhausted. I don't want it to end but could never go on like that. How can I be fake and real, i.e., how can I exist in a paradox but also experience continuity? Where is the way to knowing

DOI: 10.4324/9781003349051-1

what it is that I am as a self-reflective being? The way to knowing seems to have something to do with how I am self-constituted by others.

The way begins where we dwell. The way is found because we seek it. We seek when there is no way. The ancient Greek word *aporia* transliterates, with its alpha privative, as "without a way" or "no path" and is translated as "confusion" or "wonder." The experience of wonder can be like having something taken away, but we can't say what. It might also be like finding oneself in a place with either no way out or many possible paths. Sometimes this is how all the technological advances of our current world make us feel. We might start to feel that despite how efficient technology makes certain activities, it also removes the need to develop skills or meaningful relationships. Without certain skills, we can feel hemmed in and unable to fully engage with the world and become fully who we are. Without meaningful relationships, the kind born from vulnerability, we cannot know ourselves.

Science is stimulated by *aporia*, but in that way it is also an antidote to it. Einstein is quoted as saying, "The process of scientific discovery is, in effect, a continual flight from wonder" (Rothenberg, 2014, p. 12). When we feel like we know what something is but can't articulate that knowledge, we are in the state of *aporia*. The experience can befuddle, as the "confusion" translation suggests. There could also be a bit of frustration as we sense our inadequacy to convey what we feel we should be able to show others. However, the potentially negative side of *aporia* can also be, or become, wonder. It is for this reason that Plato and Aristotle say that philosophy begins in *aporia*. The experience of wonder, as disorienting as it may be, can also lead to the creation of our own direction as we find our way along. But fundamentally, the experience of *aporia* humbles and thus allows the questions to flow. Once we have started to find our way, by questioning, it might be possible for others to follow.

The interaction with *my* students and my efforts to remain humble and teachable myself drew me further into the teacherly way of being. A vocation is not something that can be explicitly chosen. It is, rather, a calling. And by being called to teach the wonder of learning began to be disclosed to me. That is, the truth, *Aletheia*, of what learning is began to be revealed to me and for me. Heidegger (1971) explains in his essay, "The Origin of the Work of Art," that truth for the Ancient Greeks meant to uncover. Since then, it has come to mean something more like certainty from the Latin *veritas*. But the truth of learning does not seem to be completely, or maybe even partially, graspable in the sense of certainty. Rather, learning seems to show itself, in the same way anything is revealed, sometimes in all its dazzling brilliance and at other times only partially in subtle and beautiful glimmers or in flashing moments like when light strikes a multifaceted gem.

The focus of this book is the experience of the kind of learning that takes place in institutions of higher education, colleges, universities, etc., where the face is removed completely or to some degree. The phenomenon includes aspects of various forms of technologically mitigated pedagogy, but is not concerned with *all* technology. Rather, the technology that is used for non-face-to-face learning in higher education is what I am focused on, i.e., many aspects of the Internet that facilitate interaction over space. For example, a student watching a recorded video of a professor teaching, asynchronously, is non-face-to-face learning, though it still maintains many aspects of traditional in-person learning.

In this book, I am also seeking to understand the meaning of a phenomenon that includes real-time, synchronous video interactions between professors and students, the kind of remote learning which became ubiquitous due to COVID-19. These classes allow participants to see each other in real time and are made possible through certain technologies such as Skype, Zoom, WebEx and closed-circuit cameras. However, even these classes are examples of non-face-to-face learning because the students and teachers are not fully present to each other. Some sort of screen, television, projector or computer mitigates their interaction, i.e., it is constrained to a two-dimensional plan and takes place within a usually rectangular frame. Because the experience is different, its meaning is altered. The simplest way to grasp the phenomenon I am concerned with, and the purest example of it, is to consider the learning conditions most typically provided by "online classes." However, as researchers into the topic explain,

> Online learning is hardly one thing. It comes in a dizzying variety of flavors, ranging from simply videotaping lectures and posting them for any-time access, to uploading materials ... to the Internet, all the way to highly sophisticated interactive learning systems that use cognitive tutors and take advantage of multiple feedback loops.
> (Bowen et al., 2014, p. 7)

In these classes, there is typically no synchronous face-to-face contact of any kind, either between students or with teachers. Contact is usually just between teachers and students via text and, if the class requires it, similar contact between students (e.g., message boards). In an early phenomenological account of one of the first online classes, Norm Friesen characterizes the experience in the following way, "Is there a Body in this Class?"

> In a [face-to-face] class, I can be addressed and asked a question, if not by the instructor then at least by my neighbor. This address or question, moreover, can be directed with kindness, indifference, or even hostility. All people bodily present in the classroom share this potential vulnerability, and have to be willing to trust one another to not take advantage of it. Online forums, however, present a different situation. The body is not present to indicate one's implicit willingness to participate, be open, trusting and vulnerable.
> (2016, p. 225)

"The body is not present" is a fact so obvious in an online class that the significance of embodied human presence can be overlooked. The goal of this book is to make that loss apparent so that its importance can be understood.

Education is primarily defined in the technological age (more on this below) as the ability to either retain information, find information or create information. Defining education in this way makes it measurable. By making it more measurable, education invites standardization, particularly in evaluation. How, then, does technology shape and change student learning in higher education? Primarily it sets out to solve a problem. The problem is the need to educate more people, faster, which means making more information easily available. However, "Higher education, especially in the public sector, is increasingly short of resources" (Bowen et al., 2014, p. 5). Higher education is being squeezed by demand, and online education offers a way to increase supply with finite resources.

Solutions designed, because of the exigencies of technology, to create greater efficiency in education might remove a problem by creating a worse problem or an intractable one. With every technology there are trade-offs, and it is almost always impossible to know beforehand what will be given up to receive the gifts offered by Internet innovations. As we step toward the outstretched efficiencies of online learning, massive open online courses (MOOCs) and other non-traditional, non-face-to-face learning platforms, the enormity of such changes invites us to pause and consider the unknowns of what we have already stepped into. What is known is that however inefficient and ambiguous the process of face-to-face learning may be, it has harbored and cultivated the delicate precious possibility of individualization for thousands of years. How does what is lost in order to achieve greater efficiency alter undergraduate learning? The conditions that are possible in a face-to-face class, educational phenomenologist Max van Manen says, allow us "to transform or remake ourselves in the true sense of *Bildung* (education)" (1990, p. 7).

The philosopher Richard Rorty explains our relation to solving problems involving large groups of people well when he states, "Each generation will solve old problems only by creating new ones" (2007, p. 88). Rorty is stating the insight found in the Law of Unintended Consequences, i.e., prudence dictates that we weigh the trade-offs of everything we do. This law encapsulates the greatest of all human fears. It is impossible to know the future for certain. Therefore, we don't know how our innovations will interact with other factors. Thus, merely making educational degree attainment faster, less expensive and more transportationally convenient, by moving it online, might not guarantee that it will be better. No matter how efficient the delivery of education, such standards as speed and convenience might distort learning beyond recognition, unless we alter the purpose of education.

In Heidegger's work (1977), *The Question Concerning Technology*, he explains that the purpose of his essay is to show a way, open up a path of thinking, which can lead to an appropriate relationship toward technology. The relationship is one that not only acknowledges the role of technology in our experience but also preserves what is most important about being human. Following Heidegger's thinking on technology is to strive for what he calls a "free relationship with technology." A free relationship not only acknowledges the necessity of interaction but also affirms the need for wise limitations. Ultimately, to be with technology freely requires that we understand that not everything ought to be technologized because not everything can be technologized. Not everything should be made more efficient. It is to understand that some entities are not mere resources to be maximized. To have a free relationship with technology means that certain aspects of human existence should be in-efficient by the standards of technology.

For Heidegger (1977), technology is not gadgets or devices. What it really is, its essence, is a kind of *aletheia*, a way of revealing or disclosing, which is to say, it is a way of thinking done by human beings. Since all human thinking is mitigated by language, and language is historical, all of our thinking in the present is related to the past. Our being is historical. Thus, the truth, how technology reveals the world now, is a *destiny*, though it is not a fate. The essence of technology is to set up every kind of being in the same way. Technological innovations, the Internet in particular, do of course depend on a great deal of devices, networks and gadgetry; however, none of these would have come into being without the attitude that is the essence of technology. In the experience of non-face-to-face learning, its meaning, therefore, is related not just to the computers and screens etc. Its significance, indeed its existence, following Heidegger, has to do with our way of thinking, the technological attitude.

The essence of technology is our way of thinking; it is an attitude that levels everything down to being merely resources. To level down means to constrain everything in a certain way. To circumscribe everything as a resource, standing by to be optimized, is to bind entities to one way of being and maintain that they can't be anything else. Instead of the horse being a beautiful running creature, it is instead a complex organization of protein. Protein is a resource. Thus, the horse is stripped of its possible essence and becomes dog food, or whatever other profit maximizing scheme can be imposed on wild mustang protein (this example is horrifically and beautifully portrayed in the 1961 movie *The Misfits*, written by Arthur Miller). It is the leveling of all entities to one way of being revealed that sets up the conditions of non-face-to-face learning.

To encounter a free relationship with technology, we have to have a different disposition, a different posture toward being. For Heidegger, art indicates a possible alternative to technological thinking. He takes art, understood in a non-aesthetic way, to be a key example of something that should not be understood in a technological way. Art also provides access to an alternative view of entities and experience not provided by the technological attitude. Wondering about the different kinds of thinking found in *some* art (because art can of course also be technologized as it is when it is turned into a *resource* for aesthetic enjoyment or profit) and the kind of thinking that has created our device saturated technological world opens up a way of thinking about the artistry of education, teaching and, particularly for my phenomenon, learning. Poetry, as the quintessential or highest art form, is also a way of providing glimmers of a free relationship with technology. Poems can engage with things in a way that reveals their potential to be something other than just resources. Poems can put us on a path that continues our destiny and shows a way out of the spiraling ontological cul-de-sac of technological revealing where everything is perpetually just a resource to be made more efficient.

As we currently grapple with the profound influence of Internet technology, we can learn much from how a previous age responded to the introduction of writing. Much of Plato's thought can be interpreted as a response to the conditions created by the new technology of writing. In his dialogues, Plato demonstrated a free relationship with the technology of writing. He showed that some things cannot and should not be technologized, while at the same time masterfully showing how and what should be technologized. As Plato (1997) explains in his "Seventh Letter," there is a sense in which truth cannot be written down; therefore, it cannot be technologized. Because certain aspects of art (e.g., dialogue) can be written down, certain aspects of spoken exchanges can be technologized.

Plato's work can be seen as the first sustained engagement with what it means to reduce, interrupt and diminish face-to-face contact, not just in learning, but in all human activities. In his *writings*, Plato often expresses reservations about writing because of the changes it makes to epistemology and the ability of humans to experience the truth. In his "Seventh Letter," he says, "Anyone who is seriously studying high matters will be the last to write about them" (1997, p. 1661). There is irony in that through some of the most beautiful *writing* Plato gives us questions about writing and lingering doubts about what it will do. Even though Plato chose to write, he maintained that truth could not be fully expressed in writing. Rather, arriving at the truth required dialectic, real-time face-to-face dialogue. Thus, the genius of Plato's writings is the way in which they induce conversation and are composed in such a way as to require people to come together. Plato's dialogues necessitate dialogue about them. In this way, he demonstrates a free relationship with, what was at the time, the fairly recent technology of writing.

To want to read Plato is also to want to talk about the ideas found in his writings. That was part of Plato's purpose, keep people talking and not just reading. He wanted to give people a reason to continue to work together to find truth, even if it could never be written down. He wanted to create such beautifully crafted written works that people would be knit together as they sought to interpret and create meaning from his texts.

Plato sought to keep people together, as friends really, face-to-face, even when there was a technology that could separate and atomize. He knew that reading is primarily a private endeavor and could have the power to wall people off from each other, especially if what was being read was assumed to contain *the* truth. Plato built a corpus of writing that could serve as a bulwark against the tendency to withdraw into the book and give up face-to-face oral exchanges. Plato used the danger of writing against itself to preserve something essential to being human, the non-calculative, meditative dialogue that sets out from the start not knowing how it will get to where it is going. Do our current forms of non-face-to-face learning also, like Plato's writings, consistently create opportunities for continued face-to-face engagement, unity and forms of community? Or do they become incentives for isolation and atomization, and if so, why?

Another perspective on our technological age that articulated what was fast becoming invisible is Neil Postman's 1992 book, *Technopoly: The Surrender of Culture to Technology*. Postman argues that we are often cheated by the seductive nature of technology. It is a Faustian bargain. For Postman, we are being robbed by the transformation that Heidegger elucidates:

> Because of its lengthy, intimate, and inevitable relationship with culture, technology does not invite a close examination of its own consequences. It asks for trust and obedience, which most people are inclined to give because its gifts are truly bountiful. But there is a dark side. Its gifts are not without a heavy cost. Stated in the most dramatic terms, the accusation can be made that the uncontrolled growth of technology destroys the vital sources of our humanity. It creates a culture without moral foundations. It undermines certain mental processes and social relations that make human life worth living.
>
> (Postman, p. xii)

Postman explains that the intensity of his critique is in proportion to the mostly unthinking rush to adopt any technological efficiency.

These accounts of our technological milieu, along with others, e.g. Albert Borgmann, Nicholas Carr and Sherry Turkle, frame and inform the interpretation of this book. Burdened a bit by the if not apocalyptic tone, then at least nihilistic apprehensions of these and other thinkers, I come back again to the meaning of what is lost in remote learning.

The threat to face-to-face engagement is far more prevalent than ever before. The potential for distraction and separation from others is of greater magnitude than what Plato faced with handwritten texts. It is now more difficult than ever to have a free relationship with technology. Indeed today, it is technology that distracts us away from reading a book. We hardly consider books or writing to be technology at all. Just as those who critiqued the technology of writing as containing the potential to make human beings more stupid by not requiring them to memorize as much, current critics of technology, like Nicholas Carr (2011), point to how innovations like the Internet make our minds "shallower." We can understand what critics of the technology of writing, like Plato, meant when they lamented the loss of certain mental powers such as memory and the ability to find truth in real-time face-to-face dialogues. It is harder for us to understand what can be lost today because of the Internet and powerful computer technology. According to Carr, our very ability to think at all is at risk.

Sherry Turkle (2015, 2017) has researched technology and its influence on our way of being human for decades at the MIT robotics lab. Her personal contact with the innovation and implementation of technology, as well as her close conversational interviews with those who use technology, imbue her work with a profound connection to the phenomena she explores, e.g. the introduction of robot seals into nursing homes to comfort the elderly, the response of children and adults to various robotic toys, smartphone use and social media. Turkle's diligent work has made her adept at pointing to the meaning of technology in our lives. In her book, *Reclaiming Conversation: The Power of Talk in a Digital Age*, Turkle is clear, "This new [technologically] mediated life has gotten us into trouble" (2015, p. 3). Turkle states outright:

> Face-to-face conversation is the most human – and humanizing – thing we do. Fully present to one another, we learn to listen. It's where we develop the capacity for empathy… But these days we find ways around conversation. We hide from each other even as we're constantly connected to each other … It all adds up to a flight from conversation –at least from conversation that is open-ended and spontaneous, conversation in which we play with ideas, in which we allow ourselves to be fully present and vulnerable … the conversations in which the creative collaborations of education and business thrive.
>
> (Ibid., pp. 3–4)

Turkle *shows* in her book how the seduction of technology is largely due to its promise of making most aspects of life, e.g. education, social interactions, commerce, more efficient and friction free. However, being seduced by technological efficiencies diminishes our lives, e.g. we miss out on the playful exchanges around important ideas. As human beings, we are enticed by the possibilities that technology provides. For example, it can relieve us of being bored during the random moments of the day (by turning to our smartphones for distraction), or it can reduce the friction of our interactions with other people by providing ways of not having to deal directly with their idiosyncrasies and uncomfortable differences. But Turkle's point is that avoiding boredom and the friction of reality is to opt out of life. As Nietzsche (1980) would say, such a tendency is "deadly." We live less because we become conditioned to an inadequate account of reality, as the insight from Max Frisch shows: "Technology is the knack of so arranging the world that we do not experience it" (Max Frisch, cited in Postman, 1992, p. 10). Turkle argues that just because such atomization is possible, that such a shift in perspective is allowed by technology, this provides a strong case for not giving in. Instead, we should seek, in the language of Nietzsche, what is life affirming, by holding on to what is precious in the moment of face-to-face contact. We should not reduce friction and boredom to something else, however efficient and safe it might seem to be.

If Something Is Lost from Learning, Is It Still Learning?

I have started to become preoccupied with whether I am a good teacher and what I can do to be like the teachers who helped me to learn. These preoccupations led me to begin to think about learning more and to wonder about what is happening to learning in our contemporary technological world. A 2015 study found that "relative enrollment in online classes has tripled over the last ten years… In 2002 a total of 1,602,970 students in higher education took at least one course online. By 2011 6,714,792 students took one or more online classes" (Stack, 2015, pp. 2–3). What does this trend signify? If learning happens in an online class, can it be something beyond just the acquisition of information, and if so, how does the experience differ from what can happen in a classroom? I seek, then, the lived experience of those students engaged in non-face-to-face learning for their undergraduate degrees. Within my experience as a teacher, my phenomenological question has emerged: What is the meaning of what is lost in non-face-to-face undergraduate learning?[1]

I am concerned about what is lost in online learning because of the importance of learning for my students. Typically, this loss is addressed primarily in terms of what is quantifiable about the learning experience of undergraduates. Such quantification depends on an explicit definition of learning inherently narrows and confines learning to only that which is measurable. The urge to quantify comes from a scientific attitude that strives to be as objective as possible. When this attitude becomes dominant, it is the core of *scientism*, i.e., the belief that only what can be measured has any existence at all. Due to this attitude, scientific work related to learning is considered most convincing only when it has the character of generalizability that quantification provides. It is not inherently problematic to quantify, but if that is the *only* way things are understood, something may be lost, shaved off or leveled down.

The stark and universal acknowledgment of the "necessity" of online learning was brought to the foreground after I initiated my research. When I entered this domain and cast about, what I encountered was that always the overweening pressure for efficiency brought about non-face-to-face learning. It was never a requirement or the only way that undergraduates could get an education. However, after the COVID-19 outbreak in 2020, online learning become center stage. We now live in a milieu in which it seems required, i.e., the only way forward for higher education. To question its necessity will at least raise eyebrows and at worst can mark you as one who stands against higher education.

Now that the step toward *necessity* of remote undergraduate learning has been made, it is hard to ever see online learning in the same way again. My study straddles this change from online classes being an option to a necessity. When I began work on this book, online learning was becoming increasingly available because it was considered marvelously efficient (by certain measures). My nine formal participants had their experiences during this time. The text that I created from our conversations came from a time before the necessitating of online classes. However, the interpretation and writing of the later chapters of this book took place in the new era of online learning post-COVID-19. The necessity is born from the ontology of technology. This ontology creates an attitude that diminishes learning by standardizing.

The quantificational attitude of the technological age, brought on by the urge to make everything increasingly more efficient, chokes the full possibility of what teachers do. We have not gotten to the time, yet, when teachers and teaching have disappeared. However, the full spectrum of learning, which is wondrously brought forth by teachers heeding their call, can become so radically altered that it does not exist anymore. A survey of teachers in higher education conducted by Kolowich (2012) found that when asked, "On balance, does the growth of online education excite or frighten you? (p. 1)." Fifty-eight percent "described themselves as filled more with fear than with excitement" (p. 1). On the other hand, the same survey data showed that 80 percent of administrators, those responsible for deciding to *move* classes online, were more excited than afraid. The creeping and peripheral concern that occupies my mind when I sense the urgency of an administrator asking if my class can be moved online to make it "more efficient" and help students complete their degree requirements sensitizes me to the potential fragility of learning.

The rapid increase of online classes offered at colleges and universities and the phenomenon of MOOCs as well as programs like Mindojo and online educational platforms such as Khan Academy show how modern computer technology is transforming how we learn and our expectations for learning. However, it is not clear that any of these advances are more *effective* if the goal of education is, as Rorty (1999) holds, fully formed individuals, people who can see through their socialization and even go beyond it to help shape the socialization of future generations. The role of non-face-to-face learning may expand access to information beyond any previous technology, e.g. the book. However, with such a tremendous gain there is assuredly a trade-off which might not be proportional. Thus, the concern of this book is over what is lost when the face is removed from learning.

What Is the Meaning of the Face for Learning?

For the Ancient Greeks, the word for "man" or "human being" was *Anthropos*. *Anthropos* meant "to have a human face." It is a tautology, of course, that only humans have human faces, but in the buried notion of what it *means* to be human there is a connection to *our* faces, the *human* face. For the Greeks, the face was essential to what it meant to be a human. It was through the face that the fullness of humanity manifested itself to others.

To be fully human is paradoxical. It is to be at once a being that can be an autonomous individual, a being that can, in some perennially mysterious and wonderful way, act outside of the causal order of the empirical world. However, it is also at the same time to be a material being subject to physical laws. Moreover, the human being is also inextricably part of a group, culture and tradition, i.e., a socialized being. The experience of freedom is likely due to language, something immaterial and unconstrained by physical causality. It is through the face that we most fundamentally express language. The face, a portion of our bodies, reflects our conscious life more than anything else, is like a tablet for our emotions and is a scaffold to hold up and emphasize what we communicate. Because of what it can communicate, "There is a power in the human face, a power that is different and that is more than just that which is shown" (Picard, 1930, p. 102). The students I talk to do not "notice" the absence of direct face-to-face contact in their online classes. What they do notice is whether their preconceptions about learning are being met or not.

Students mention that they are often inclined to select online classes where they are most concerned about the course content. When they are concerned with other aspects of the learning that is typically considered to take place at colleges and universities, i.e., social skills and building relationships, they adamantly pursue face-to-face classes. They usually have a distinction in their mind between classes they would take online and classes they would take in a traditional setting. For example, Josh, one of the preliminary students I spoke with from the University of Maryland, explained that in his major, computer science, most of the courses are taught non-face-to-face. Partially because of that format, Josh made the rare choice, for a computer science major, to minor in English. He tells me that most of his peers minor in math. When I asked him why he would seek out face-to-face learning for his minor when his major was mostly non-face-to-face learning, he said, "When you have something like philosophy or history or writing, talking with other people and experiencing the ideas in general is very important. In computer science it is not the focus; it is more mechanical and functional." Students, like Josh, seem to recognize that they are consciously compartmentalizing aspects of learning, e.g. social and/or emotional versus content and/or methods. However, even in their choice of face-to-face classes, students also acknowledge their desire to attain information, but the same cannot be said of their selection of non-face-to-face classes. They know MOOCs and other forms of online learning will not lead to social skills or relationships. Particularly since the COVID-19 outbreak, non-face-to-face learning is no longer a rare experience. Many people expect learning to happen in the absence of face-to-face contact.

When questioned about online learning, students do not immediately say, "I don't see anybody in class" or "there is no direct face-to-face interaction." The lack of ready reflection on the experience seems to be due to the expectations about the experience. Students take the online class and go into the experience of non-face-to-face learning already understanding what will not be there. Therefore, to many, what is lost in online learning does not stand out as especially significant or meaningful, because these losses were expected. The losses were already considered part of the experience.

Students are already conditioned by our current technology to know what to expect from learning without the embodied presence of others or real-time face-to-face encounters. They seem prepared to be able to cope with the lack of face-to-face contact. Students hardly find the difference remarkable, unless they are asked questions about efficiency and flexibility and if these are major concerns for them in attaining their education. Questions about efficiency connect to the underlying and technological attitude toward education manifest in non-face-to-face learning. Student expectations of learning are already shaped by the technological outlook. They accept implicitly both the ontological assumptions of the technological age, that everything is just a resource to be used efficiently, as well as the epistemological prescriptions, i.e., knowledge is just information. Thus, it may come as no surprise that students and many professors as well as administrators naturally think of learning as strictly circumscribed "means-end" activity (Heidegger, 1977). It is in the technology age, for Heidegger, that the means-end distinction collapses, i.e., there are no ends or stable teleological concerns except those that are just additional means.

The essence of modern technology changes how we think about everything. Changing our thinking alters the way in which entities are revealed. Things, activities and systems stand out differently when our thinking is altered. We can even come to circumscribe ourselves to the narrow domain of consumers. When education is thought of primarily as a tool, an instrument for getting something done (e.g., making money), instead of something beautiful or just a human endeavor done for its own sake (i.e., an end in itself), how one learns and the means of education, make little difference as long as a grade is received and a credential granted. "If the ultimate utility of schooling for the educational consumer is to provide him or her with the credentials that open doors to good jobs, then the content of school learning is irrelevant" (Labaree, 1997, p. 67). Grades, degrees and earning potential are examples of how the ends of education are defined in the technological age.

Much of what we know about remote learning depends on the context in which the discussion takes place. For example, if I ask students what their all-time favorite class was, I have never heard mention of an online class or even a hybrid class, even if they earned a high grade in those courses. However, if the context of the discussion is efficiency and I am asking what a student liked best about their online MBA program, they will probably go on and on about the convenience and flexibility in getting the credential. They will probably not refer much to their learning in this later example because of the strict instrumental nature of learning in a non-face-to-face setting. It seems like when learning becomes merely a means to an end, it is not the means that are valued but the end, getting the degree that gets them the job that gets them the money, i.e., a collapse of all ends into means for some further process and on and on.

Phenomenology of the Face

Emmanuel Levinas offers us a phenomenology of the face. He seeks to find the context in which we encounter a face as a face and determine the meanings that that experience has for us. Levinas has the insight that the face is the foundation of the ethical. "The face of a neighbor signifies for me an unexceptionable responsibility, preceding every free consent, every pact, every contract" (1998, p. 88). It is the face of the other that requires me to consider what is right and what is wrong. It seems then that, for Levinas, without an encounter with faces we do not become human. To be human is to be socialized into the infinitely expanding net of linguistically mitigated references. A large portion of that relational ontology that substantiates our human-ness is due to our direct contact with other humans. Somehow, without that connection, our freedom is jeopardized, and we cannot become ethical (Turkle, 2017).

What is it to have a human face? Is it merely the appearance of our visage, our countenance? How do we have, make, wear or "put on" a face? Levinas calls the face the "infinity of the other" (Levinas, 1961/1969, p. 213). The face could only be fully considered infinite if he was referring to the real encounter with the other's face, not some merely abstracted conceptual ideas of a face constructed in the mind from fragments of text or even a still photo. "A face is an anachronous immediacy more tense than that of an image offered in the straightforwardness of an intuitive intention" (1998, p. 91). When Levinas is talking about a face, he is talking about the living skin, the flickering and roving eyes, constantly changing mouth and lips. He based his ethical idea of the responsibility we feel when we encounter the face of the other not just on an abstraction of what a person is, but their real presence in a body right in front of us.

> A face approached, a contact with a skin – a face weighted down with a skin ... The skin caressed is not the protection of an organism, simply the surface of an entity; it is the divergence between the visible and invisible.
>
> (1998, p. 90)

It is from our encounter with the outer layer of the other, their skin, and its most meaningful, and usually most exposed portion, the face, that we begin to know others.

When considering the phenomenon of the face, what we notice is its flexibility and fluidity, and yet it is also stable and fixed. Van Manen says, "In the constant volatility of the face lies the vulnerability of each person" (1991, p. 180). Faces tell us things; they convey information – that is why we say that clocks have faces. The human face tells other humans that they are looking at a human because of what it reveals to them about possible intentional states. We know that we are looking at a human face by the way it moves, flexes, sags and changes or does not change. Dr. Paul Ekman's research suggests that there are over 10,000 facial expressions, only 3,000 of which convey emotion (Ekman, 2021). There is a saying that 80 percent of communication is non-verbal; if this is even partially true, then much of what we communicate is by way of our body, and our face in particular.

In order to gain access to undergraduate experiences of non-face-to-face learning, I had some preliminary conversations through some individual meetings with four students. For example, the computer science student Josh, mentioned above, was one of these. I met with the students individually to find out how they experienced online learning. In this chapter, I quote anecdotally from these four undergraduates and use pseudonyms.

Sean, a vibrant student who loves to interact with people, who has also taken over 20 online classes or MOOCs, said this about face-to-face classes:

> There is so much you pick up from people not in what they say but the underlying meaning of what they say and how they act when they are talking and how they carry themselves. If you see someone always standing up straight and confident and looking at the teacher, you know, a confident person - or you see someone else slouching and never answering questions there is so much you can understand.

Sean learns from watching others, not just what they say, but how they comport themselves with their bodies. He goes on to explain his experience with remote learning, "With online classes you don't develop that social understanding of how individuals act when they feel certain emotions that you have from everyday interactions. It's so superficial, from a computer. You don't have that bond." What Sean wants to learn is more than just the information related to the subject matter in the class. He wants to learn what might be called emotional intelligence, how best to listen and understand so that he can connect with others. He says, "Emotional intelligence builds soft skills that everyone neglects." Based on his experience, he knows that he cannot learn this kind of intelligence or these skills from non-face-to-face classes. He understands that he needs to learn as much as he can about the subtlety of human communication just as much as course content in order to achieve his long-term goals when he wants and in the best order.

A subtle way of rejecting someone, though usually obvious, is to avoid face-to-face encounters, e.g. we avoid eye contact. By not looking at someone's face, we may seek to slightly diminish the demand that their humanity has on us or at least the call, or duty, that it has on us to act a certain way. Avoiding face-to-face encounters is a way of not allowing the other's humanity to grip our own. In this context, consider the way students tended to turn off their cameras during synchronous Zoom classes during the COVID-19 outbreak. By avoiding the regard of another's face by looking down, or only showing our profile when talking and not meeting their eyes, we may also communicate things about ourselves, e.g. shyness, vulnerability and weakness. However, it is possible that in looking away from the human face we can also be taking the first step in dehumanizing. When we look away, with certain intentions, we take away the human face; we refuse to acknowledge what Levinas would say it requires of us. The face of the other calls on us to do and be, to act and become, in certain humanizing ways. The face is probably vital to all socialization. The call of the face might be the foundation of all learning.

Ignoring the face transforms our interactions with others by freeing us to do other things. In Sherry Turkle's (2017) book, *Alone Together: Why We Expect More from Technology and Less from Each Other*, she tells of a young woman who, when communicating with her grandmother, does not look at her face even though she appears to. The young technologically savvy and efficient professional admits that during Skype conversations (video phone calls), she is free to "do email" because her grandmother does not seem to notice the difference. The young woman realizes that she is not able to connect fully with her grandmother through the technologically mitigated conversations. From the example provided by Turkle, we can learn that face-to-face means more than just seeing someone else. It also means more than just seeing their face in real time, as Skype makes possible. Face-to-face is about the directness of the contact that allows all of the details possible from immediacy of presence, e.g. the subtle facial cues and expressions that are non-discursively understood in our relations with others.

Not having to deal with the face can be acceptable because it is efficient. Without encountering an immediately and fully present face we can dispense with the time needed to interpret and process complex information communicated by facial expressions. Relieved of the need to understand the meaning of the face or faces around us, we can focus our minds more narrowly on the task at hand, the course content, for example.

Because faces are immensely complicated, given the range of what they can convey, they are also profoundly ambiguous and can also show up as objects of great confusion and frustration. Ambiguity is found when simplification is impossible or ongoing. When we are up against ambiguity and the possibility of confusion, it is then that we are also likely to experience what is meaningful. The meaning of non-face-to-face learning is nestled in the complex context provided by the technological age.

The face-to-face encounter tells us about the other. It is not merely the shape of the face, its angles, colors, wrinkles and contours; it is its ability to make human expressions. It is the potential of the face to do so many things that makes it so meaningful. Our faces can shine our humanity. It is in the encounter with another's visage that one's humanity is delineated. Their visage is the outward sign of their humanity. Humans are what they are because of their exposure to human faces. That exposure is made most evident to us through what we see and by watching the eyes of others.

In George Sheehan's philosophy of running book (2014), *Running & Being: The Total Experience*, there is a summary of philosophical explorations of the importance of eye contact and/or what Sheehan calls "the look":

> Seeing, looking into another's eyes, can be a total revelation. The look, wrote [José] Ortega [y Gasset], is an act that comes directly from an inwardness with the straight-line accuracy of a bullet. Erving Goffman described it as "the most direct and purest reciprocity that exists anywhere." The look, then is in the present tense. It has nothing to do with past or future, with where or will be. The look is now. It is direct. Like a poem it must not mean, but be. We look through, not with, our eyes. Our eyes, therefore, are what we are. My eyes are me. The eyes, then, reveal, and in revealing appeal for revelation. The eyes, then, reveal, and in revealing appeal for revelation … The look, then, tells no less than who I am. It says, "This is the real me." It tells truth in the sense the Greeks used the word: to bare. The look, that subtle yet tenacious look, does just that. It bares me down to the submerged inner landscape of my soul.
>
> (pp. 28–29)

The look of our eyes happens in the real-time moments of our meeting and is unmediated. Eye contact is powerful because it is direct.

Van Manen explains:

> There is little doubt that we experience the presence of the other person most strikingly by way of the eyes. Through the eyes we may sense the innermost being of the other person, his or her soul. They literally provide me a "glance" of the other person's essence. And through the eyes the other person also has access to my being. Eye-to-eye contact is being-to-being contact. And through the eyes we are able to speak to each other about things that words may not adequately convey. It matters not so much what is said than how: the openness or vulnerability that makes it possible for eye-to-eye contact to be a genuine encounter – an encounter in which I know myself addressed at the heart of my existence.
>
> (1991, pp. 179–180)

It may just be that our being as humans is constituted by these profoundly tiny optical interactions aggregated together over years.

We always seek eye contact to know as much as possible about the inner intentional life of others. A full understanding of such intentionality and how we achieved the wonder of our level of consciousness may always be a mystery (Tallis, 2016). However, from the evidence of feral children, it seems that we do not have human consciousness if we are left alone (Steeves, 2006). "Did you know that it is really important to look at your baby's face?" cyberpsychologist Mary Aiken asks. "They need your eye contact. There is no study of early child development that does not support this" (2016, p. 90). There are crucial developmental stages that cannot be reached if the child's brain is not exposed to the proper stimulation (Ibid.). The same requirement must surely be sustained throughout all levels of education.

Even children understand what the face and eyes in particular convey. As van Manen says, "Children know intuitively that the eyes have a more direct connection to the soul than the words which flow from the mouth" (1991, p. 179). The soul, the inner life of subjectivity, consciousness and freedom, is mysteriously manifest in the subtle movements, dilations, flicks, blinks, squints and myriad other shapes that don't even have names. Once my two-year-old daughter said to me, "Why you have angry eyes?" I told her I was not angry, but I knew what she wanted to see. Happy eyes.

The face is not completely lost even when it is gone. In online classes, there are vestigial remnants of the face, but these leftover halfhearted traces of real-time embodied human presence are not effectual. Students may provide a picture of themselves or choose an image to represent themselves. However, as one student I talked with in my preliminary probing of the phenomenon, Sean, said:

> Yes, you [might] have a picture but you don't have those little nuances that come from everyday conversations and seeing that person. You don't get to see what type of person they really are, what they are trying to present about themselves.

Obviously, a picture is not the same as interacting with the actual person even if it helps to get to know them. But often there is not even a picture. If there is no visual image, only the student's comments and written responses may provide some of what is conveyed by the face when we communicate with each other. Emotional word choice and punctuation, even emoticons, help to make the absent face of the student or teacher more present in the imaginations of those who are communicating. However, textual representation can be more conscious and even more contrived than how we might act when we are physically present to each other in a classroom. As Sean says, "Even with introductions in online classes and group projects – you never see someone for who they really are – you just see a glimpse into what they are trying to portray." The highly curated and mostly anonymous presentation of self by others in a faceless online exchange can substantiate the lurking intuition of a solipsistic world.

When letters were the main form of long-distance communication, recipients imagined the face of the sender as they read, or looked at pictures of the sender propped-up next to the letter. As Nietzsche (1974) says, "The style and spirit of letters will always be the true 'sign of the times'" (p. 259). His comment should pull us up sharply. Do we even send emails, let alone letters anymore, or do we just occasionally text? Does the loss matter, and if so, why does it matter? The other, pre-Internet, form of long-distance intercourse was made possible by the telephone. The phone does not show a face, but in some way it brought us closer to the face than just text. We could hear the movements of the face, the whiskers of a beard, the click of teeth, a cheek rubbing on the receiver. Hearing the voice emitted from the body in real time was a much closer approach to the other than their written words. Even though with FaceTime, Skype and Zoom it is impossible to experience eye-contact, defined as gazing into another's eyes as they reciprocally do the same, these are, however, surely wonderful approximations to real-time face-to-face contact. Screen-to-face or face-to-screen is not the same thing as face-to-face even if there is real-time face presented on the screen. Because the face is so fundamental to what it means for human beings to interact, as long as human interaction exists so will the human face. However, the face does not completely afford itself to the demands of technological efficiency.

The ambiguity of the face, and thus its inherent meaning-fullness, cannot be entirely captured. The face, and all the meaning that it is able to convey, requires presence, real-time exchange. Removing it completely, recording it or allowing it to be present only partially, as in a photo, makes the face, if not totally then at least partially, absent. When it comes to the face, partial absence is a significant alteration because of how delicate, fluid and expressive is the phenomenon of face. The face is usually the first thing to be traded for faster, more flexible delivery, not just of communication but now, also, learning.

With every gain in efficiency, whether in massive lecture halls or online classes, something is also lost. Sometimes the gains of introducing technology into certain classrooms in certain situations may outweigh what is lost, but not always, e.g. a professor who uses PowerPoint may be able to cover more material, but students may not learn as much, especially if learning is understood as more than just exposure to content. Crucially, it is very hard to know beforehand what the outcome balance of efficiency gains will be. The epistemological uncertainty is particularly palpable if technology subsumes a whole course as it does when a class is moved to a non-face-to-face learning format.

Lecturing to the anonymous hundreds in a large auditorium seems only analogous to what learning could be like, indeed what it was once like. Worse, by my biases, when a class is "moved" online and there is no face-to-face contact whatsoever between teacher and student, this relocation is only recognizable as education because narrow quantifiable outcomes are met. Learning, then, ceases to be a strictly human activity and becomes a technological endeavor. The project is exemplified by the collapse of the means/ends distinction with regards to learning, i.e., it matters less (or not at all) how the ends are achieved as long as the ends are met. However, that does not mean that it is all bad; there are advantages to non-face-to-face learning.

One student I talked to, Ken, explained that the experience of non-face-to-face learning in his undergraduate learning helped to build his self-confidence and improve his study skills. He said that if the course had been "a regular psych[ology] class I'm not sure I would have enjoyed it any more or any less." He went on to say, "I think also that satisfaction [comes from] knowing that I learned all of that on my own." Ken's comments show how non-face-to-face learning made him feel empowered. "It was pretty satisfying," he said, knowing that he had not been "tugged along" as he normally would have allowed himself to be in face-to-face classes.

Perhaps non-face-to-face learning can provide a positive experience with independence. Rather than being an experience that is only fraught with loneliness and uncertainty, it can give certain students at certain times the opportunity to mature and maybe even the conditions to learn things they wouldn't face-to-face. Online classes can be, as they were for Ken, a chance to take responsibility within the context of the experience to learn for themselves. Another student I talked to, Josh, said,

> As I keep accomplishing stuff [in my online class] I get more assured I can actually do it if I put the work in … It takes a lot of discipline to sit there for an hour and just grind through the videos and not just do other things on the computer.

The experience may have the potential to highlight their role in learning. That is, in an online class students may not feel that they can blame the professor or other external conditions as much if they do not learn. However, this may ultimately depend on the outcome.

Ken told me, "I got an A in the class. I was pretty happy with that result … it helps getting good grades." Students like Ken who earn a good grade in an online class may tend to evaluate the experience in a positive light. They may tend to overlook the aspects of the course that they did not like. Certain shortcomings of the class may be ignored or forgotten, e.g. lack of face-to-face contact and relationships that transcend the course. They might even conclude that all the parts they did not like were actually for their benefit since the *outcome*, the grade, was good. On the other hand, students who earned a low grade may not think non-face-to-face learning was good even if we can assume that the conditions of the experience are comparable. Students who earn a low grade may complain about all the things that their counterparts with higher outcomes don't worry about. Indeed, Ken said that if he had gotten a low grade, he would have "hated the class." Of course, these considerations reveal nothing *essential* about non-face-to-face learning because they could apply equally to traditional classes.

The Methodology: Hermeneutic Phenomenology as Philosophical Inquiry

The need for the type of methodology used in this book is due to the nature of the question about the meaning of what is lost in remote learning. Since it is a question about meaning, it is an inherently non-quantificational and interpretive project. To support such research, consider this quote from computer scientist Jaron Lanier:

> Here are some tough truths: We currently don't have a scientific description of a thought or a conversation. We don't know how ideas are represented in a brain. We don't know what an idea is, from a scientific point of view … We can pretend that we will understand them any minute, so it is as if we already understand them, but then we are just lying to ourselves.
>
> (2018, p. 131)

With such fundamental questions about ourselves still open, interpretive methodologies are a crucial way for understanding how we experience a complex phenomenon like online learning.

Phenomenology is one of the ways that we can become aware of our ontological assumptions, e.g. the technological attitude that all beings are resources. It is concerned with finding out what exactly things, entities, really are, by understanding how we interpret them. Becoming aware of how we understand the way entities exist for us can dispose us to think about our own way of being as humans in the world. We should not be ontologically naïve and become swept along by a commonsense view of entities, especially technological ones (Adams & Thompson, 2011). If we don't understand the ontological foundations of technology and how it influences education, we will not be able to solve problems with technology, e.g. how it reduces the need for skillful human engagement with the world (Thomson, 2005). Without understanding what technology really is, in its essence, we will also not be able to know what problems it can cause in education when it is used as a substitute for teachers or other more human forms of learning. As one phenomenologist explains, "It is important to ask not *only* what a given technology enhances but also what it simultaneously reduces or diminishes both experientially and hermeneutically" (Adams & Thompson, 2011, p. 742). The point is technology is never neutral. There are always trade-offs when education is made more efficient by the faster transfer of information via MOOCs or iPads. The work of phenomenology is intensely observational, but it must also be of the real lived experience, not experimentation or the setting up of unrealistic or idealistic conditions.

Phenomenology is not a method in the sense of an algorithmic recipe for proceeding toward a conclusion. There are things a phenomenologist might do to unpack the meaning of a phenomenon, but there is, strictly speaking, no method. It is very sensitive to observation but is not generalizable. It does not present or advance an argument. Its purpose is not to provide a conclusion that can be abstracted to other situations in order to provide answers to problems. Phenomenology does not seek to establish a theory. Therefore, in examining the phenomenon of non-face-to-face learning, a simplification (i.e., a theory) will not do. Rather the aim, or hope, is to achieve a possible view of the experience in its complexity as something complex.

Phenomenology is able to study things that normally escape quantification and research that depends on measurement. Phenomenology explores, for example, moods, the experience of time or relationships. It is particularly focused on identifying the meaning of something, e.g. eye contact, dispositions, affordances and pathic engagement between entities (Ihde, 1990; Introna & Ilharco, 2006). Phenomenology is philosophical and is a human science not a social science (Adams & Thompson, 2011). It asks lots of questions and tries to formulate the best questions relating to the phenomenon studied. However, this does not mean that the questions are always completely answered. The emphasis is on asking questions and providing answers that illuminate possible interpretations. Of course, phenomenology does not disparage answers.

Emphasizing the context is very much the phenomenological project because context is what makes meaning possible. For example, as the technological humanist Jaron Lanier puts it so well, in his book *You Are Not a Gadget*, "Meaning is only ever meaning in context" (2011, p. 136). Lanier gives the meaningfulness of words in a natural language as an example. He explains that each word has meaning, precisely because of the limited number of words found in a language. It is the ambiguity provided by context and the extra work each word has to do that makes languages meaningful. A language with an infinite number of words would have no ambiguity, context would be irrelevant and, therefore, it would be meaningless. Determining the context is thus an exploration of the ambiguous bounds of the phenomenon.

Just like with finding the meaning of a word or a sentence, at least part of finding the meaning of a phenomenon is examining the context in which it is possible to experience that phenomenon. Each feature of the context impacts the phenomenon in a different way and to a different degree. Thus, asking the meaning of something is like asking a good question. As Plato showed, when we ask a good question (or maybe even just any question), "What is justice?" we are also explicitly or implicitly asking *every other question*.

My experience as a teacher has led me to a concern for face-to-face learning. However, the phenomenological project of this book is to work to reveal the meaning of what is lost in remote or non-face-to-face learning. The networked nature of questioning, how one question draws and pulls on others endlessly, is due to the contextual nature in which our human meaning is made and understood. It seems that nothing can be defined or known independent of a relation to other things, maybe even everything else. The relational nature of all our concepts is captured in the view that we, according to Heidegger and others, inhabit a world structured by a relational ontology, i.e., what entities are is just how they are related to other things. Presenting the meaning of something requires the observation and articulation of the context of that thing, which is itself the many multiple relations to other things. A quest for meaning is about showing how the part is related to the whole.

Part of the value of my phenomenological study will be the detail to which I am able to describe non-face-to-face learning. To make the description detailed means the painstaking articulation of the relation of parts to whole (Adams & Thompson, 2011; van Manen, 2007). Phenomenology seeks to answer, to varying degrees, the question of how a certain segment of reality, a phenomenon, a part, relates to the whole of reality. In this way, meaning can be approached. The work of hermeneutic phenomenology is thus to show how a certain situation relates to the wider context, the whole, in which the situation takes place. These questions are mirrored in the hermeneutic phenomenological concern with language. The context in which a word or a phrase is used can transform what the word or phrase means. Thus, careful interpretation of what my participants say means being sensitive to the context not just the literal meaning. For this reason, sometimes normally unhyphenated words may be hyphenated so as to draw attention to relational significance carried in the world, e.g. response-ability.

Phenomenologists place great emphasis on language and words, so these become part of the study. A great deal of the hermeneutic work is working out the interpretation of texts that are produced through direct phenomenological research. Etymology of crucial words becomes vital to the project of revealing meaning because "Attention to etymology fosters a critical awareness that instrumental speech is but the veneer of language. Instrumental speech facilitates communicative transactions, yet hides the layers of meaning below" (Thiele, 1995, p. 118). To regard language as more than its instrumental veneer is to already work outside of the technological attitude toward language. Thus, phenomenology seeks to see things as they are, to let them be, and not constrain them to one "enframed" way of being understood.

The phenomenological focus on language connects it with poetry and the kind of knowing and meaning that poetry provides. To show what the components are, and how they not only constitute the whole but are also interrelated, depends on rich descriptive language. A detailed description explains by showing what happens to the people and things involved in the phenomenon using experiential language. It is only the pre-reflective experience that concerns phenomenology (Adams & Thompson, 2011). The point is to show the *meaning* of a specific phenomenon. To show the meaning is to elucidate the significance of something. Anecdotes are used in phenomenological research because they contain meaningful experiential language. Descriptive language reveals the phenomenon. The revelations of a good phenomenological study can provide non-trivial understandings, or insights, that can deepen our questioning and perhaps change our thinking and actions. They can lead to profound gestalt switches where, like Wittgenstein's "Duck/Rabbit," our understanding of something is completely changed in a moment (Thomson, 2011). If that occurs, educational policies may be questioned and changed. It is possible for there to be convincing power in a phenomenological description and hermeneutic rendering. That conviction might overlap with certain arguments or positions about how to define education and how to bring about learning. However, the phenomenological description can never be constrained to one conclusion.

Hermeneutic phenomenological work is an end in itself. It is not the means to some other purpose. The process of studying, interpreting and writing about a phenomenon are as important as the finished product. Analogously, for you the reader, the reading of the study is as important as whatever may come as a result of that reading. The reading of this book works to open up the phenomenon, to elucidate an essence, to present a path or a way of thinking.

Participant Introductions

I had conversations with students who have had varying exposure to remote learning. They fell into three groups. First were those who had taken some online classes and were currently enrolled in one. Another group had recently taken online classes but were not currently enrolled in any. The last group had taken online classes several years before our conversations.

I found participants from differing groups because of the varying temporal perspective they provide on the phenomenon. It helped illuminate a retrospective disposition toward non-face-to-face learning as compared to those who are actually engaged in it now. None of the groups are representative, and there are experiences other than time that shape recollection and the quality of the experience, e.g. maturity, type of non-face-to-face class and necessity of the material. However, it seems that temporal exposure to the phenomenon was an important aspect of how re-collections of the phenomenon were given, and that is why I sought this kind of diversity of exposure.

To explore the meaning of what is lost in remote learning, it does matter where my students come from. Participants had to be, or have been, undergraduates. I went to their schools to find them. I solicited participants from institutions of post-secondary education in the D.C./Maryland/Virginia metro area. I advertised for participants by posting at schools in the area.

While Creswell (2013) suggests five participants as an adequate number to conduct a phenomenological inquiry, I settled on a range of seven to ten because I hoped to get a multiplicity of perspectives in order to do in-depth work. I was able to get nine participants. All of my participants had completed at least one online class as undergraduate students. My participant selection was informed by Mobley (2015), who says, "The intent of these criteria [is] not to 'sample' different aspects of the phenomenon in order to generalize, but, a diversity of perspectives is needed to provide rich textual accounts of the lived experiences that are then interpreted" (p. 145). By getting nine participants, I was able to get a rich array of facets of the lived experience of non-face-to-face learning. Phenomenology aims to get at diverse perspectives but not in a compare and contrast manner. This was not about being able to make generalizations or diversity for the sake of diversity. I was able to get a rich descriptive view of the phenomenon by engaging with the differences presented in my participants' tellings.

Creating a Text to Interpret

I got to know my participants well to create an ease and freedom that allowed for free-flowing conversation. There was then a certain willingness on the part of the participants to enter into an examination of their lived experience of remote learning. The willingness sprang not just from goodwill and incentives (e.g., gift certificates) but also from a genuine interest in the phenomenon itself. It was possible that some who participated did not feel a sense of *aporia* as they took online classes along with their traditional courses. However, all of them did describe moments of confusion or expressed curiosity and wonder as to how both formats were in some way equivalent.

I did not take online classes myself as an undergraduate. My principal encounter with the phenomenon of non-face-to-face learning was by having conversations with people who took online classes as undergraduates. It is important to emphasize that these were conversations and not interviews. There were no predetermined questions or set course or time limit for our encounters. In this I followed Gadamer's philosophical insights about conversations:

> It is called dialectic because it is the art of conducting a real dialogue … What emerges in its truth is the logos, which is neither mine nor yours and hence so far transcends the interlocutors' subjective opinions that even the person leading the conversation knows that he does not know.
>
> (1975/2004, pp. 360–361)

I had initial conversations with all of my participants individually. At the end of the first conversation, I invited the participants to write a reflection piece before our second conversation. After completing the two conversations with each participant and collecting each of their writing assignments, the collection of data was complete. I had over 260 pages of material to study and interpret. Throughout this study, all of my participants are only identified by pseudonyms.

I personally recorded and transcribed all of the conversations. The laborious task of transcribing the conversations was not a chore to get out of the way, but actually a vital way of conducting the human science research.

Facets of the Phenomenon

Like the sides of a cut gemstone, each of my nine participants provided a facet of non-face-to-face learning. There are of course many more facets to the experience, as many as there are those who take online classes. Moreover, unlike a gem, the facets that my participants show me often overlap. Indeed, where their accounts overlap are sometimes areas that I find most important. Sometimes the face of online learning that they show me is very similar. Each of these people who have taken the time to participate in conversations with me about online learning comes at the experience in different ways. Yet, they also have many things in common about themselves and the experience they describe. What I receive from them is something like an enneahedron that I can turn, examine, probe and try to interpret. Like a gem, what they have offered up is precious.

The various perspectives of my participants helped form the overall showing of the essence of non-face-to-face learning for undergraduates. They have things in common about what they bring forth. They also express some contrasts which help to highlight aspects of the overall phenomenon. The facets of my participants are grouped into four "edges" showing commonality.

Hindsight: Memory and the Temporal Distance of the Phenomenon

There is an important remembered quality to phenomenological inquiry. To get inside the experience, to understand how it was lived for an individual, is to delve into memory. As Gadamer explains, "What can be called an experience constitutes itself in memory. By calling it such, we are referring to the lasting meaning that an experience has for the person who has it" (1975/2004, p. 58). To ask for the meaning of an online class calls on my participants to enter their experience through memory. As Gadamer notes, this is part of how phenomenological work is made possible. "The human sciences arrive at their conclusions by an unconscious process. Hence the practice of induction in the human sciences is tied to particular psychological conditions … e.g., a well-stocked memory" (p. 5). Thus, the nature of my participants' memories is an inherent quality of this book.

Their early memories were often most distinct, and their first exposure to the phenomenon resonated deeply. However, it was impossible to know how much of their memories were impacted by their more recent experiences. It was never explicitly my task to uncover what they may have forgotten. Instead, the conversations guided what was revealed by participants. On the whole, despite what may look like significant changes to online classes over the last two decades, my participants' accounts of what was meaningful to them in none-face-to-face learning did not vary greatly.

Mary is the participant who had the second longest memory of the experience. Online courses had become available at her university while she was a student over seven years before we met. Because the online format was new back then, her school had been concerned with whether or not the classes would be academically rigorous. Thus, students were limited to only one online class per semester, and they could only take a certain number as part of their degree.

Expectations dominate how students perceive the experience of non-face-to-face classes. Mary's perspective was important because, unlike students with more recent exposure to online classes, she had almost no idea what to expect. Thus, her expectations leaned more toward apprehension of the unknown, rather than matching reality to what she had thought it would be like. This was before such conditioning experiences like exposure to online learning platforms, e.g. Khan Academy. However, since the classes were so new, Mary's facet elucidates the difficulties of realizing the consequences of the loss of face-to-face contact after she was already in the experience. Mary felt the loss as it happened, even though she knew it would not be there. It wasn't until she took the class that she encountered what was lost in non-face-to-face learning.

Mary happily dove into her online classes. She was glad to have the opportunity to have greater control of her schedule and knock off some "easy" required courses for her degree. She knew the classes would be easy because she already knew how to write a research paper (her first online experience was an advanced writing course). She was grateful for the experience and did not seem to have any regrets or especially impactful consequences due to her online classes. Mary was satisfied that it had helped her learn to be more of an adult by learning to manage her schedule and more efficiently fulfill degree requirements.

In our conversations, Mary's account of the discussion boards laid out the paradigm of this most loathed aspect of online classes. The discussion boards are one of the aspects of online classes that are meant to most overlap with a traditional class. However, in this similarity the difference is poignant. Like many other participants, she found the discussion board reading and posting tedious. Mary, as with most of my other participants, could "see the point" but wished she didn't have to "post one comment and give two replies," i.e., the standard weekly assignment for many online classes. For her, the discussion boards did not help her feel connected to other students but were just another hoop to be jumped through to complete the course. At one moment in our conversation, she captured the essence of this sentiment by saying, "I did not see the reason of putting in my maximum effort when I was not going to get anything in return from the professor or in my grades."

With Travis, I was able to receive the perspective of not just an undergraduate but also a member of the military. Travis started his undergraduate work while he was still in the Marines. He took classes through a school that catered mostly to members of the military and had online classes designed with an understanding of the special situation their students faced. It was fascinating to learn that an American member of the military deployed in a combat zone might also be worried about a due date for an upcoming homework assignment or looming exam. Such is the pressure to get a degree. In these circumstances, non-face-to-face classes provide a way for military students to work on their studies.

Unlike some of his peers, Travis did not have to juggle active duty and his online classes. He was still in the military but had an extra six months in Europe and wanted to use his education stipend before returning home. So he went into his experience of online classes hoping to get something out of his "free education" but not really sure what he would learn.

Travis took two classes and did the work in coffee shops in Germany. He despised both classes. He and his fellow military students often expressed their disdain for the busy work associated with discussion boards and the diluted quality of the education he was receiving. As he said about the online classes, "It's not a journey of self-experience that I feel as though is monumental or significant to me." However, he was happy to be able to complete some course work that he thought would enable him to transfer to a good school. Travis completed his undergraduate degree at the University of Chicago, a school that is apparently so good, or at least has such high standards, that they did not accept any of his online classes.

Lane was older. He was one of three participants who was "non-traditional" when he took his non-face-to-face classes. Lane had already had two successful careers, married and had a daughter before he returned to finish his undergraduate degree. He had worked as manager of a veterinarian hospital. Lane had also been a professional chef. It was fun to hear his stories of helping to save pets and construct cheese caves and deal with restaurant investors. Being closer to middle age, Lane brought a mature perspective to the experience he offered of non-face-to-face learning as an undergraduate.

Given his age and life experience, Lane approached all his undergraduate education in a different way from other students. His expectation for all of his learning, including online classes, was different. He didn't *need* a degree. As he told me once, he was already living the life of someone in the 1 percent. Therefore, when he took a class, he delved deeply into the material and dedicated hours to study, re-reading and pondering. He took two online classes because they were upper-level courses with specific content he did not want to miss. He wanted to be changed by his education, so he allowed himself to be pulled and challenged. Lane explained it in his own words:

> As a student in the modern age it requires you to be flexible and open to new experiences. I have known people my age that have done similar things, taken classes or done a second degree or been with people that are much younger than them and they make no attempt to kind of try to blend in. They make no attempt to understand what their other classmates are really kind of going through in their current life or the current atmosphere. And I feel like that is something that I always try to do. I always try to at least understand.

Unlike the other participants, Lane was different because he was actually seeking to alter his online classes. "I try to take that position of another kind of leader in the class because the professor can't do it all." He wanted to make it better by increasing effective exchanges between students on the discussion board. He was able to bring about specific improvements to the structure of the course because he knew the professor from a previous class. Lane seems to have the personality where if he sees a way for improvement, he is going to exert energy to bring about that change.

Lane seemed to have a much higher tolerance for what other students might perceive as busy work, because to him he could turn it all into a beneficial experience. However, Lane was also an unflinching critic of both professors and students. There was tension in his relation to both. He saw himself as apart from the other students because he was far older and had such a different perspective. For the same reasons, age and experience, he also had an affinity with the professors. For example, he was the only student in one of his online classes who created the course material for one of the readings. That is, he taught part of the class.

The Synchronous and the Asynchronous Online Class

I consider any undergraduate class that does not take place in a classroom to be non-face-to-face. As I have explained in earlier sections, even a video call is not face-to-face. Real-time interactions where the other person's face is visible may seem to go a long way to filling the gap left without direct physical presence. I hope that after having to use Zoom and other synchronous videoconference programs, most teachers agree that what is lost is too precious to go without. Simply seeing someone in real time is not the same as being face-to-face. For example, while I am grateful to be able to see my children's faces moving and smiling through the screen when I am away, it does not replace my presence at home. The mere thought of such logic turns my stomach. Videoconferencing, for all its necessity at times, is not the same thing as embodied presence with others. There is so much that we are not able to share if we reduce our interactions by removing eye contact and imposing a small, framed, two-dimensional perspective on each other.

If non-face-to-face learning is the genus, there are many species. Two of the main divisions in non-face-to-face classes are between the synchronous and the asynchronous. Only two of my participants, Danna and Evan, had any experience with synchronous online classes. However, this type of non-face-to-face learning has become the dominant exposure of all undergraduates to non-face-to-face learning. Due to COVID-19-related restrictions, most undergraduates now have had to take some kind of synchronous non-face-to-face class, made possible through different types of videoconferencing programs like Zoom.

Interestingly, COVID-19 college policies seemed to imply that there is a difference in quality between asynchronous and synchronous classes. For example, my college offers many asynchronous classes that count the same on a student's transcript as an in-person or synchronous class. But when COVID-19 hit and in-person classes were moved online, the college required teachers to teach synchronously. One can infer that administrators at least noticed that something is unique and important in synchronous elements of a class.

Danna's experience with online learning contrasted with all of the other participants for two important reasons. First, she had taken only one non-face-to-face class over five years before we met. Her facet of the phenomenon allowed for no comparison among online classes. Second, the one class she had taken was completely synchronous. However, unlike many of the synchronous Zoom classes offered during the COVID-19 restrictions, hers did not show the other members of the class. The main component of the synchronicity of the class was the audio of the professor as she taught the class with a shared, real-time PowerPoint presentation. Another synchronous aspect of the class was the ability to chat with other students and hear their comments when they were unmuted.

For Danna, making the class synchronous was an added frustration. She thought the course material was remedial and her time was wasted listening to the professor read material she had just reviewed in the book. She was frustrated that the real-time interactions were marginally helpful. While she understood the theory that she would learn from her peers by listening to their comments, Danna believed she did not did not benefit because the function was too slow, and it did not seem like an efficient use of her time on the off chance that some random comment might help her. She explained that it was clear the other students felt the same way and the teacher was frustrated with their lack of attention and participation.

Like Lane, Evan was an older non-traditional student. He had returned to get an undergraduate degree to facilitate a career change to nursing. He was also the only other participant, besides Danna, who had a synchronous component in his non-face-to-face class. Similar to Zoom students today, part of his course was a videoconference call. Once or twice a week, the students engaged in a work study program in a hospital would all log in to share experiences from their studies and work. They had different shifts, and the required videoconference was a time to gain insights and support from the experience of others.

Evan's was the only participant able to consider the phenomenon of video interaction and how it altered the phenomenon of non-face-to-face learning. He noticed a more casual nature and body language. Most of the other students were typically at home, and, since the meetings took place in the evening, they were either in their pajamas or some other informal attire. Many sat on their beds, laid on the floor or otherwise assumed a posture that would be unusual in a normal face-to-face meeting.

What was particularly striking was Evan's comments about his own body language. He explained that during a videoconference he often found himself striking a pose of putting his interlaced fingers behind his head while talking. Upon consideration, he felt that this was odd behavior on his part.

> It is something I would never do in person. You will never see me do this [he does the gesture] generally with someone because it feels weird. I feel like you are a car salesman or something, but if I feel like no one is there I can kind of just go like this and I don't know why that is.

For Evan, the fact that he performed this innocuous, but, to him at least, unusual, body language indicated that though he could see the other people, he was not *with* them; they were not really *there*. The absence of the other was shown to him by his tendency to do something with his body that he would normally constrain himself from doing around others.

Another insight from Evan's facet into the synchronous video interactions was the doubt as to what others could and could not see on their screens. There was a great deal of epistemological ambiguity about whether what was being perceived was shared or not. The concern also extended to what was being heard. Especially problematic was when multiple people would begin speaking. This usually happened in response to a general question posed to the entire group. As everyone started to answer, they realized there were others speaking and so nobody could listen to anybody. Realizing what was going on, everyone would usually stop at the same time. Then silence would pervade as all former speakers would be unsure of who should continue. Evan's description showed that relaxed, spontaneous and less-moderated discussions are lost even in synchronous remote courses.

Current Non-Face-to-Face Undergraduates

Some of my participants were in non-face-to-face classes during the time we had our conversations. They could refer to what was happening to them right at the moment. However, each participant could also reflect on former non-face-to-face classes as well. Our conversations usually began by examining the first experience with non-face-to-face learning to see what had stood out. The a priori attitudes and perceptions seemed to be distinct in ways that cast a shadow over their current experiences.

These participants seemed to be the least naïve about their experience with non-face-to-face learning. Their attitude was the most nonchalant and mature of all the participants.

> All the classes start the same way. You have a week to post an introduction of yourself on a discussion board, and then depending on the class give examples of things in your daily life that relate to the class.

In general, these participants had a franker attitude. They did not feel they had to probe their memory in order to offer up something about the phenomenon. As I asked them questions about their place of learning or their interactions with professors and other students, they could speak directly without an effort of memory.

Carl had "wasted" time before getting serious about his undergraduate learning. He had spent time working, and he said his blue-collar background had made him somewhat suspicious of the need for a degree. However, once he had resolved to move his education forward, he was a committed and dedicated student. Part of the reason he enrolled in non-face-to-face classes was the sense that they were easier. If he could get higher grades, then it would help to compensate for his former low GPA. He was also drawn to online classes because of necessity. The additional offerings allowed him to complete required courses faster. He was anxious to rehabilitate his GPA and transfer to a top university.

Carl had spent significant time trying to self-educate. Some of his first experiences with non-face-to-face learning were with free college courses offered online by MIT and other universities. He took the time to use Khan Academy, too, and took a course online that was designed to teach students how to learn. At one point, he revealed the startling fact that in one of his online classes the professor sent an email saying she would be on a cruise for six weeks. She wished them all well in the course and hoped they would be okay because she could not guarantee her access to reliable Internet access.

A precious component of what Carl offered in his facet of non-face-to-face learning was the level of preoccupation he felt. He explained that while online classes were more efficient and offered greater flexibility, this came at a cost. The self-scheduling of non-face-to-face classwork created a noticeable burden. "The online classes are on my mind more than the not online classes. Unless I am sitting [in a class] or I am on campus the thing that I am thinking about is online classes." Carl never felt like the class was over. It had no boundary; it just kept on going. No matter how much work he got done, there was always more. The pressure to keep up with the class was constant. There was nobody else to share the burden of keeping track of assignments with or the relevant thread of learning that was being offered by the course. For Carl, the non-face-to-face learning seemed to blur and meld into all of his other normal everyday concerns. They occupied his mental energy in a way that traditional classes did not.

Of my participants, Nathan is the third and last non-traditional student. Like Carl, he had "wasted" time when he was the normal undergraduate age and then had spent 15 years working. Among other things, Nathan was a published author. He had written for a pro-wrestling blog and was a professional poker player. Now that he was focusing on his undergraduate degree, he was living at home with his traditionally minded Hindu mother and younger brother.

Nathan is a devoted son and fond of his boisterous brother, whose loud infectious laughter was a constant background distraction while Nathan tried to complete his online course work on the shared family computer. At one point, he described the difficulty of getting any work done while his brother and mother watched a football game in the other room. His mother, now in her 60s, had also returned to school. Nathan was excited to be taking one of his future online classes with her as they both completed general university required courses. He explained that he often found himself giving his mom advice about learning, that it was not just about completing the class to get the credit, but that she should seek to really learn.

Nathan worked very hard as a student. Like Lane, he did not *need* a degree. He expressed frequent frustration with any class where the professor was not willing to thoroughly correct him. He remarked that he was always trying to become a better writer, so he was anxious to get substantial feedback on his written work. There was much for him to be frustrated about in the hyper efficient atmosphere of non-face-to-face learning.

Nathan emphasized the feeling of being on an island in online classes. He quickly learned that it was up to him to get through the course. "It's you. It's you or bust. You won't learn the material unless you make yourself learn the material." For Nathan, learning the material was not all he was after. He wanted to improve, learn new skills and increase his abilities. However, his experience with online classes was often disheartening. Nathan realized that some professors in his online classes were clearly using templated answers cut and pasted for multiple students. That was bad enough, but even more aggravating for Nathan was when he asked a question genuinely hoping for a personalized learning experience, only to be referred to the syllabus and other course materials.

Nathan offered the following assessment of his experience:

> A teacher can usually assess the feel of the class in an in-person setting. Online there is none of that. All they see are grades and by that point you've moved on to the next bit of material. There is no lecture where there is back and forth with questions, so you can't break things down in a simpler way. You can't simplify it for whoever needs it, so everyone has to learn just what's put out there. And they might have the opportunity to ask questions but you can only communicate so much through text. Sometimes just gauging the classrooms mood or how they do on exercises during the lecture. There is none of that before you get to the grade. It's just a grade and that is it.

Nathan's concern was that the grades were given without there being an opportunity to receive help learning, without there being anything added to the individual student's efforts. He thought the professor's role was to provide guidance and help students learn. Then their grades would reflect the professor's role in their learning and not just their own individual might. As he described it, the experience boiled down to a student's own work ethic. They could not depend, as he thought they might in a normal class, for assistance from the teacher.

Taking Many Online Classes: The One Versus the Many

The whole is composed of many parts. There are many facets to a three-dimensional shape, but it is still one thing. The issue of the relation of the one to the many is ancient. In *Republic* 596a, Plato says, "We customarily hypothesize a single form in connection with each collection of many things to which we apply the same name" (1997). Phenomenology is an engagement with the relation of multiplicity to something singular. Phenomenology dives into the limitless possibilities of experiences in or with a phenomenon and strives to articulate the meaning of that phenomenon. The meaning is not singular either. However, the multifaceted account has a kind of unity, a sort of one-ness.

Originally from Virginia, John had gone far into the Midwest to do his undergraduate learning. Far from home for the first time, he got into trouble. After two years, he dropped out and came back home to live with his parents and recover. Although clearly intuitive and charismatic, John struggled to figure out his academic path. Once he decided to complete his bachelor's degree, he was demoralized to find out that he would need to re-take many required courses. He needed to raise his GPA to qualify for transfer, and the school he wanted to go to would not accept some of his classes. John could not stomach the idea of sitting through so many classes again. Thus, he embraced the opportunity to complete many online classes at his own pace. The experience of repeating classes and taking them in different formats made him an example of a kind of expert student who knows just how much work to do to get the best outcome.

John was the opposite of Lane and Nathan. For him, it was all about necessity. He *had* to take the classes in order to transfer. He *had* to raise his GPA. He was dedicated to efficiency maximization rather than learning. He was thrilled to excise professors and other students from the experience of undergraduate learning.

> Online teaching is taking the power of learning away from the teachers and [gives it] to the students. Because teachers have limited access to their students, they cannot impact their studies in traditional ways. I have never spoken with one of my online teachers.

With online classes, he found the closest one-to-one correspondence between what was required in the class and what he would be expected to do. He knew that he did not need to learn anything in these courses. He had no incentive, because he had already taken most of these courses before.

John was a savvy online student. His experience taking several online classes every semester gave him experience. He learned how to navigate the classes with increasing efficiency. He knew how to figure out the least possible amount of effort the course would require of him to get the grade he wanted. This was perfect for him. It was just what he wanted from his experience. He did not want to learn anything new, convinced as he was that he had already learned it all. As he put it:

> Listening to someone prattle on and on about something I already know, just for them to say the one thing I didn't, and I miss it because I was bored out of my mind. [This] has happened to me more than once. I already know most of the stuff being discussed.

The student who takes many online classes like John becomes better at taking them. Becoming better at online classes makes the student an even more efficient "learner."

In the way that John's facet helped shows the perspective of someone who has many experiences with non-face-to-face learning, Scott represents "the one" because he had only taken one online class. Scott is similar to John in that his attitude toward online classes was almost completely positive. However, for Scott the reason was not due to the efficient format. Scott was the only participant whose experience of non-face-to-face learning was totally by choice. It was an upper-level elective that he chose to take strictly because of his interest in the course content, Russian History.

Scott is a typical undergraduate. In addition to his studies, he works and is involved in school clubs. Part of the reason he loved his online class was because he came to respect not just the professor ("for treating me like a real historian") but also the other students. He really appreciated what he learned from them through their shared reports, thoughtful discussion board posts and group work. Despite his unreserved enthusiasm for the online course, he also gives one of the most unintentionally haunting insights into what is lost in remote learning I will discuss later.

Scott's experience highlighted an important distinction in online classes. The distinction connects to Lane's facet as well. Both Scott and Lane had taken upper-level major courses online. When the non-face-to-face learning is an upper-level course, it usually has some distinct features. First, it is generally a smaller, more intimate class that is constituted solely of majors. All of the students are there because they are deeply interested in the course content and want to be successful beyond just the course requirements. Second, the teacher is usually dedicated to the subject rather than being a "proctor" as John calls them. Third, the students often already know each other and the professor from previous face-to-face classes. Knowing each other outside the non-face-to-face context

36 Introduction

changes the dynamic of anonymity that many online classes slip into. And even if they don't know each other, there is a sense that they may have future face-to-face classes together.

Note

1 To get a sense of the interpretive aim of this book, consider the following. "The words 'meaning' and 'interpretation' are ambiguous, both in philosophical circles and in ordinary conversation. In one very important sense of these two words, they are quite closely related to each other: an interpretation of something aims at answering the question what the thing means. It is in this sense that I will be using these words" (Gillon, 2012, p. 81). In this book, I will be presenting an interpretation in order to show the meaning(s) of my phenomenon.

References

Adams, C., & Thompson, T. L. (2011). Interviewing objects: Including educational technologies as qualitative research participants. *International Journal of Qualitative Studies in Education*, 24(6), 733–750.

Bowen, W. G., Chingos, M. M., Lack, K. A., & Nygren, T. I. (2014). Interactive learning online at public universities: Evidence from a six-campus randomized trial. *Journal of Policy Analysis and Management*, 33(1): 94–111.

Carr, N. (2011). *The shallows: What the internet is doing to our brains*. New York, NY: Norton and Company.

Creswell, J. W. (2013). *Qualitative inquiry and research design: Choosing among five approaches* (3rd ed.). Thousand Oaks, CA: Sage.

Ekman, P. (2021). *Personal website*. Retrieved January 25, 2021, from https://www.paulekman.com/

Friesen, N. (2016). Is there a body in this class? In V. M. Manen (Ed.), *Writing in the dark* (pp. 223–235). New York, NY: Routledge.

Gadamer, H. G. (2004). *Truth and method*. New York, NY: Continuum. (Original work published 1975)

Gillon, J. S. (2012). *On the nature, interpretation, and value of artworks*. (Unpublished doctoral dissertation). Princeton University, Princeton, NJ.

Heidegger, M. (1971). *Poetry, language, thought*. New York, NY: HarperCollins.

Heidegger, M. (1977). *The question concerning technology, and other essays* (W. Levitt, Trans.). New York, NY: HarperCollins. (Original works published 1962, 1952 & 1954).

Ihde, D. (1990). *Technology and the lifeworld: From garden to earth*. Bloomington, IN: Indiana University Press.

Introna, L., & Ilharco, F. M. (2006). On the meaning of screens: Towards a phenomenological account of screenness. *Human Studies*, 29, 57–76.

Kolowich, S. (2012, June). Conflicted: Faculty and online education. *Inside Higher Ed*. Retrieved January 21, 2020, from https://files.eric.ed.gov/fulltext/ED535214.pdf

Labaree, D. F. (1997). Public goods, private goods: The American struggle over educational goals. *American Education Research Journal*, 34(1), 39–81.

Lanier, J. (2011). *You are not a gadget: A manifesto*. New York, NY: Vintage Books.
Lanier, J. (2018). *Ten arguments for deleting your social media accounts right now*. New York, NY: Henry Holt and Co.
Levinas, E. (1969). *Totality and infinity: An essay on exteriority* (A. Lingis, Trans.). Pittsburgh, PA: Duquesne University Press. (Original work published 1961).
Levinas, E. (1998). *Otherwise than being or beyond essence* (A. Lingis, Trans.). Pittsburgh, PA: Duquesne University Press. (Original work published 1974).
Mobley Jr., S. D. (2015). *Difference amongst your own: The lived experiences of lowincome African-American students and their encounters with class within elite historically Black college (HBCU) environments* (Doctoral dissertation). Retrieved from Digital Repository at the University of Maryland (DRUM).
Nietzsche, F. (1974). *The gay science: With a prelude in rhymes and an appendix of songs* (W. Kaufmann, Trans.). New York, NY: Random House. (Original work published 1887).
Nietzsche, F. (1980). *The advantage and disadvantage of history for life* (P. Preuss, Trans.). Cambridge, UK: Hackett Publishing Company. (Original work published 1874).
Picard, M. (1930). *The human face* (G. Endore, Trans.). New York, NY: Farrar & Rinehart Inc.
Plato. (1997). *Complete works* (J. Cooper, Ed.). Cambridge, UK: Hackett Publishing Company.
Postman, N. (1992). *Technopoly: The surrender of culture to technology*. New York, NY: Alfred A. Knopf Inc.
Rorty, R. (1999). *Philosophy and social hope*. New York, NY: Penguin Books.
Rorty, R. (2007). *Philosophy as social politics*. Cambridge, UK: Cambridge University Publishing.
Rothenberg, A. (2014). *Flight from wonder: An investigation of scientific creativity*. Oxford, UK: Oxford University Press.
Sheehan, G. (2014). *Running & being: The total experience*. New York, NY: Rodale. (Original work published 1978).
Stack, S. (2015). Learning outcomes in an online vs. traditional course. *International Journal for the Scholarship of Teaching and Learning*, 9(1), 1–20.
Steeves, H. P. (2006). *The things themselves: Phenomenology and the return to theeveryday*. Albany: State University of New York Press.
Tallis, R. (2016). *Aping mankind*. New York, NY: Routledge Classics.
Thiele, L. P. (1995). *Timely meditations: Martin Heidegger and postmodern politics*. Princeton, NJ: Princeton University Press.
Thomson, I. (2005). *Heidegger on ontotheology: Technology and the politics of education*. Cambridge, UK: Cambridge University Press.
Thomson, I. (2011). *Heidegger, art and postmodernity*. Cambridge, UK: Cambridge University Press.
Turkle, S. (2015). *Reclaiming conversation: The Power of talk in a digital age*. London, UK: Penguin Press.
Turkle, S. (2017). *Alone together: Why we expect more from technology and less from each other*. New York, NY: Basic Books.

Van Manen, M. (1990). *Researching lived experience*. Albany, NY: The State University of New York Press.

Van Manen, M. (1991). *The tact of teaching: The Meaning of pedagogical thoughtfulness*. New York, NY: SUNY Press.

Van Manen, M. (2007). Phenomenology of practice. *Phenomenology and Practice*, *1*(1), 11–30.

2 The Withdrawn or Lost Face of Online Undergraduate Learning

Beginning to Offer: The Showing and Revealing of Themes

To open the thematic rendering of my phenomenon, I begin with long summarizing quotes from some of my participants over the next few chapters. The long passages show the range of experience within the phenomenon of non-face-to-face learning. More importantly, the detail and comprehensiveness of these passages helps to begin the revealing of the essence(s) of what is lost in non-face-to-face undergraduate learning. By starting to think about the facets of the experience revealed by my participants, I can begin to understand its context. Once I can situate myself in the context of their experience, I am able to begin to feel my way toward an articulation of its possible meaning(s). After some individual examination of these long passages, subsequent chapters progress by presenting primary themes. These themes and their sub-themes can be roughly introduced by having in mind the following four questions about what is lost in online learning: (1) Can those in non-face-to-face classes be called upon to interact with others in that experience? (2) What calls on students in their being-in-the-world to put themselves into non-face-to-face classes? (3) What does the technological attitude do to the learning experience of my participants? (4) What do my participants do to search for faces where there are none?

There is so much unarticulated or unarticulatable understanding that we have of human embodied communication. In our being-with-others there is at least as much non-discursive knowledge as there is with any of our most advanced skills. The professional baseball player can no more explain how to hit a homerun than he can diagram it or provide insight into how to create an algorithm for it. In the same way, a professional chef, a musician or a mechanic cannot fully articulate (i.e., make explicit) how they are able to solve problems or be creative. In all of our being-in-the-world, we act toward things and engage with others in ways that we cannot fully explain. An example Hubert Dreyfus (2008) uses is the differences between cultures in how far is normal to stand from others. How to social distance according to familiarity or the purpose of the interaction

DOI: 10.4324/9781003349051-2

is never something that is explicitly taught, and yet individuals in every culture learn it, and since COVID-19 our sense of social distancing has been changed. Thus, when my participants recount their experience of non-face-to-face learning as they lived it, they recognize the absence of something. They are able to connect the experience to the withdrawal of something that is normally present in their average everyday engagement with the world.

It is not merely the faulty formatting of remote learning or technical issues that elicits the overwhelming negative focus of the characterizations of what is lost from remote learning. Instead, for my participants, it is most often the non-face-to-face nature of these classes. To wit there is no technological solution or equivalent remote compensation that can make up for what is lost in online undergraduate learning. It is the expression of the participants' experiences that leads to the interpretation that remote classes are a compromised form of learning.

The Work and the Normal

I begin here with one of the most positive accounts of remote learning. Even in this happy and glowing account what is lost in online learning can be noticed. Indeed, it is one of the principle insights of this book that positivity toward the experience of remote learning is no indication that nothing is lost from education. As is shown here, it is often what is lost from learning that makes students feel like the experience is positive. Here is some of what John presented to me in conversation about how he experienced online learning:

> The work itself honestly does not change from an online class to a non-online class. Actually doing the work itself is relatively the same. … All of the reading that's done essentially would be the same reading you'd be doing in normal studying. You just find a nice spot and you sit down and read. That part of the experience is just the same. A lot of the experience from an in-person class to an online class is the same. The big difference is just not being there with everyone else. I think that is honestly the best way to describe the experience. I want you to imagine being in a normal class, having a normal class, you have to go every single day to get the assignments, the teacher tells you about it, he gives you assigned reading. I want you to just take away the classroom part entirely, the teacher part entirely and all your classmates entirely. Just take all that away, that's an online class. That's the simplest way to describe it. It's not entirely accurate because there's a couple less stringent parts to it, but that is like 90% of it. All of that classroom stuff is not there. That's what I would describe as the best part of the experience. Not having. The rest is the same. Nothing else changes when it comes to the actual work itself.

The Withdrawn or Lost Face of Online Undergraduate Learning 41

John has taken many non-face-to-face undergraduate classes. In the last few years, he had to transfer back home from a "party school" in the Midwest. As he is preparing to complete his degree at a new university, he has discovered that many of his classes are not accepted for transfer credit, so he has to re-take them. John takes the classes online as a priority in order to get through the repetition and redundancy of courses and content as efficiently as possible. He explains to me that with the flexibility and saved time he is able to work as a lead salesperson, even becoming a manager. He lives at home and is a top-level competitive "gamer" on par with those who play video games professionally. He has a special keyboard and double monitor computer setup in his basement where he plays. He also uses the keyboard to type work for his classes because of how satisfying it is to press the keys; they give a "satisfying" click, with each depression. Since he is taking so many non-face-to-face classes, he spends more time in his familiar environment with his favorite equipment than he would be able to if he were in traditional in-person classes.

In the passage above John describes the experience of non-face-to-face learning in comparative terms. He consistently links his description by using words such as "normal," "non-online" or "in-person" undergraduate class. His description bounces back and forth from the non-face-to-face experience and what he assumes is understood and shared, i.e., traditional learning. He grasps the conceptual tool of contrast and comparison with vigor, as he defines it, by using the differences between the two experiences to highlight what is essential to the online experience. As we talk, I can tell he is sensitive to my reactions; it often seems like he is trying to figure out what I want.

Heidegger (1962) uses the term *Dasein*, typically left untranslated to mean the kind of being that we humans have. Its literal German meaning can be translated as "being-there." It is precisely "being-there" that John says is gone in a non-face-to-face class. What John's experience shows me is that something that is lost in remote learning is the place of our being, the ability to be there. I interpret him to be saying that there is no human being-ness in an online class. Not only is there nowhere to be, even if there were, nobody is there. It is perhaps an extreme interpretation of the increasingly more common and thus mundane experience of online classes that perhaps they do not allow the human being to be. Without a "there" for our being, the specifically human way of comporting to the work is truncated in the online virtual space. To take away the place, the there of our being, is to displace our sense of beings who dwell (Heidegger, 1971).

John uses "the work" to denote what is shared between the two types of classes, i.e., the course content. Presumably, "the work" must be equal between the two formats of instruction; otherwise, the courses would not be equivalent, the online version would not fulfill what is satisfied by completing the other. Here John uses "the work" to mean basically the required reading, something that he understands as essential material that must be covered. It does not seem to capture assignments related to the readings, e.g., papers and quizzes. Even if there may be some reading he could skim or skip, there is still some that is just work that can't be avoided. What makes it work is the time it demands, being integral to the course. That material, he shows, has to be the same no matter what the course format. But this work has an aspect of choice to it. He has to decide how much of it is *really* essential and required for him to get what he wants out of the course. Getting these readings done is on him. In order to complete the course, it is something he has to figure out. He is always trying to figure out how much of the course really is this kind of "work." "The work" implies the part of the course that no matter what will be his responsibility.

Since John strives for the greatest efficiency, he is gratified that he does not have to be burdened by the need for much interaction with others, professor or students. The efficiency is found at the cost of withdrawing the face of others. It is to de-personalize the experience by removing the delicate and intricate complexity inherent in other persons. For as O'Donohue says, "The human face is the subtle yet visual autobiography of each person" (1997, p. 39). None of that subtle individuality is necessary to John's goal of completing the work. He *could* engage with some aspects of the individuality of his fellows, but he does not have to.

John's frequent use of "normal" is meant to connect to the traditional notion of a face-to-face class. For him, normal also seems to carry with it a burden, the weight of fullness or completeness. It is meant to show that with the normal comes a comparative decrease in efficiency. For John, the primary cause of inefficiency is other people. He understands that online learning rewards those who are looking for the withdrawal and loss of face-to-face contact with others. Efficiency is gained because, as phenomenologist of technology and education Catherine Adams puts it, "The mediatic veil of technology fails the test of pedagogic immediacy and meaningfulness" (2011, p. 270). A more efficient class is the product of what is left over after technology filters out inefficient aspects of experience such as personal immediacy and shared contextual significance; these are two important aspects of what are lost in remote learning.

To be a student in a normal class, John shows that you have to *get ready*; you have to *go there* and *pay attention*. In his account of the normal interaction with the professor, it is of an intermediary, someone who is superfluous, but who is necessary to get what is needed. The teacher stands as one who distributes what is needed according to a predetermined schedule. What John says shows that for him, in an online class, he has more control, he can get the material and the instructions and do the work without any mediation. Removing the personal immediacy of being with a professor in-person and sharing the same contextual significance of the classroom allows the student to have more control over the learning experience. The diminished form of learning that remains is more easily subject to the personal mastery of the student. It is less of a social process and more of an individual conquest.

John says that to do the work, which mostly refers to reading, he finds a "nice spot." In one of our conversations, I ask him, "What is your physical place of learning?" He describes this as "Sunroom. I sleep and then I wake up. I need a sunny area with a nice chair and a cup of coffee." What a nice place indeed – a room bright with the clear light of the sun. I know that John is a bit of an insomniac. Sleeping during the day is one of his biggest impediments to academic work, so getting a good nap removes one major cause of procrastination. The place he learns in sounds much better than a stiff public classroom, hard chairs with lots of other people under fluorescent lights. Alone, fully rested and with plenty of caffeine, he says, "I could do a weeks' worth of online classes in three hours." As he establishes this routine and applies a degree of self-knowledge, he has found himself to be very proficient at completing online classes.

What Is Withdrawn and Lost Along with the Absent Face

John's description of non-face-to-face learning shows that more than just the faces of other people are removed. He asks me to imagine a normal class and start removing all of the things that I encounter there: the professor, classmates, the room, the desks, the place, everything. He is asking me to pull all these things away and look at what I have left. His thought experiment leaves me with nothing physical or significant, like Gertrude Stein said, "there is no there there" (more on this later). As I imagine, I suppose there could still be a required text or two, but even that could be in a file on the course website. The technological efficiency of the online class is to withdraw so much of what is normally expected in a class and to leave behind strange new vestigial traces. In his extremely thorough analysis of Heidegger's phenomenology of technology, philosopher Richard Rojcewicz explains,

> Technological things do not present themselves in a reticent way or even in a neutral way. They are insistent; they work upon us insidiously, and relentlessly, until they make a claim that excludes all other claims. That is to say, technology fascinates us and claims our undivided attention.
>
> (2006, p. 218)

It is this sense of seduction by the advantages of technology that I get from John. For him, he is drawn to defining his learning by how efficient non-face-to-face learning is.

The faceless class is a kind of no-thing and no-place. As might be expected by anything mitigated by the medium of the Internet, it is essentially immaterial. John does admit that his thought experiment definition is not "entirely accurate." The non-face-to-face class would of course, for example, still require a computer and all the physical things and space they need to access the online class through the Internet. However, even in 1997 John O'Donohue could say, "Technology and media are not uniting the world" (p. 17). The sense that all the things that are gone from an online class do not in fact matter for learning is a potentially hasty misstep that John accepts. O'Donohue continues, "They pretend to provide a world that is internetted, but in reality, all they deliver is a simulated world of shadows" (Ibid.) John is asking me to imagine shadows; it is all immaterial and mutable. This shadow world of remote learning is what we are left with when the faces of the professor and other students are lost.

The narrative of virtual connection rings hollow. The more we live with the notion of online "connection," the more we know it is inadequate. The narrative rests on the factual inability to experience the world when it becomes highly technologically mitigated. Heidegger (1977) noted that it is correct to define technology as a "human activity." So, in a sense everything we do is a kind of technology. However, with the advancements of computer technology our innovations are becoming nested, efficiencies inside of efficiencies. As technology becomes more mysterious and essential, we become further removed from the natural environment and traditional constraints of existence. For John, non-face-to-face learning is *an* experience but is it *the* experience he really wants or needs? How do students know what they need aside from the imperatives placed before them?

Norm Friesen's (2016) phenomenological analysis of online discussion boards taps into the same level of physical absence that John notices. John is enthusiastic about the efficiencies offered by immateriality and absence. These gains in efficiency come with a trade-off. Friesen observes, "An online discussion has a structure that is much less disorderly and amorphous than a regular classroom conversation. The interruptions, lack of clear order, and 'un-repeatability' of face-to-face discussion are deftly circumvented" (2016, p. 230). To make something repeatable is an important aspect of efficiency. Like Heidegger's (1977) distinction between ancient and modern technology, one of the key differences is the kind of uniformity that comes from machine manufacturing, i.e., exact repeatability. However, learning how to fall into a conversational mode or attitude about important topics is an important part of undergraduate learning. Thus, one of the most vital things that is lost from remote learning is conversation. Students in online classes do not have real or what we might consider "full" conversations. Moreover, the loss of conversations means that undergraduates learning non-face-to-face have less proficiency and skill at engaging in the sort of high-level dialogical exchanges we typically might expect from fully educated undergraduates.

References

Adams, C., & Thompson, T. L. (2011). Interviewing objects: Including educational technologies as qualitative research participants. *International Journal of Qualitative Studies in Education*, 24(6), 733–750.

Dreyfus, H. L. (2008). *On the internet (thinking in action)*. London, UK: Routledge.

Friesen, N. (2016). Is there a body in this class? In V. M. Manen (Ed.), *Writing in the dark* (pp. 223–235). New York, NY: Routledge.

Heidegger, M. (1962). *Being and time* (J. Macquarrie & E. Robinson, Trans.). New York, NY: HarperCollins. (Original work published 1926).

Heidegger, M. (1971). *Poetry, language, thought*. New York, NY: HarperCollins.

Heidegger, M. (1977). *The question concerning technology, and other essays* (W. Levitt, Trans.). New York, NY: HarperCollins. (Original works published 1962, 1952 & 1954)

O'Donohue, J. (1997). *Anam cara*. New York, NY: Cliff Street Books.

Rojcewicz, R. (2006). *The gods and technology: A reading of Heidegger*. Albany, NY: State University of New York Press.

3 The Irksome Face of Online Undergraduate Learning

Danna described her synchronous non-face-to-face class as a kind of annoying and tedious chore:

> We had to figure out how all of the technology worked and so the teacher had to tell us what platform we went to, how to make sure the audio was working, projects we would have in class, and it was interesting to get to understand that this was how we were going to get to communicate if we were not in a room together. But I found it really annoying the whole time. It was all this extra stuff that really had nothing to do with the content of the class and you just had to do it for the sake of getting connected to the class. If the Internet was not working you would have to get up and move to adjust those conditions. And then the first class there was of course a lot of technical difficulty. The woman [the professor] was all the way in Colorado and all of your classmates, well you don't know where they are. And I would always go to this classroom in one of the buildings that wasn't being occupied during the time. So I was just in there with a very quiet room. But the first class she ran through the syllabus and I think she projected it on the screen and anytime she did PowerPoints she would put it on the screen and underline it so we could follow along and contribute to the conversation. I remember thinking it was all really tedious. She would read from the slide and underline here and there, and occasionally she would randomly call students to ask questions. And she would get frustrated because it was like, "So Britney what are the three…? It's on the slide and I had just went over that." Britney was probably doing something else and really was not in the moment. I really felt the whole time that I wasn't learning. I wasn't learning. It was just, here is a bunch of information. She was reading it to me and she would try and make it engage with a conversation but again with everyone being god knows where and you could not see her face either it was just the PowerPoint and whatever materials she had and would read off of or try and summarize. I just

remember it being kind of tedious and I think it was twice a week and we had to meet for at least an hour to just sit around.

Synchronicity and being able to hear the voices of the professor and other students during a specific weekly class time helped Danna's experience appear more like a face-to-face class. However, what comes to mind for Danna in her memory of the only non-face-to-face class she took as an undergraduate is primarily negative aspects of the experience. The fact that it was synchronous and connected by audio did not manifest itself to her as enhancing the course. Indeed, she spends some time describing how these aspects required "annoying" preliminary complications unrelated to the course content. The overall result was a class that she found "tedious" in which she "wasn't learning." When I asked her why she wasn't learning, she said that "fact and recall" are "not intellectually stimulating." She tells me that the class could have been done without the synchronous part since most of the material covered during that time was what she read in the text. For Danna, the synchronous class time was experienced as blatantly redundant, even in some sense punitive.

Tedium

Danna says "tedious" instead of "boring." It seems like she might have said boring but looking a bit at the etymology shows that "tedious" does reveal more of what she was experiencing. With tedious, as opposed to boredom we get the sense of *unnecessary* lengthening out, connected in meaning to the word "prolix": "of long duration, lengthy, protracted; overlong, overextended" for example "that which has flowed beyond its bounds." Tedious is related to the "humdrum," something that is "tiresome, from length or slowness, irksome." In comparison, boredom picks out those times that are not always lengthened for no reason. We can be bored of efficiency. We can feel bored "with" something even when what is happening is important or engaging (Heidegger, 1995/1929).

Interestingly, an etymological exploration connects two of her words. Tedious is connected to annoy by "irk." That is to say overall Danna is irked by the experience. It seems overlong and bothersome specifically because it didn't seem to need to be that way. The irksome quality of tedium is manifest in the experience of unnecessary obligation. She feels required to do that which should not be necessary. It is easy to pick up on her frustration. Part of her negative sense is due to a judgmental stance toward the class even while in the class. That is, it is not just in her memory that she now considers the class annoying and tedious; those were her feelings as she took the class. She really felt that she was being imposed on in an unnecessary way.

Even without being able to see the other students in the class Danna was aware of their similar annoyance with the tedium of the course. She recalls that at one point someone had forgotten to mute their microphone, and everyone could hear sounds of cooking. The long pauses after the professor asked questions were not attributable most to hesitation in not knowing the right answers, but rather in the need for students to take time to go back over the recent slides to be able to parrot back what was being requested. The tedium led to a palpable sense that for Danna her time was being wasted. "I am just sitting there having an audiobook read to me kind of thing." She tells me:

> I am the type of person who likes to prioritize efficiency so in a lot of my classes if I did not feel like I was receiving the information I would just not go to the class and read the textbook.

However, for this class she was required to *always* "show-up" by being present via her logged-in computer and availability to participate in the synchronous presentation. For an intelligent and dynamic student as Danna, it was not tolerable for prime hours of the day to be used inefficiently at school. Her experience shows that the often-stringent login and participation requirements for some synchronous online classes may make them less efficient for some students and push them toward distraction.

Efficiency

Danna told me that because the class was tedious, it made her feel like, "I could be using my time more effectively." Within her description of the experience, she shows that it drew herself out of it. She started to evaluate it by a standard of what she considered effectiveness, and it fell short. It was clear that what she meant by effectiveness was efficiency. She felt like the time was not effective because she was not getting enough done during that time. To make the experience more effective, she wanted to utilize the time more thoroughly to complete more of what she felt needed to be done.

Students, of course, could get this sense in any class, but something about this one non-face-to-face class made her sense that something was not measuring up, that there was a fullness, richness or completeness that was missing. As Glen Mazis explains, in his 2016 book on Merleau-Ponty's phenomenology of perception, "If one thinks of the face-to-face exchange with another person, we can recognize a different kind of back-and-forth energetic exchange of sense than occurs in other types of expression" (p. 82). The missing encounter of the energy of other faces in the classroom seemed to render the synchronous online class fairly pointless to Danna. Without the full encounter of face in her class, its purpose seemed to be diminished or missing. With less of a point, it was harder for her to justify the time she was spending with the class. Danna's unarticulated grasping at what was missing led her to fill the void with something.

To remedy the gap in effectiveness (best understood as efficiency), Danna spent her synchronous time doing homework. She said she tried to keep her multitasking to working on material for the class for two reasons: it made her feel less guilty, and if she was called on to respond to a question or contribute in some other way, she might be a little bit more prepared. However, since being called on was a comparative rarity in a class of about 30 students, she could make the time more effective by multitasking on non-class-related work as well. Danna said she was sure other students were doing the same. She said she could just tell by the occasional background noises and delayed responses. Sherry Turkle (2017) extensively reviewed all of the cutting-edge research on multitasking and concluded, "When psychologists study multitasking, they do not find a story of new efficiencies. Rather, multitaskers don't perform as well on any of the tasks they are attempting" (p. 163). If online classes encourage multitasking, even under the synchronous conditions that Danna experienced, something is being degraded. Either students like Danna are not paying attention to what is going on in the class or the homework they are doing suffers.

Multitasking

Khan Academy is one learning platform that helps to condition students to non-face-to-face learning before college. One of the main things that makes Khan Academy, and most online learning presentations, so convenient is that they allow for multitasking. Of course, sitting in a classroom listening to the teacher could be construed as a kind of multitasking if students are taking notes. However, the kind of multitasking afforded by the experience of online learning is different. For example, here is a recent anecdote from *ScienceDaily*:

> Kent State University Professor Andrew Lepp, Ph.D., remembers the incident well. About two years ago on campus, he encountered a student entering data into a spreadsheet using a desktop computer. Next to the desktop computer, the student had a laptop computer open with Netflix streaming. Beside the laptop was the student's smartphone, which the student was listening to through a pair of wired headphones. Being curious about the simultaneous use of three screens, Dr. Lepp asked the student what she was listening to on the headphones. "Oh, that's my online biology course," the student replied to Dr. Lepp's complete amazement. This phenomenon of multitasking across three or four internet-connected devices simultaneously is increasingly common. Dr. Lepp was curious to know how often this happens during online education, a method of delivering college and even high school courses entirely via an internet-connected computer as opposed to a traditional face-to-face course with a teacher physically present.
>
> (Kent State University, 2019)

How often indeed? Given the convenience afforded by online classes, it is not hard to imagine that students get up to all sorts of other activities while simultaneously doing non-face-to-face learning. Dr. Lepp went on to say, "This question is important to ask because an abundance of research demonstrates that multitasking during educational activities significantly reduces learning" (Ibid.). Based on his research, Dr. Lepp (2019) and his colleagues found the obvious: students multitask far more in non-face-to-face classes as compared to traditional classes. What is lost in remote learning allows students to practice at divided attention, not mindfulness.

Students online could be taking notes about asynchronous video lecture or they could be listening to the presentation on Khan Academy while scanning their email, writing a reply, monitoring the news etc. There really is nothing to check how much students can divide their attention from a specific learning task. It is completely up to them to be responsible with how much deviation, distraction and interruption they allow into their non-face-to-face learning experience. A study titled "Effects of Multitasking on Retention and Topic Interest" showed that for most students the temptations offered by the Internet itself are often too distracting to keep focused on the task and effort required to learn in an online class (Dindar & Akbulut, 2016). Taking account of the distractions of the Internet and the many other responsibilities undergraduates juggle, the ease and convenience of non-face-to-face learning is practically designed to slip into a highly degraded form of learning because it is so easy to become unfocused.

Taking notes in a traditional class divides attention, but only about the same topic or intentional issue at hand, i.e., learning from what is going on in the classroom. Students in a traditional classroom are there to learn; they intend, to one degree or another, to get something out of the experience. If taking notes deviates students' attention from listening, then so be it, as long as it helps them to achieve the purpose of taking away some learning that was intended by the professor for the course on that day. Though taking notes, strictly speaking, is a form of multitasking, it is nothing compared to the radically disparate activities facilitated by the convenience of non-face-to-face learning.

Students in a traditional classroom can divide their attention between sundry topics unrelated to the content of the course or the current discussion the professor may be conducting, e.g. their minds can wander and daydream. Adding to that possibility we have introduced an array of distracting devices into the classroom. The contemporary computer technology that washes around us seems to be the source of so much ease and flexibility. It particularly allows us to divert our attention in ways impossible before. Many teachers today lament having the experience of students who brazenly, or in a clandestine manner, use their smartphones or computers to scan the Internet, e.g. Facebook, Twitter and WhatsApp (recently, one of my distracted students confessed to repeatedly monitoring his stock trades). These students are in class bodily, but they are switching their attention back and forth between a chat with a group of friends, online updates from their social network and shopping. This diversion of attention has been roundly criticized when it happens in the classroom, but there is nothing to stop it from happening for solitary online learners alone in their bedroom or sitting in a coffee shop.

One reason the in-class multitasking with electronics is criticized is that even if it is argued that the students only harm themselves and their own potential learning, and grade on the exam for example, they are also almost guaranteed to be causing a distraction to others in the class (Fried, 2008). The broad multitasking allowed by computers in the classroom seems to dilute the intentional outcome of the classroom. If students are not committed to paying attention, with those they are with, to the matter at hand, then the overall learning experience is diminished. If it is a problem in traditional classes, then how much more of an issue is it in online classes? As Dr. Lepp (2019) found, it is a huge factor.

Once I saw a fellow classmate, sitting next to me, scanning the Internet and shopping for shoes. Seeing the shoes flash by as she scrolled through the colorful online catalog completely took away my attention from the small seminar we were supposed to be participating in. It was not that I cared that she was looking at shoes or that I was reminded of some of my own shoe shopping that I needed to do. Rather, when I saw her scanning the Internet, I felt that it disparaged what was happening in the class. To me, it seemed that she was making a judgment, "I have more important things to do than give my undivided attention to this class." It was also a potential judgment about what she felt was required to pass the course. In her mind it is possible she felt the course was structured in such a way that the lectures were linked only loosely to the assessments, and, therefore, applying the attitude of efficiency, she was disposed to divide her attention. She probably had experience and knew that in this type of course she could succeed according to her standards without always giving full attention to the lectures. However, the shock for me was that the thing she had found to replace attention to the class was footwear. That realization made me begin to wonder also if the class was not worth my attention. Here was someone I respected, sitting right next to me, who had made the determination that what was going on did not *really* matter. As I thought, I then became distracted by trying to figure out what was important about the class, when my clearly intelligent neighbor didn't think it was. I wondered if I was being duped. Was it silly for me to be giving my full attention? I wondered, "Should I be doing something else while in this class so as to maximize my time and not waste it?" I was able to get my attention back on class, but it seemed to be less focused. I had lost something by being distracted. The experience of witnessing someone else's distraction not only distracted me – I joined them – but it also degraded the learning experience by sowing doubt.

By being able to move about, jumping from one task to another and then back, students might feel that they are using their time more efficiently because they are getting more tasks done in the same amount of time. However, this seems reasonable only if they define the learning they are intent on gaining as somehow equivalent to getting through a task, e.g. a recorded video or online task. Indeed, the completion model of education seems to invite the pressure to multitask during non-face-to-face learning. Students in online classes often have an intense urge to complete the task so as to mark it done. Their expectation is that mere exposure will be enough to learn the content. But, in their urge to finish the discussion board post or online article, it is hard to say how multitasking impacts the effectiveness of their learning. How can they know that missing a few questions on a review quiz would not even have happened if they had given their full attention? If they do consider the outcome to have been due to their own divided attention, it still might be considered a worthwhile trade given if they feel they were being more efficient. Thus, what is lost in online learning due to the opportunity and even incentive to multitask is the sense that the learning task matters at all. As long as it is completed, it is all that matters, not whether the student knows more or feels they have learned.

References

Dindar, M., & Akbulut, Y. (2016). Effects of multitasking on retention and topic interest. *Learning and Instruction*, *41*, 94–105.

Fried, C. B. (2008). In-class laptop use and its effects on student learning. *Computers & Education*, *50*, 906–914.

Heidegger, M. (1995). *The fundamental concepts of metaphysics: World, finitude, solitude* (W. McNeill & N. Walker, Trans.). Bloomington, IN: Indiana University Press. (Original work published 1929).

Kent State University. (2019). Multitasking increases in online courses compared to face-to-face. *ScienceDaily.* Retrieved February 4, 2020, from www.sciencedaily.com/releases/2019/02/190214153135.htm

Lepp, A., Barkley, J., Karpinski, A., & Shweta, S. (2019). College students' multitasking behavior in online versus face-to-face courses. *SAGE Open*, *9*(1).

Mazis, G. (2016). *Merleau-Ponty and the face of the world: Silence, ethics, imagination, and poetic ontology*. Albany, NY: State University of New York Press.

Turkle, S. (2017). *Alone together: Why we expect more from technology and less from each other*. New York, NY: Basic Books.

4 Experiencing the Synchronous but Absent Face

One of the participants in my study, Danna, tells me, "In this class we did not really discuss and it was not face-to-face so you could not really gauge reactions. You couldn't gauge – you couldn't tell the emotional expressions so I honestly was doing other work." It is through encounters with the faces of others that we are able to normally gauge reactions. Danna's sense is that she is there with others in the class but their absence means that they are not her neighbors. She cannot fully depend or relate to them. To help draw out the meaning of this experience, I am reminded of Heidegger's work in the phenomenology of language. In his essay "The Nature of Language," he works out the relation of neighborliness and the lived nature of language, i.e., poetry. Heidegger explains:

> Neighborhood, then, is a relation resulting from the fact that the one settles face to face with the other. Accordingly, the phrase of the neighborhood of poetry and thinking means that the two dwell face to face with each other, that the one has settled facing the other, has drawn into the other's nearness.
>
> (1982, p. 82)

When we are face-to-face, we have been "drawn into the other's nearness." To draw into their nearness is to allow yourself to become partly them, and they become partly what you are. In the face-to-face encounter, we reflect the other back to themselves. We also experience ourselves reflected back to us. To be face-to-face is to settle into mutual self-revealing.

Before proceeding, it is important to note a word that Danna used in her last quote, mentioned above. For Danna to use the word "gauge" shows that she is getting at a comparative notion, "to ascertain by exact measurement." To measure is to understand by a standard, to discover what something is in relation to something else. Deep in our philosophical consciousness is the phrase from Protagoras echoing down through the millennia, "Man is the measure of all things." As a fragmentary sentence, we do not have the full context of what Protagoras may have been trying to reveal. However, it seems that individuals, to some degree or another, determine how we will understand something. That is, what we encounter in experience, to a certain extent, is ours to make of what we will. Danna's point is that she could not make the experience fully her own because she was not given that with which she might gauge, i.e., the emotional expressions that would come from the face of her professor or classmates.

Synchronous but Lost

For Danna, it didn't matter that her experience of the other people in the class was synchronous because she could not receive what their faces could convey. Losing contact with the others in this way was too much. It was impossible for her to find a bridge over the gulf between others created by their lost faces, so she multitasked.

> I didn't feel like it was the best discussion ever, even though it was virtual and we were all there. You almost couldn't keep someone accountable because you didn't know what they were doing – [whether] they were listening – for all you knew they could have just turned it on and muted it. You could do other work and engage once and awhile enough to meet the basic requirement.

For Danna, when face-to-face contact is lost she does not feel accountable. Full contact with others pleads with her and calls forth the need for her to give her attention. She knew that the synchronous virtuality of the experience was an attempt to bridge the dis-placement of physical presence, but it was insufficient.

Thinking about what her professor might have been trying to do with her non-visual presence, I ask Danna, "If you had face-to-face contact you feel you could have seen the professor's emphasis?" Danna explains:

> We could not see her so it made it very hard for us to really take it seriously … when you are a classroom teacher, one of the strategies to get kids to pay attention is just proximity, just get close to them, to the kid. We did not really have that; she did not see us face-to-face so we did not know what she took seriously or not.

Danna seems to be explaining that without the physical presence of her teacher, without seeing, for example, raised eyebrows, widened or narrowed eyes, hand gestures or a quick turn of the head etc., she could not readily distinguish the relevance of the information being presented. For her, it would have been the teacher's embodiment and particularly her face that would communicate what should be emphasized. It would have been the way Danna interpreted the face of her teacher that would have helped her to see the texture of the material in such a way that she could more fully grasp its relevance and make it her own. With the loss of her teacher's face, it was as if all the information were uniform. The uniformity of the presentation was related to its facelessness.

The uniformity and monolithic absence of the living presence of a face in her synchronous class did not just create annoyance for Danna, it also frustrated her teacher. The teacher's frustration became part of Danna's learning experience. She explains:

> There were times that she got frustrated ... she would ask a question and nobody would answer because I am sure everyone checked out. You would hear her say 'So what's the answer?' and you could hear her increase her voice level.

The increased voice level is something that would be meaningful in a recorded lecture but even more significant in a synchronous online audio exchange. It communicated to Danna the emotional state of her teacher and how she was experiencing the students' engagement with her presentations. Danna notes the voice here, a vestigial element of real face-to-face interactions, only to highlight how it conveyed frustration. She never tells me that the sound of the voice helped her to know what the professor was excited about or even if it helped to convey notes of caring. The disembodied voice of her teacher was only noteworthy because it revealed negative emotions that Danna felt too. Maybe if she had felt less frustrated by the course the synchronous encounter with the lost face but heard voice would have sounded positive.

The Virtual: Failed Simulacrum?

In conversation with Danna, it is possible to become aware of the various tensions in non-face-to-face learning formats. I notice that the tensions develop around the parts of the experience that are meant to be like normal in-person classes. Students, especially those like Danna, who have only a few online classes, or don't want to take them, call out these attempts of copying or replacing. I notice for Danna the virtual failed because it created loss. It did not make her feel more responsible or less anonymous. Indeed, though her experience had the live synchronous aspect of the teacher's voice and the sounds of her classmates, it did little to make her feel like the class time was worth her attention. Compared to the asynchronous experience of most of the other participants, her attitude about the teacher and her classmates was similar.

In Sherry Turkle's book, *Alone Together: Why We Expect More from Technology and Less from Each Other* (2017), she says, "Sometimes people experience no sense of having communicated after hours of connection" (p. 12). Turkle goes on to say that this results in "a nagging question: Does virtual intimacy degrade our experience of the other kind and, indeed, of all encounters, of any kind?" (Ibid.) Virtuality can be understood as the attempt to make a partial copy or simulacrum of an experience, whether it is for learning, business or pleasure. The virtual is very close to fantasy. When we become so accustomed to virtuality, as with fantasy, we can start to feel frustrated with the non-virtual. Our frustration may be due to altered and unrealistic expectations.

The experience of non-face-to-face learning disturbs our typical sense of what is relevant. For undergraduate students like Danna, in an online class the normal cues of what is relevant are removed. For example, computer screens are the primary means by which the simulacrum of the classroom is recreated. However, unlike a classroom, a lived environment filled with ambiguity, risk and vulnerability (as well as the possibility for human contact, friendship and caring), the screen is always starkly naked and relevant. In Lucas Introna and Fernando Ilharco's article, "On the Meaning of Screens: Towards a Phenomenological Account of Screenness" (2006), they use a Heideggerian insight related to the "ready-to-hand" to explain, "Because the content in front of us [on the screen] always shows up within our involvement ... [being in a class and trying to complete the requirements] it is already presumed relevant, as deserving our attention" (pp. 64–65). They go on to say:

> This aspect is crucial. The content in front of us is not just presumed relevant, but is *already presumed* relevant. In soliciting our attention its relevance does not depend on its specific content but on a particular involvement in-the-world in which we dwell.
>
> (Ibid. emphasis in original)

The same goes for the voice of Danna's teacher and the sounds of her fellow students. Only she is frustrated that the relevance of these things goes unquestioned. The relevance, like that of what we encounter on a screen during our engagement with it, is presupposed and imposed. The simulacrum of the virtual fails in some sense because its relevance is always presumed.

The Space of the Present Absence

In an asynchronous class, the absence of the face is also made present. Instructors for these types of classes, where there is never any real-time interaction, make vestigial elements of their embodied presence knowable by "coming online" to check on a discussion thread posted to an Internet-learning platform such as Blackboard and Canvas. Professors' faces are not seen in these classes, though sometimes students are shown a photo next to a brief profile. Usually, students just have a name and an email address to identify their online professor's presence. But the name and symbols of the email stand in for the face in a non-face-to-face class.

When this slight remnant of presence is left online, as when the professor's name or username accompanies a typed comment or reply, students are able to experience the presence of their absent teacher. What does it mean to experience absence?

In *The Question Concerning Technology* (Heidegger, 1977), the translator explains that "the German noun *Gegenwart* means both 'presence' and 'the present.' It thus speaks of presence expressly in the present" (p. 158, fn.3). Becoming familiar with how Heidegger understood presence helps to see that the type of presence that the students experience in a non-face-to-face class is typically *not* of a presence in the present. When they experience the presence of the professor, or other students, it is through what they have left behind in what they have written, but they are no longer present in the moment that the student reads the words. It is a kind of partial presence or a lingering trace of what was *Gegenwart*. Full presence, in Heidegger's sense of *Gegenwart*, is not possible in the asynchronous online class.

> That which 'does' in such a sense is that which works; it is that which presences, in its presencing. The verb 'to work' understood in this way – namely, as to bring hither and forth – names, then, one way in which that which presences, presences.
>
> (Ibid., pp. 161–162)

Thus, the full presence of teachers is lost in a remote class. Teachers are present only to students when they are working. When they are "performing and executing," teachers appear only by direct actions; they become real when they perform as teachers. In meaningful striving and engaging, the professor of an online class becomes present. In a normal class, there is the possibility for passive or restful presence in the sense that the mere appearance, the embodied presentation of the professor, in whatever capacity, during class time is a presencing.

As Danna's experience shows, the place or space of non-face-to-face learning is a fraught issue. The idea that the cyber world is an actual place or the space where students "go" when they learn online is a metaphorical transfer of location even when there is in fact no real spatial differentiation. However, as with all powerful metaphors, there is the tendency for slippage. The metaphor can become *the* reality. The metaphor can be literalized erroneously; such a mistake leads to a faulty understanding of space. According to van Manen's account of the existential of space, it is impossible to define the cyber world as an actual place.

> We know that the space in which we find ourselves affects the way we feel. The huge spaces of a modern bank building may make us feel small, the wide-open spaces of a landscape may make us feel exposed but also possibly free, and just the opposite from the feeling we get in

> a crowded elevator. As we walk into a cathedral we may be overcome by a silent sense of the transcendental even if we ordinarily are not particularly religious or churchgoing. Walking alone in a foreign and busy city may render a sense of lostness, strangeness, vulnerability, and possibly excitement or stimulation. In general, we may say that we become the space we are in.
>
> (1990, p. 102)

Because non-face-to-face learning can happen in any space, the space in which it happens can, following van Manen, make the experience what it is. Unlike the classroom that is a certain kind of space, the cyber world or space of online learning is everywhere and thus, in some way, nowhere.

Even though Danna could hear the others in her class, she was not with them in the same space. Somewhat ironically the place that Danna chose to do her remote class was in an empty classroom. She put herself in a place designed for learning face-to-face with others. In that space of learning, alone, she was not able to share the place of learning because she was not there in that empty room with anyone else. Danna's body was not with the others in her class. This spatial disconnection also has a temporal aspect.

We cannot be in time, subjective or otherwise, if we are not bodies, and "we are always bodily in the world" (van Manen, 1990, p. 103). In the same way, talk of the lived experience of space is meaningless without the underlying fact of our bodies. But as corporeal beings, we are also fundamentally in relation to others. We exist in time and space with others because of our bodies. The setting of non-face-to-face learning is relational. However, the setting of non-face-to-face learning filters out aspects of lived space, corporeality and, to a great extent, directs relation with others.

> When we meet another person in his or her landscape or world, we meet that person first of all through his or her body. In our physical bodily presence, we both reveal something about ourselves and we always conceal something at the same time.
>
> (Ibid.)

How can we come to know others without an encounter with what we most share with them, our corporeality? No doubt there is much that can be related to through text, images and video, but these only convey traces of the body. Real-time embodied encounters with others are the least efficient and thus antithetical to the driving impulse of technological thinking.

References

Heidegger, M. (1977). *The question concerning technology, and other essays* (W. Levitt, Trans.). New York, NY: HarperCollins. (Original works published 1962, 1952 & 1954).

Heidegger, M. (1982). *On the way to language* (P. D. Hertz, Trans.). New York, NY: Harper & Row, Publishers, Inc. (Original work published 1959).

Introna, L., & Ilharco, F. M. (2006). On the meaning of screens: Towards a phenomenological account of screenness. *Human Studies, 29*, 57–76.

Turkle, S. (2017). *Alone together: Why we expect more from technology and less from each other*. New York, NY: Basic Books.

Van Manen, M. (1990). *Researching lived experience*. Albany, NY: The State University of New York Press.

5 Writing to No Face and Everyone
The Present Absence

Presence-ing of the Face during Online Learning

In my conversations with a participant named Lane, I was presented with instances of careful naming of the phenomenon of non-face-to-face learning. He is an older-than-normal student who returned to school after two short but successful careers as a chef and managing a veterinarian hospital. His course was designed, as are many online, with a significant portion of time required posting and replying to other students. Another participant, Evan, described these online "discussions" in this way, "The message board was to try and give you the experience of having, you know, a dialogue with other students about the content." The posting of comments or questions and requiring a degree of interaction or reciprocal replies is a vital part of most of my participants' experience of asynchronous online classes.

Lane felt that the teacher's online activity catalyzed the whole experience:

> Her presence would come at the end of the class and that is when everyone else would actually start responding. So responses would come at the very end of the week after initial responses had been put in at the beginning so then it would just be, everyone would be rushing. So that's the way the classes work. She would show up and – hey what's going on? And then it was like everybody was trying to put their responses in.

Lane felt his teacher's presence in the remote class but something was missing. It could not have been what we typically mean by someone's presence. Her embodied, synchronous and lived presence was not manifest in his online class. However, she did make her being and personality known. It mattered that she engaged with students and that they knew she was there. She was not there in a physical sense, but by interacting with them via text online they had a sense that her physical presence was somewhere.

DOI: 10.4324/9781003349051-5

One of the primary ways that Lane's teacher made her face-less presence known was through her textual replies to students' online posts. The manifestation of her engagement with the textual material heightened the importance of the assignment for the students. The teacher's presence, such as it was, was the whole point of the effort and was looked to as the primary means by which students could be evaluated for their efforts. In Lane's class, there was a lag between when students could post an initial response to a reading or viewing assignments and when they were *required* to reply to the initial postings of other students. Lane explained that this caused a procrastination and rush pattern that made it hard for him to get into the flow of the class, or to really take the posts of other students as seriously as he would have liked.

Lane noticed that the teacher's entrance into the flow of textual "discussion" gave a distinct temporal dimension to the experience. It caused the students to wait till the last minute. The effort expended was seen, for Lane, as only relevant if it came right before the moment the students knew the teacher would have a view on their work. The absence of the teacher meant that if the students knew that nobody was watching, in any meaningful and apparent way, they would just wait until they knew it was about time for the teacher to "come online."

Learning Discussion Boards

The justification for the discussion board posting assignments is that they bring the students together and increase learning (Cho & Tobias, 2016). It is as close as many online classes can come to having an actual discussion. Online course designers acknowledge the power of discussion for learning, but the version created by online posting and the accompanying rules go a long way toward radically altering the nature of the exchange (Lieberman, 2019). For example, it becomes a task to check off and complete instead of something that you are drawn into naturally due to curiosity or because of a desire to engage in thoughtful reflection with other students. The assignment also seems, like many heavily technologically mitigated exchanges, to dwell primarily in the realm of safety rather than allowing for risk. It is hard to know why one should be bold when all that is really required is the posting of text. Many of the complaints students have with the assignment relate to the superficiality with which it is engaged with and evaluated by professors. Even if teachers do read all the exchanges, students know that the posts do not really matter much, i.e., it will not alter their grade. So long as there is evidence that they did the assignment, presented some required quantity of text, at the right time, the quality can only be commented on and is generally never penalized.

Friesen's phenomenology of the discussion board posting in online classes shows how they fail:

> There is an experiential gulf ... that separates what happens in online forums from what can happen in the classroom. The existence of this gulf is all too often ignored by experts who study and make recommendations for the use of these online forums. Experts ... quite explicitly characterize the activities that these technologies facilitate as 'discussion'.
>
> (2016, p. 233)

Friesen's point is that they are not discussions. The posting of comments online can be called a conversation, but doing so requires such a narrow understanding of that phenomenon. It is an utter distortion, one that is allowed because asynchronous learning that also requires interaction must be done with textual material created and left behind by faceless others.

As noted in Chapter 1, the ancient Greek word for human being, *anthropos*, is defined as that which has a human face. The loss of face-to-face pedagogical encounters is definitive of most online learning. The exception is video lectures, but even this is not truly face-to-face since it is not fully reciprocal and is almost never in real time. Even real-time video contact via Skype or Zoom is a diminished face-to-face experience since shared eye contact is impossible (Dreyfus, 2008; Turkle, 2015). On a Zoom call if I *appear* to be looking you in the eye, all that I am seeing is the small circle of my computer's camera. On the other hand, if I look directly at your eyes, if I try to meet them on the screen, I will appear to you on the other end of the Zoom call to be looking down, i.e., to explicitly *not* be making eye contact. Face-to-screen is not face-to-face. The screen is not and can never be *anthropos*.

Similar to the ethical phenomenological call found in Levinas much of John O'Donohue's discussion of the face turns on the following point, "[face] is the most amazing thing in creation. In the human face, the anonymity of the universe becomes intimate" (1997, p. 37). Here O'Donohue is trying to explain that the value of the face, what makes it special and precious, is its ability to reflect, or show, *better than anything else* immaterial consciousness in matter. The face is the outward physical expression of freedom. The "anonymity of the universe" is the mute dumbness of material reality – it does not speak, only something with a human face can speak. The human face is capable of unmatched subtlety of expression. No other animal has as expressive a face as human beings, and it is a vital component of our experience of the world:

> You can situate human beings entirely in the world of objects. In doing so you will in all probability reduce them to animals whose behavior is to be explained by some combination of evolutionary psychology and neuroscience. But then you will find yourself describing a world from which human action, intention, responsibility,

freedom and emotions have been wiped away: it will be a world without a face. The face shines in the world of objects with a light that is *not* of this world – the light of subjectivity.

(Scruton, 2014, p. 42)

The face is one of the definitive conduits to our essentially subjective lived experience. It is the clearest manifestation of our transcendent freedom as *persons*. Even narrowly partitioned portions of the face are immensely complex in the range of information that they can convey. How much is communicated by the eyes and lips separately? *Anthropos*, the entity with a human face, has the ability to demonstrate such great flexibility; it therefore is imbued with hermeneutic richness. The face of a person is the most amazing thing in the world. It is precious.

Dependent on the Absent Other

Because of the nature of the assignments in his online class, Lane was made dependent on others to get them done. What he describes is something like a "first mover problem." If he posted first, he didn't have the advantage of reading what others had already posted. He would post without the benefit of possibly incorporating their insights or avoiding mistakes. However, if he waited too long, then the really good points, the original insights, could be used up. Moreover, Lane was free to post his initial reply as soon as he wanted, but he could not complete the assignment without engaging with at least two other responses. To post his replies, he had to wait for those other responses to be posted. But nobody was willing to post until they knew the professor was going to log in and start examining the various exchange threads posted online. Then, at that point, there would be a flurry of initial posting and responses. Lane thought that this distorted the purpose of the online text conversations that were supposed to be happening. He was so concerned that he even helped the teacher to change the assignment dates so that this would not happen. More recently, online course design researchers have come to the same kind of solution to solve the procrastination and rush pattern of required online conversations (Lieberman, 2019).

For thoughtful students like Lane, the discussion board posting assignment was confusing from a pedagogical perspective. He understood the purpose of the assignment. He wanted to learn from it. However, in its current design, especially the timing of posts, he found it to have an ambiguous relation to his learning. On the other hand, without being asked to reflect on the experience or for those not too concerned with what they are actually learning, many other students might be grateful for an "easy" assignment that can be completed without much scrutiny. The design of the discussion board assignment seemed to increase the possibility that it would not be taken seriously. Whether a student decides not to take an assignment seriously is possible in any format, but the anonymity and lack of a direct connection to their grade made it even more likely that those Lane would be interacting with were just going through the motions. The possibility for them to not take responsibility for their own learning was heightened. They were also set up to not feel like helping to take responsibility for the learning of the other students. Instead, they just rushed to complete the assignment. Whether it was done in good faith was hard to tell, but Lane sensed that the work was not genuine.

What Written Language Cannot Do

Being able to type the comments means they can be edited. Indeed, a great deal of filtering and thought can go into the comments that students post in an online class. Such work, if done, has the value of helping students convey written ideas better. But obviously it is nothing like a face-to-face conversation. As Mary explains:

> You are forced to reply to posts but that does not create the same in person bond. Because somebody posts one thing and you would post a reply and that is just it; there is no back and forth. There is no personal-ness to it, it is just about that topic.

Online classes try to copy, mimic or create a simulation of in-person classes but they cannot really do that; they are something else.

The intimacy and the risk of error are reduced in text-mediated exchanges. When text becomes the medium of communication, it can be blamed. As Sherry Turkle's research in *Reclaiming Conversation* shows: "The students keep returning to the idea that digital conversations are valuable because they are 'low risk.' The students talk about how, when they are online, they can edit messages before sending them" (2015, p. 36). The possibility for careful editing and anonymity create the conditions for what Turkle calls, in another book *Alone Together*, "the emotional affordances of digital communication." One of these affordances that matches the default coolness of written language "is that one can always hide behind deliberated nonchalance" (2017, p. 198). Text is a more controllable medium than conversational speech. For example, "Through speech ... there is a taking up of the other person's thought, a reflection in others, a power of thinking *according to others*, which enriches our own thoughts" (Merleau-Ponty, 2014/1945, p. 184). In contrast, the typed word is a narrowed form of language. It is not embodied. It is difficult for it to carry the same temporal weight, e.g. punctuation can only go so far. There is even some evidence that typing itself changes the content of what is communicated. Nicholas Carr (2011) relates the story of how Nietzsche's close friends could recognize a transformation in his writing style when he began to use one of the first typewriters. Nietzsche himself even said, "Our writing instruments contribute to our thoughts" (Nietzsche, 1882, cited in Ihde, 2001, p. 97).

Text is simultaneously more ambiguous and precise than language conveyed face-to-face, i.e., conversation. Since Plato, the spoken word has been privileged for obvious reasons, but the distinction has not been without criticism. For example, in *Margins of Philosophy*, Jacques Derrida (1984) works to collapse the distinction between written and spoken language. His notion of polysemy applies equally to spoken and written words. However, text is generally thought of as being more precise and thus potentially carrying less significance than spoken language. If those who read what is written and understand it mostly in the way the author meant, then its meaning is precise though its interpretive significance may vary (Hirsch, 1967). Moreover, whatever is posted online can be typed in a document first, carefully edited and fashioned before it is presented. On the other hand, if a student's typed post on a discussion board is misinterpreted, it can be amended and/or explained with more typed comments. The sense that every typed word matters is heightened by the fact that the readers on the other end know that the words *could* have been carefully chosen. Thus, they assume the words must mean exactly what it seems to the reader that they mean. However, language is inherently ambiguous; that is what makes it meaningful, its openness.

It is not the same with face-to-face conversation. Every moment is risky. Breakdown is eminent. Even if we go back and try to re-say what was said, the impact of the moment it was heard cannot be fully reencountered. In a non-face-to-face class, where there is so much non-verbal communication of what we mean, text is open to a profound font of ambiguity and thus interpretive uncertainty. It cannot be clarified in the moment. It is always understood by a solitary reader. To reach understanding, the students engaging in a discussion board interact only asynchronously, each in their own time and place, reaching back and forth to each other for a sense of what is meant. However, this only happens if they care enough to do so, if they feel called upon to clarify what they have read. It seems that such expenditure of effort is more often than not a fantasy in the domain of efficiency and optimization.

References

Carr, N. (2011). *The shallows: What the internet is doing to our brains*. New York, NY: Norton and Company.

Cho, M.-H., & Tobias, S. (2016). Should instructors require discussion in online courses? Effects of online discussion on community of inquiry, learner time, satisfaction, and achievement. *International Review of Research in Open and Distributed Learning, 17*(2).

Derrida, J. (1984). *Margins of philosophy* (A. Bass, Trans.). Chicago, IL: The University of Chicago Press.

Dreyfus, H. L. (2008). *On the internet (thinking in action)*. London, UK: Routledge.
Friesen, N. (2016). Is there a body in this class? In V. M. Manen (Ed.), *Writing in the dark* (pp. 223–235). New York, NY: Routledge.
Hirsch, E. D. (1967). *Validity in interpretation*. New Haven, CT: Yale University Press.
Ihde, D. (2001). *Bodies in technology*. Minneapolis, MN: University of Minnesota Press.
Lieberman, M. (2019, March 27). Discussion boards: Valuable? Overused? Discuss. *Inside Higher Ed*. Retrieved March 4, 2020, from https://www.insidehighered.com/digital-learning/article/2019/03/27/new-approaches-discussion-boards-aim-dynamic-online-learning
Merleau-Ponty, M. (2014). *Phenomenology of perception* (D. A. Landes, Trans.). London & New York: Routledge. (Original work published in 1945).
O'Donohue, J. (1997). *Anam cara*. New York, NY: Cliff Street Books.
Scruton, R. (2014). *The face of God: The Gifford lectures*. London, UK: Bloomsbury Publishing.
Turkle, S. (2015). *Reclaiming conversation: The power of talk in a digital age*. London, UK: Penguin Press.
Turkle, S. (2017). *Alone together: Why we expect more from technology and less from each other*. New York, NY: Basic Books.

6 Solitude and Inauthenticity

The discussion board assignments show that the often-imagined solitary experience of the online learner is dependent on the absent presence of others, the professor and the students. Even though he never saw them, talked with them or even really knew much about them, Lane's success in the class was intertwined with the others in a way that is not usually the case in a face-to-face class. When non-face-to-face classes are designed in this way, with a heavy emphasis on discussion board participation, in making both initial comments and responses to others, the class is unified asynchronously. A web of comments and replies is formed from one student to the next. And knowing that the teacher will be reading the threads can heighten the effort. The degree of scrutiny that the professor expresses by way of this "virtual" listening determines how seriously students take their work. However, even in a small class keeping track of the constant interactions and exchanges can be daunting for the teacher. Unsurprisingly, according to my participants, the outcome of these enforced interactions is lackluster. Of course, enforced or required classroom conversations that happen face-to-face can also fail and turn out to be dull, uninteresting and merely performative. However, the possibility for learning in a conversation in-person seems more likely given the descriptions of my participants. Lane and several other participants went out of their way to lambast the required student discussion boards, the one part of their experience where the absence of others was made present. In a moment of clear phenomenological naming, Lane says:

> So this is the thing, some responses are purely masturbatory. It's like what I used to call with one professor "high-fives." And I actually called the class out in one of these talks, in one of the forums in saying, "we are just giving high fives to each other, we are not actually giving a true response of what we think or a counterpoint." It's like "that's a great idea" "good job" so that's not a response, it's a verbal emoticon – you know. Its not real.

DOI: 10.4324/9781003349051-6

Lane highlights the superficiality of the so-called discussions between students. It's just like a teacher who does not take the time to be thoughtful in giving feedback on an assignment. The issue for Lane is that they are "not real" and somehow they can't be real. If a comment or reply consists only of agreement and support, it is not genuine. Emoticons are supposed to convey meaning, but in their overuse they become less meaningful. Lane is getting at the point that if over used, encouragement, though it technically fulfills the requirements of the assignment, does not help others learn. To make the exchanges real, those reading the response must encounter something besides obsequious approbation. To make a post "real" must mean to find a posted comment or question that is inherently different, something that helps the reader learn by encountering the texture of difference. To learn from the other students, their posts should by genuine articulations of personal thoughts. Even if the post is given primarily in agreement, it needs to be supported, qualified and questioned in order to make the reader sense the authenticity of what is being expressed. The post should not be given, if inauthentic, just to provide evidence to the professor that a box was checked and the assignment was completed. However, estimations of authenticity are usually problematic, especially without a face-to-face encounter.

Conversations thrive in the atmosphere of hope. In *Pedagogy of Hope: Reliving Pedagogy of the Oppressed*, Paulo Freire argues that we have an ontological need for hope (2014). He goes on to say that when we converse with others, even those we might consider combatants, we do so in a "climate of hope" (p. 186). Conversations born of hope lead to the conviction that something will be achieved in the exchange with another. But what exactly will be achieved cannot be completely determined or known beforehand. To make the outcomes of a conversation explicit is to remove the conditions for genuine conversation. To be real then, the exchange of reciprocally posted text for other students has to overcome the sense that the receiver has of knowing that the response was only done because it was a requirement. Such a hurdle may be insurmountable because in a remote class authentic engagement is lost. All actions are primarily understood as fulfilling requirements. Curriculum theorist William F. Pinar is emphatic that "Authentic conversation requires 'going beyond' the surface to take into account 'unspoken' and 'taken-for-granted' assumptions, including 'ideology'" (2004, p. 157). Pinar's hope is Socratic in that learning is understood as self-knowledge, where what is gained is the ability to have coherent beliefs (Siebach, 1995). Such a hope is lofty, and even in a face-to-face class this deep encounter is rare. However, it is not just more likely to happen in a traditional class than it is to happen online, it probably cannot really happen at all non-face-to-face. Conversations, and the kind of learning that teachers hope will come from them, are most possible when there are no requirements or rules. It is hard to image how to set up a non-face-to-face conversation without many intrusions of the explicit.

Only a genuine effort to really engage and be authentic can make the posted replies seem like they are done in order to help the other student learn. There has to be some element of surprise that shows what was offered in the response was not just done to check a box. That means what is written has to be similar enough to be relevant but also different or creative enough to be additive to what is already there. Lane's main concern was that the teachers of online classes needed to make sure that there was the right amount of friction caused by the encounter of difference in the discussion board exchanges. He thought students should step up and do it, but they needed to be encouraged to open up to the risky possibilities of real conversation.

Of Online Learning and Onanism

Lane, a professional man of the world (married with a daughter), uses a potentially vulgar and mechanical word to describe and assess his experience of learning from online student posts. His word choice captures the sense of the disturbance to learning he experienced. It expresses his sense of the degraded or defiled learning that was produced. The masturbatory, whether explicitly sexual or not, is that which is not necessarily done alone but is rather that which is done only for the self. It is an act that should involve others deeply but instead excludes them by using them. In the masturbatory others are objectified, or as Kant (1964) would say, they are used as merely a means to an end and not as ends in themselves. For Lane to not fully engage with the discussion board requirement is to be an inauthentic student. It creates inauthentic learning.

The archaic word "onanism" also names the same kind of selfish wasting and attitude. However, it taps into another sense in which the self-indulgent can become pejorative. It derives from the name of a man in the Bible, Onan, who avoided his responsibility. Onan was one who did not fulfill his duty. Lane happens to be one of those students who takes his learning extremely seriously. He is not in the class and seeking a degree because he has to. He is already financially and professionally secure, so he seeks learning for its own sake. Because of that perspective, it is easier for him to see how others are cutting corners and doing as little as possible; he does not accept such behavior as pragmatic or the way learning should happen. Lane takes responsibility not just for his own learning but can also notice when others aren't. He has somewhat of a tragic image of himself, like a quixotic hero who others do not understand; he might even seem a bit absurd. Lane knows that he does not fit in with the general attitude of going through the motions to appear like he is a good student. He wants to actually be a good student. He wants to be changed by his learning experience.

Lane shows that the desired course objective to have students interact in an online discussion board is achieved by making these types of simple, self-satisfying "high-five" comments. The ends are achieved. However, the way this requirement is fulfilled is a farce. It is carried on as a mechanistic response and not due to genuine need or respectful engagement with others as might happen in a face-to-face conversation. In fact, the exchanges become a kind of defilement where all parties are degraded by the objectification of the other. Similar to Lane, Norm Friesen's deep consideration of discussion board posting for online learning comes to a similar kind of conclusion. "It does not seem to be a real response to what I am saying … many of the replies in the forum do not seem to have much to do with the messages they supposedly respond to either" (2016, p. 230). The posts are done without a wider concern for whether they are fulfilling the purpose of learning. They don't appear to take responsibility for what is being created. If education is growth, as John Dewey (1997) argued, then these posts are not educative. They do not contribute to, "growth in general." Which is to say, it does not "create the conditions for further growth" (p. 36). The reason someone would take responsibility is precisely to create those kinds of conditions. That is what an engaged teacher would hope to achieve through the discussion board assignment.

For non-face-to-face learning, the point seems to be that to call the posted comments educative is to accept a sort of degradation in place of the real thing. The posting of comments and replies has the same sort of final outcome of what a normal classroom exchange is supposed to be, and it certainly fulfills the requirements of the syllabus. However, the experience is only a simulation of the real thing. Lane is showing that the learning he would like to experience from these online discussions is "disturbed" or "confused" by their forced and self-flattering nature. Ultimately though, it is not the requirement itself that is the inherent issue. Instead, it seems to have more to do with the level of attention that the instructor gives to these exchanges. To not just feel that the posts are done to "check a box," students need consistent feedback on every post; otherwise, what they write quickly degrades. They need to be shown how to fully respect others in a purely text-based format. The reason that the exchanges are degraded seems to be that it is hard for professors to demonstrate or guide students in how to authentically engage with others. The root of the issue might be the massive amount of careful time and attention that this would require of instructors.

A Faustian Benefit

As with all technological innovations there are always trade-offs. Catherine Adams and Terrie Thompson (2011) put this clearly in their articles about the use of technological devices in education: "The more intimately we embrace and become intertwined with a technology, the more vulnerable we are to its breakdowns, and to it responding unexpectedly otherwise than our desire" (p. 741). They explain that "A given technology both enhances and disrupts and ultimately reshapes current practices in often unexpected ways" (p. 743). If non-face-to-face classes create the kind of degradation that Lane pointed out, there are, of course, gains elsewhere in some form of efficiency. We don't enter into the Faustian bargain of technological innovation for no reason. For example, in another one of her articles, "Technology as Teacher: Digital Media and the Re-Schooling of Everyday Life," Adams says, "Becoming accustomed to using PowerPoint for teaching *opens up new ways to construct knowledge*" (2012, p. 268, emphasis added). She goes on to say, "Habituating to PowerPoint (or *any* technology) harbors other implications, including unwitting subscription to its prescriptions, as well as a retreat of critical discourse regarding its presence" (Ibid., emphasis added). Although there might be unintended consequences of every technological solution, we usually get something we want.

Mary, who took two online classes as an undergraduate more than seven years before our conversations, points out one of these gains in efficiency:

> I also really enjoyed that there were no – I mean every now and then you get a classmate who likes to talk, who likes to chime in, and it's not something helpful but it's about something personal, that kind of derails and they go off on a tangent. And you are just sitting in class thinking, "I am not paying to hear about your whatever." I did not think about paying attention at the time but, "I am not wasting my time to hear about your one-on-one conversation with the professor" ... that does not happen online.

For Mary, you of course miss out on some bad things too when you don't have to sit in a classroom. These bad things are the seemingly irrelevant, tangential and perhaps overly personal or those comments from individuals who seem to monopolize class time. It might be good for students to manifest a personal connection with the professor in class but sometimes it crosses over the line, particularly if it happens repeatedly from one or two other students. That problem is eliminated in a non-face-to-face class. It might even be one of the greatest inefficiencies of traditional classes, the time wasted by other students on unrelated or trivial questions and comments. These exchanges take the professor's attention away from the class or other students. It is time that could be spent during office hours one-on-one but which now requires that everyone's time be involved. Perhaps that is not the liability it seems, but for Mary at least, that was her impression. Picking up on the efficiency of online classes, avoiding this problem shows how Mary regards her experience with the lens provided by the technological attitude, leveling everything down to the one distinction of what is the most optimal use of the scarce resource, i.e., time.

References

Adams, C. (2012). Technology as teacher: Digital media and the re-schooling of everyday life. *Existential Analysis: Journal of the Society for Existential Analysis, 23*(2), 262–273.

Adams, C., & Thompson, T. L. (2011). Interviewing objects: Including educational technologies as qualitative research participants. *International Journal of Qualitative Studies in Education, 24*(6), 733–750.

Dewey, J. (1997). *Experience and education*. New York, NY: Simon & Schuster. (Original work published 1938).

Freire, P. (2014). *Pedagogy of hope: Reliving pedagogy of the oppressed*. New York, NY: Bloomsbury Academic.

Friesen, N. (2016). Is there a body in this class? In V. M. Manen (Ed.), *Writing in the dark* (pp. 223–235). New York, NY: Routledge.

Kant, I. (1964). *Groundwork for the metaphysics of morals* (H. J. Paton, Trans.). New York, NY: Harper Torchbooks. (Original work published 1785).

Pinar, W. (2004). *What is curriculum theory*. Mahwah, NJ: Lawrence Erlbaum Associates.

Siebach, J. (1995). *Self-knowledge in Socrates and St. Augustine: A consideration of Alcibiades 1 and Confessions book 1* (Unpublished doctoral dissertation). The University of Texas at Austin, Austin, Texas.

7 Vulnerability and Community
Body and Conversation

All of the non-face-to-face classes that my participants took as undergraduates started with an assignment that required them to introduce themselves. Sometimes this was a short perfunctory note. Other times it was more involved and required that they answer certain questions related to an initial prompt. Mary says, "In the first week, everyone was assigned the task to write a post to introduce themselves. You had to say what year you were in, what your major was, and give a fun fact." None of my participants seemed to care for this assignment because they didn't think it contributed much. It didn't help them to connect to anyone else, i.e., it did not really break the ice. They seemed to be expressing the sense that they were being forced to try and pretend that the online class was like face-to-face environment. Copying the type of thing done in an in-person class was not the same thing for them. My participants could sense the loss of the possibility for vulnerability and full human connection.

Phenomenologist and dancer Celeste Snowber explains that "Vulnerability comes from the word, *vulnere*, which means to tear open" (p. 50). In her book *Embodied Inquiry: Writing, Living and Being through the Body* (2016), she tells us:

> Vulnerability often reveals itself through our bodies; the tension in the shoulder, the butterflies in bellies or heartache in the chest. There is no absolute map to the places where one opens up to the fragility or vulnerability. Yet this is what makes us human, what deeply connects us to each other.
>
> (Ibid.)

When we are exposed to others, there is the *possibility* of being torn. It is the risk inherent to exposing our bodies to others that heightens the experience. And when we are not torn by others, we could become bound to them. The paradox is that when we are most vulnerable, we enter the possibility for the greatest strength as we might become bonded to others. These meaningful bonds are possible because of our bodies, as neurosurgeon and philosopher Raymond Tallis explains, "We deceive ourselves if

DOI: 10.4324/9781003349051-7

we forget how we remain fastened to our physical body and, through embodiment, are vulnerable to pain and suffering from within and without that body" (2003, p. 5). In the supposititious virtual future where we have somehow escaped embodiment,[1] there is nothing really at stake, no vulnerability and thus no possibility for meaning within that domain.

Aletheia of the Face

The visceral embodied feelings of vulnerability were never directly mentioned by my participants. In their experience, it is lost or obscured. With the withdrawal of the face, its nakedness and accompanying invitation to ethical regard is yanked. O'Donohue's account shows what is withdrawn: "While the rest of the body is covered, the face is naked. The vulnerability of this nakedness issues a profound invitation for understanding and compassion" (1997, p. 42). The cyber face, what is presented online, is incapable of fully nurturing the ethical response. Students in an online class find themselves in partial loneliness. This is because the "Body is the common texture of all objects and is, at least with regard to the perceived world, the general instrument of my 'understanding'" (Merleau-Ponty, 2014/1945, p. 244). Without their body being present to others, the understanding that comes from the body cannot happen. Instead, the body alone at a computer screen understands something else. Whatever that is, it is not what would be understood when physically present with others.

Related to nakedness of the face is Heidegger's etymological fascination with the Ancient Greek word for truth, *Aletheia*. He makes the point that the true is not the correct, the certain or the verifiable. With *Aletheia* Heidegger is trying to show that truth means access to the essence of a phenomenon or entity (1977). The face, the re-vealed and un-covered is fundamental to our vulnerability in interacting with others. It is not usually behind a mask. Likewise, the face on a Zoom tile or in a profile picture is just a kind of image impervious to being "torn." As Catherine Adams says about remote learning, "Students are encountered as icons on a screen" (2011, p. 269). Icons, no matter what they are made of, represent permanence, not change, growth or fragile humanity.

Without a sense of risk and the chance to really connect, Mary goes on to say:

> I read most of the posts, but other than that I didn't learn anything else about my peers. Even though the class is structured to promote interaction between students, I didn't talk to them further unless there was a group project and even then, it was minimal communication.

Mary and most of the other participants did not see these initial introductory posts as a chance to get to know their classmates and form bonds with them. They did not learn more from them or form relationships that could extend beyond the class. Instead, they thought it was administratively imposed busywork, something a bureaucrat, not the teacher, had decided was important. They knew that part of the rationale for the assignment was to give them something to do the first week of class to verify their enrollment.

Conversations and Efficiency

From listening to my participants, it is clear that they come to the experience of non-face-to-face learning with definite expectations. Education online is primarily understood as information transfer. Assignments that seem unrelated to this purpose are unrelated to what students expect from their online classes. However, as J. Glenn Gray explains in his very Heideggerian philosophy of education, *The Promise of Wisdom*, "Education is more than information" (2017/1968, p. 13). He goes on to ask, "Where is the wisdom we have lost in knowledge? Where is the knowledge we have lost in information?" (p.17). The point of higher education cannot be just gaining information or skills; it must also be about wisdom. Wisdom allows us to live well and hold on during the repetitive, mundane day-to-day reality of our existences. Wisdom comes from understanding others. We come to know others through our relationships with them. As Gray says, "Unless our youth find in formal education the time and leisure for that unhurried building of relationships which modern living makes increasingly precarious, they are unlikely to find them later" (p. 55). During the undergraduate years, the conditions for relationships can be created and allowed that are not found anywhere else. And in this way the wisdom born of community is formed.

Gray (2017/1968) explains that education always takes place within a concern for broader goals and purposes. What education, and the learning that constitutes it, is for, matters. Like John Dewey, Gray agrees that education is ultimately about the wider concerns of the group, its culture and success. The conversations that can take place as part of undergraduate learning are integral to the formation and sustaining of community.

> We can only regain community in education if we learn that communication is near its essence. And communication is only possible where individuals are able to speak directly to one another, with enough intimacy to assure understanding beyond the logical sense.
> (p. 48)

Speaking directly means face-to-face, in real time with full embodied human presence. Unmitigated conversation is being present with others in the conditions that allow for subtle, potentially friction filled, vulnerability pregnant interactions. It is to enter into the working out of meaning and purpose (s) with others. One good characterization of what I mean is this description from Arthur N. Applebee (1996) in *Curriculum as Conversation*:

> In a lively classroom environment in which real conversation are being engaged, this process of challenge and extension will be generated in part by the press of the conversation itself. Disagreement, divergent interpretations, alternative viewpoints should require participants to clarify and extend their own insights rather than capitulate to someone else's view. Teachers play a central role in ensuring that such high standards are always maintained. Through the questions they ask and the challenges they pose, effective teachers help students to focus, clarify, and raise the level of their contributions.
>
> (p. 115)

I hope it is clear that this does not sound like the description of something that can happen in an online class. Moreover, if this type of exchange is even possible in a synchronous video class, it is very difficult to achieve. To create such an environment requires the immediacy of direct embodied presence. That means what is lost in remote learning is the possibility for liveliness. To be alive means to be not fully predictable or controlled. Remote classes are therefore less alive than face-to-face classes.

Any infringement on conversation (e.g., the need to unmute as is usually required in a synchronous video class like on Zoom) and altering it to make it more efficient can radically alter the possibility of gaining wisdom from education. The seductive urge of technological innovation is always to make things more efficient. When technology approaches conversations in order to make them more efficient, the result depends on assumptions about the purpose of conversations imbedded in the technology. For example, it might be a common assumption that conversations are for exchanging information. Technology is then utilized which can maximize information exchange in conversations. We are left to wonder if standards of efficiency can apply to a conversation and if the purpose is really to exchange information. We may become especially hesitant if we accept that with all gains in efficiency there is a trade-off; something is lost. That is, not only might we wonder if the assumptions imbedded in technology about conversations are correct, we may also be unwilling to accept the costs for such maximization. Sherry Turkle gives an interesting way of thinking about this. To examine what can possibly be wrong with efficiency, she gives a paraphrased version of Shakespeare. She says, "We are 'consumed with that which we are nourished by'" (2017, p. 207). Turkle is showing that the reason we demand efficiency, even from things like conversations, is because living efficiently requires increased efficiency. It is a vicious cycle. When it comes to conversations, what is lost in making them efficient is too much. However, as conversations become compromised, the response, from Turkle's point of view, is only to redouble efforts to make conversations more efficient.

Technological innovations keep drawing us in further, like a mirage. Neil Postman's work (1992) sensitizes us to the consequences of the allure of efficiency. He shows that efficiency is one of the principles by which innovation succeeds and efficiency depends on conceiving of people as consumers. Postman's point is that students are now thought of as consumers, and universities businesses. For the technocrats, this is the most efficient arrangement. "The bureaucrat considers the implications of a decision only to the extent that the decision will affect the efficient operations of the bureaucracy, and takes no responsibility for its human consequences" (p. 87). Once that becomes accepted, that schools are a kind of business, whenever an innovation promises efficiency, the seductive power to make the trade-off is strong. I wonder how often we stop to ask if students are consumers? Are we aware enough to even realize that they are treated this way? And if they are not consumers of education, how should they be understood?

Beyond the Logical

When Gray (2017/1968) says, "beyond the logical sense," he seems to mean that there must be something non-discursive that happens in conversation. To fully commune with others is to enter into a kind of *conveyance of being* itself during conversation. Speakers in a conversation work out their mutually self-referential realities in a joint project. The "convers" of conversation goes beyond the logical sense, a sense that cannot be found fully in a one-to-one correspondence between words and their meanings. To go beyond the logical is to enter the sense of poetry. Like the sense found in T.S. Eliot's 1963 poem, *The Love Song of J. Alfred Prufrock*, where "the yellow smoke that slides along the street." Such effluvium makes me think of the burning of unsavory wet things, probably unnatural stuff like plastic, the product of advanced modern chemical technology. Even in its destruction and disposal it leaves behind its mark. Under the conditions of our technologically mitigated world, we are still called upon to care and to take responsibility in hope. In the necessary conversations that are the fabric of community we present our face. As the poem says, ours is a face that we have prepared to be met by others in vulnerability and intimacy. It takes time to create, to prepare and to meet. And time is part of the meaningful net of existence. As Merleau-Ponty (2014/1945) says, "The ambiguity of being in the world is expressed by the ambiguity of our body, and this latter is understood through the ambiguity of time" (p. 87). Our existence is made potentially meaningful because of the layers of ambiguity. And as in Eliot's poem, "works and days" constitute our being as humans, which is constituted by the trillions of "cognitive handshakes" (Tallis, 2016) that we enter into with others through all of the necessary trivialities of life. The creating and destruction, the eating and the drinking, all taking place against meaning making possibilities of language. As Gray (2017/1968) says, "We are human beings largely by virtue of language" (p. 173). All natural languages are inherently ambiguous (Wittgenstein, 2009). The ambiguity of language mirrors the ambiguity of the body and reality itself. We can see that for Merleau-Ponty language reflects the human beings' experience of reality. "Ambiguity is essential to human existence and everything that we live or think always has several senses" (2014/1945, p. 172). It is the ambiguity of language that creates the possibility for meaning.

Note

1 For example, the influential futurist Ray Kurzweil explores and advocates for this idea in his 2005 book *The Singularity Is Near: When Humans Transcend Biology*. New York, NY: Viking. His view seems to depend on the reification of the metaphor that the human brain (and thus the mind) *is* a computer (concern for the potential consequences of forgetting that "the brain is a computer" is just a metaphor was examined at length by Postman (1992)). This error leads Kurzweil from a fear of mortality to the disparagement of embodiment. Besides Dreyfus' book *On the Internet*, another excellent antidote to this faulty technological thinking about the body is Robert Epstein's article "The Empty Brain" in *Aeon*, May 18, 2016. "Your brain does not process information, retrieve knowledge or store memories. In short: your brain is not a computer." https://aeon.co/essays/your-brain-does-not-process-information-and-it-is-not-a-computer. As Tallis puts it so well, "We would not, for example, wish to be etherealized into words; or live in a world where all interactions are mediated through symbols or electronic or optotronic communication systems. The 'lightness' of our being would become 'unbearable'" (2003, p. 7).

References

Adams, C., & Thompson, T. L. (2011). Interviewing objects: Including educational technologies as qualitative research participants. *International Journal of Qualitative Studies in Education*, 24(6), 733–750.

Applebee, A. N. (1996). *Curriculum as conversation: Transforming traditions of teaching and learning*. Chicago, IL: The University of Chicago Press.

Eliot, T. S. (1963). *Collected poems 1909-1962*. Orlando, FL: Harcourt Brace & Company.

Gray, J. G. (2017). *The promise of wisdom*. Middletown, CT: Wesleyan University Press. (Original work published 1968).

Heidegger, M. (1977). *The question concerning technology, and other essays* (W. Levitt, Trans.). New York, NY: HarperCollins. (Original works published 1962, 1952 & 1954)

Merleau-Ponty, M. (2014). *Phenomenology of perception* (D. A. Landes, Trans.). London & New York: Routledge. (Original work published in 1945)

O'Donohue, J. (1997). *Anam cara*. New York, NY: Cliff Street Books.

Postman, N. (1992). *Technopoly: The surrender of culture to technology*. New York, NY: Alfred A. Knopf Inc.

Snowber, C. (2016). *Embodied inquiry: Writing, living and being through the body*. The Netherlands: Sense Publishers.
Tallis, R. (2003). *The hand: A philosophical inquiry into human being*. Edinburgh, UK: Edinburgh University Press.
Tallis, R. (2016). *Aping mankind*. New York, NY: Routledge Classics.
Turkle, S. (2017). *Alone together: Why we expect more from technology and less from each other*. New York, NY: Basic Books.
Wittgenstein, L. (2009). *Philosophical investigations* (G. E. M. Anscombe, P. M. S. Hacker, & J. Schulte, Trans.). West Sussex, UK: Wiley-Blackwell.

8 Reciprocal Voyeurism
Hiding from Others Together

Despite the lack of attention or importance that they seemed to give their introductory discussion board assignment, several participants like Mary mentioned that they *did* read all the other introductory posts by their fellow students. They explained to me that they did not put much into their own posts because they knew nobody was going to read them. When I asked "Why?" they said that it was because nobody was required to read them. When I pointed out to a few participants that *they* had taken the time to read the others, they still didn't think anyone else had done the same. There was a voyeuristic sense of their view toward the others in their class. They felt anonymous but were curious about the other students. However, they did not seem to impute this feeling to the other students, even though the other students potentially felt just as anonymous and curious and were therefore just as likely to be voyeuristically engaged. The lack of reciprocal awareness seems to demonstrate the way that non-face-to-face classes cut students off from fully realizing the other.

The voyeuristic aspect was that my participants expressed a curiosity with the other students, enough to read their short biographies, but never enough to really engage and get to know anybody. They avoided crossing the line past anonymous voyeur. Like the character played by Jimmy Stewart in Alfred Hitchcock's *Rear Window* (1954), students in online classes often experience themselves as set off from others, unable to really interact with them but still fascinated by them. Much of the disconnection is due to the limited means of interaction. A line from the movie that aptly captures the conditions of voyeurism is when the character says, "You don't know the meaning of the word neighbor. Neighbors speak to each other" (Hitchcock, 1954). Without being able to fully speak to each other, students in non-face-to-face classes are potentially less neighborly. They don't rely on each other as much as they could in a traditional class.

As in *Rear Window*, students in online classes peer out at others, but the fact of their observing activity is mostly invisible, though not impossible to notice. The paradox of not fully being in contact with others but

DOI: 10.4324/9781003349051-8

still enamored with the idea of knowing them without their knowledge is alluring. However, if you cannot come to full contact with others, what is the use or interest in partial contact? Is it a sense of power and control? Being able to observe others without them knowing is something that students in online classes sense they are able to do in secret, like a spy through a crack in the wall. In *Rear Window*, when one character asks to use the protagonist's huge telephoto lens, she says, "Mind if I use that portable keyhole?" A keyhole is usually something fixed. But with a mighty lens we can peer into the windows of homes far away. The Internet can be a kind of portable keyhole too.

When we observe others, when we think they do not notice, we assume the posture of the voyeur. The English translation of the French word "voyeur" is instructive. *Scopophilia* is the deep love of observation, watching. The modern world of screens makes us all scopophiliacs. We all look out at the world like Jimmie Stewart's character with a telephoto lens to focus and observe others. We imagine we will be unnoticed and safe within our own protected confines. From movies to our phones, technological innovations consistently play to the human preference for the visual, i.e., what can be read instead of heard, seen instead of felt. The voyeur is not fully connected to others. In the film *Rear Window*, the difficulty of full ethical responsibility is tested.

There is also the pointlessness of voyeurism. It is something done from curiosity during the conditions of leisure. The voyeur is born of idleness. The degree to which we become watchers and not actors seems to depend on how much free time we have. It could also be related to how familiar we are with the conditions of engagement with others. The voyeuristic aspect of online classes could also relate to how comfortable or unengaged students feel. For those more familiar with the format, they might be only peripherally concerned with how others are watching them and how curious they are about observing others. The voyeuristic tendency seems to be related to the level of vulnerability students feel in an online class. The more secure they are, the less they are concerned with the sense of being watched.

Lurking

In his account of online textual exchanges, Norm Friesen is able to name this mostly hidden activity of observing others online through what they write. He says he is "lurking." By keeping out of sight, one is able to be sneaky. The lurker is one who can potentially be getting away with something, whether it be avoiding work, taking something without permission or evading full responsibility. The etymology of the verb "to lurk" even connects to frowning, the facial expression of displeasure. The perception could be that even in an online setting lurkers have something to hide or are otherwise discontent. For example, what do we think of those in a

Zoom meeting, or other type of group videoconference, who leave their camera off without explanation? In the lurking condition Friesen says:

> I cannot share the same openness and vulnerability that those already posting to the forum do. At the same time, everyone in the conference is still able to suppose that I am still able to see everything that they are doing and saying.
>
> (2016, p. 229)

There is a perception of unfairness to lurking. Others might think that a student who is lurking is taking advantage by not fully paying the price in vulnerability. They are not sharing in the same level of exposure that everyone else is allowing. There is a sense in which this is also true of face-to-face classes. Students who do not reveal what they are thinking or engage fully but instead watch or mimic other statements can be viewed as not fully investing in the in-person learning experience. However, they are still there. They communicate many things non-verbally, and their mere physical presence makes them vulnerable even if they shelter their thoughts behind silence and lowered eyes.

There is tension in students' perception of anonymity. As Friesen points out, the other students in an online class discussion board know who is lurking. Lurkers are revealed by their absence from textual exchanges because they have not posted yet. However, everyone knows that they can still read what everyone else has posted. In this way, the voyeurs in an online class know that they are also potentially being observed and watched as much as possible. Students in my synchronous Zoom classes are acutely aware of this. During my first experience teaching in a non-face-to-face Zoom lecture, students emailed me to complain about having their image copied. Apparently, word had gotten out among some of the female students that one of the male students was a "Simp" and was likely using screenshots to save their images. Soon many of the women were requesting that they be allowed to turn their cameras off during class.

For students in an online class that requires any sort of interaction or engagement online, it is not really anonymous. The lurker's absence is noticed. Students quickly learn that even though they might feel like they are alone, they aren't. They know that others can perceive their online presences, whether it is by the text they leave behind that is linked to their name or the professor's view of the online course that tracks engagement on the course platform. They also know that even their absence can be conspicuous. Moreover, they know that what they do online is permanent. They cannot erase their comments or their logins. Danna tells me, "On the platform anything you write online gets tracked." Students tend to hold back in the exchanges. What they write is often not fully genuine since it is constantly being hedged and curated. They seem to behave like someone being watched, like they are the objects of other voyeurs.

Faceless Efficiency

My participants seemed to project onto the facelessness of the rest of the class their own attitudes about the course. The main thing they project is their own attitude with regard to efficiency; it is their goal. In *Technics and Praxis: A Philosophy of Technology* (2012), phenomenologist Don Ihde considers efficiency a value. The implications of Ihde's view for online learning become apparent when we see that Heidegger connects values and purpose.

"The essence of value has an *inner* relation to the essence of aim" (Heidegger, 1961/1984, p. 16). Our purposes become or just are what it is that we value. The intense valuation of efficiency springs from the technological attitude that levels everything down by removing all meaningful distinctions, i.e., standardization. In so doing, we come to increasingly "aim" at efficiency. One participant, Evan, explained that the online format, particularly the reliance on platforms such as Blackboard and Canvas, made all of the courses "cookie cutter." They were all of the same form even if their content was totally unrelated. "That is just the nature of the tool that they are using. So you don't necessarily feel like you are experiencing something that is really content specific or created by the professor for you in some particular way." Efficiency depends on removing special, individualized differences. The standardization that is required for most online courses requires the loss of most of what can be considered characteristic of a specific individual. Students in non-face-to-face classes experience the format as diminishing the possibility for the creative expression of their teachers and themselves.

The attitude of efficiency, and the extreme value it is given, is most manifest in comments by participants pointing out that unless something was required, they would not do it. Moreover, they saw this valuation and the decisions that flowed from it as one of the few things they knew for certain about the other face-less students in their classes, i.e., nobody was going to do anything that was not required. Only what was explicitly related to their grade, in a sort of one-to-one correspondence, was worth any student's time and effort. For example, in reference to extra material posted to the course website, Evan remarked, "I am sure there are some of those links that have interesting and valuable information but you don't end up going to those." He certainly would if it were required or if it would help him finish an assignment.

Oriented toward efficiency, the students still have to make an introductory post that they regard as a waste of time. But since it is required and contributes to their grade, they do it. Mary showed that the "get to know you" assignment did little to help her connect with others. Throughout the class, the students are required to continue to interact with each other via posts. Mary gave me some details as she recounted her experience:

> Writing a weekly post was the one task that took up the most of my time. There was always a prompt that reflected that week's topic and you had to write one original post and then comment on two of your peer's posts. I tried to write my original post as soon as possible. Waiting for others to post as well so you have another post to comment on took time. I would have to log into Blackboard a few times a week just to check and comment on that week's posts.

Via the comment assignment, a reciprocal burden is placed on students in online classes. Indeed, the implicit, if not explicit, purpose of the assignment seems to be designed to foster learning among peers. Discussion board posting, as described here and by other participants, creates tension between the students' autonomy and their dependence on others. The burden comes to each student on their own, needing to do their part, and how they must wait for others. Students are free to make their original post, and, in doing so, they create the conditions by which other students can complete the other aspect of the interactive assignment. The mutual dependence is the source of the reciprocal burden. They carry this burden by apprehension for the future, i.e., they are left in expectant waiting until face-less others post textual comments. Until others post, the assignment cannot be completed. They are also required to keep checking back in to see what others have posted about what they wrote and to find places to add their other required responses.

The imperative of efficiency seems to dominate the possibilities for exchanges with Mary's fellow students. When she wrote her posts, she did it to fulfill the assignment and not to build anything else. Her posts were there, on the Internet, for the rest of the class and professor to read, but she was absent. In the *Absent Body*, Drew Leder beautifully draws our attention to all that we overlook about embodiment because we are so familiar with it. "My body ... is fleshed out by a ceaseless stream of kinesthesia, cutaneous and visceral sensations, defining my body's space and extension and yielding information about position, balance, state of tension, desire, and mood" (1990, p. 23). Thus, there is the sense that for Mary it seems her words were only like a trace of what her full embodied presence would have been, only a slight whisper.

The text of Mary's comments appeared just as the text of everyone else. There was nothing remarkable about it. All of the comments and replies were leveled. The manifestations of presence could only come in one way. It's easy to imagine the special individuality with which our comments in a regular class are conveyed, e.g., tone, speed, amount and mistakes. As Leder (1990) explains, "My expressive face can form a medium of communication only because it is available to the Other's gaze" (p. 11). Withdrawing the facial medium of communication makes informational exchange more efficient. In his careful research comparing oral and literary cultures, Walter Ong shows how this efficiency is made possible: "Written words are isolated from the fuller context in which spoken words come into being" (1982, p. 101). Context is what creates meaning. Meaning is inherently dependent on ambiguity. Writing inherently removes *some* of both context and ambiguity.

Preoccupied by Absence

The discussion board goes a long way in tying students to the class, constantly bringing their minds back to it. Lane remarked, "I actually have alerts on my phone." The alerts let him know when he needs to log in and check what others have written in response to his posts. Moreover, another participant, Carl, told me: "The online classes are on my mind more than the not online classes. Unless I am sitting or I am on campus the thing that I am thinking about is online classes." The design of non-face-to-face classes is often effective at becoming a priority in the minds of the students I talked to. Carl explains:

> I think a big part of it is there is no professor reminding you that these are the due dates and you constantly have to be your own kind of reminder. And even if you have a professor who is not really good about it, just going to class everyday kind of reminds you.

Knowing that they have to depend on others to complete assignments puts mental pressure on them to keep checking in with their class. At least for some of my participants, the format creates a sense of ownership. They have a sense that they are in control because of requirements for more contact and consistent mental attention.

In pragmatic yet poignant language, Mary brings forth some of what the present absence of her fellow students meant to her:

> There's no seats online. There is no person to person, so you are missing a lot of the small interactions that are just human. I weighed the pros and cons and so for this class because I knew it was an easy A and the content, I was ok giving up that interaction.

It's not that there are empty seats, they just don't exist. There isn't a place next to you, like there is in a classroom.

Norm Friesen (2016) makes the same observation as Mary in his careful phenomenological essay about early forms of online learning "Is there a Body in this Class?" He says, "Students cannot be arranged" (p. 225). There is no physical manifestations of fellow students to which one can orient or respond in a spatial manner. In Friesen's description, he shows how the lack of a physical manifestation of the bodies of fellow students draws attention to the spatial character of embodiment:

> In 'ordinary' classrooms, when we speak of 'sitting next to someone,' we do not differentiate between the person's identity and his or her body. My body, in this context, is who I am – it is my identity. Our bodies are the medium through which we reveal our identity ... we are immediately present to each other as embodied beings.
>
> (Ibid.)

Embodiment is lost in remote learning.

To be embodied means that our bodies are identical with who we are. However, in an online class the body is conspicuously absent, while our identity is strongly implied. This means that often in an online class it can feel like our identity is not fully revealed. Instead, it becomes manifest to others in a way totally separate from our body, i.e., through text on a computer screen.

Mary never found herself in bodily proximity to other students. She knew there wouldn't be physical encounters with others when she took the class. And she knew that without that physical presence something would be lost in her online class. When she experienced the absence, it was acceptable because it accorded with her expectations. It would be very disconcerting to be alone in a class when you expected others, but knowing that there won't be anyone makes the experience generally unremarkable.

For non-face-to-face classes, one of the only distinguishing features was not who had posted but which posts already had received the requisite comments from other students. Evan remarked that he felt sorry for those posts that hadn't received replies. He would seek out posts with no replies. Evan did this knowing it meant he might be missing out on a more interesting discussion taking place on a longer thread. He sort of rooted for the underdog, trying to find the neglected posts so that he could help them out. He seemed to adopt a pedagogical attitude much like Lane, in trying to help others learn. This teacherly tendency may have come from being slightly older than the other students. I asked if it was ever the same student he tried to help, Evan said no, it was just whichever post thread was shortest.

I asked participants if they ever tended to just comment back and forth with a few students. They said no. It was not something they did, mostly because they thought the professor might not like it, though it was not something specifically prohibited. In this case, in the realm of explicit instructions and clear tasks, participants describe making up an additional rule. Somehow, they felt that it was an unwritten requirement of the experience that they not pair off with other students in order to fulfill their reciprocal posting and commenting assignment. Where did they get this sense and why did they impose it on themselves? Not pairing off was, for one thing, a way of not forming any relationships. It was a way of remaining anonymous precisely where it would have been possible to become more personally known. It seems to be part of the essence of what is lost in remote learning that students feel they should try to remain as anonymous as possible.

References

Friesen, N. (2016). Is there a body in this class? In V. M. Manen (Ed.), *Writing in the dark* (pp. 223–235). New York, NY: Routledge.
Heidegger, M. (1984). *Nietzsche volume two: The eternal recurrence of the same* (D. F. Krell Trans.). New York, NY: HarperCollins. (Original work published 1961).
Hitchcock, A. (Director). (1954). *Rear Window* [Film]. Patron Inc.
Ihde, D. (2012). *Technics and Praxis: A philosophy of technology*. Dordrecht, The Netherlands: Springer.
Leder, D. (1990). *The absent body*. Chicago, IL: The University of Chicago Press.
Ong, W. J. (1982). *Orality and literacy: The technologizing of the word*. New York, NY: Methuen & Co. Ltd.

9 Narrowed Purpose

Text, Money and Efficiency

It strikes me that the more explicit the reason is for the existence of an activity or institution, the more likely it is that it will be regarded with a quid pro quo attitude, e.g. government, nature and education. This is surely not what Aristotle meant when he said, "Every craft and every inquiry, and likewise every action and every choice, seem to aim at some good" (1999, p. 1). The good to which we aim at in education cannot be based merely on fair exchange for an explicit outcome. We must hope for some synergistic outcome where the whole is more than the sum of the parts. What is lost in remote learning could be a sense for such a notion of the good, an outcome beyond an exchange that is agreeable to all parties involved.

One of my participants, Travis, a former Marine, tells me, "The online classes that I have taken felt more transactional because there was a clear purpose." Superficially, the purpose of an online class is the same as a face-to-face class. When John tells me, "All I want is this piece of paper" (i.e., a diploma), he could be referring to a traditional class. But then he continues, "I don't need this [face-to-face interaction] because I can get all that stuff doing literally anything else." Like Mary, and the other participants, John expected what would be missing in an online class: there would be no faces. In contrast to some of the others, he does not miss it, and the educational purpose of the class was clarified and made more efficient by this absence. John is grateful for this void in the traditional face-to-face learning experience because he is allowed to focus on just what needs to get done in order to get what he wants. Yet, as the purpose or goal of non-face-to-face learning becomes clearer, it also, paradoxically, becomes potentially more ambiguous (Olt, 2018).

Online classes promote the kind of learning that happens when students are *exposed* to information, and that is all that my participant John, for example, expects from the experience. In *Reclaiming Conversation: The Power of Talk in a Digital Age* (2015), Sherry Turkle illuminates the kind of learning made possible by online classes. By her view, too much can be lost when something is reduced to mostly textual exchanges, like email. When students in a non-face-to-face class read the teacher's

DOI: 10.4324/9781003349051-9

instructions or lecture slides along with the textbook or other written materials, the non-face-to-face pedagogical exchange "boil[s] down," according to Turkle, "to an exchange of information. In acting, in law, in business, the loss of a face-to-face meeting means a loss of complexity and depth. A younger generation may be getting accustomed to this flattening of things" (p. 264). The flattened or leveled-down experience is just what John is seeking. He wants the maximally efficient learning experience.

In his book *Elucidations of Holderlin's Poetry*, Heidegger (1981/2000) provides the philosophical background for the leveling tendency of technology:

> The men of this earth are provoked by the absolute domination of the essence of modern technology, together with technology itself [devices, algorithms, and systems] into developing a final world-formula which would once and for all secure the totality of the world as a uniform sameness, and thus make it available to us as a calculable resource. The provocation to such making-available orders everything into a single design, the making of which levels the harmony of the infinite design.
>
> (p. 202)

The technological attitude unites the essence of technology and powerful innovations like the Internet. They are swept up together in an unrelenting drive to unify and homogenize. The action of the technological attitude is the great leveling tendency that infuses so much of contemporary experience. Thus, it is the very nature of the Internet to shape our interactions with everything, including each other, by leveling. Internet mitigated interactions seem to level by removing meaningful distinctions. In the article "Dwelling in the Classroom: A Phenomenology of Distance Learning," Koukal et al. explain: "On the Internet, Others can *only* appear as text *within* the text that is the Internet, and so every Other appears in more or less the same way" (2002, p. 31). And this way of appearing as an other to be encountered is itself "superficially indistinguishable from the text generated by the various programs that make up the Internet system itself" (Ibid.)

Text Flattens the Experience to One Level

When education is conceived of as just the exposure to and acquisition of information, a faceless format is more efficient. Non-face-to-face classes are attractive to John because they remove what he regards as superfluous to his goals. The extraneous is removed by reducing the pedagogical encounter to the merely *textual*. Norm Friesen's (2016) phenomenological analysis of online classes makes this point as well. The reduction brings the purpose of the class more in line with the imperatives of John's educational efforts. As Heidegger says in his lecture course *What is Called Thinking* (1954/1976), we live in a time when everything becomes "leveled to one level" (p. 33). Learning, limited to the textually expressed, becomes what can be learned from reading. Learning is then not what can be learned from modeling the examples of the face of teachers and other students. Heidegger thought the uniformity and potential homogeneity of textually mitigated communication can eventually lead to the situation where, "The burden of thought is swallowed up in the written script" (Ibid., p. 49). In his *Parmenides* lectures (1982/1998), Heidegger says:

> In the time of the first dominance of the typewriter, a letter written on this machine still stood for a breach of good manners ... Mechanical writing deprives the hand of its rank in the realm of the written word and degrades the word to a means of communication ... The typewriter makes everyone look the same.
>
> (p. 81)

However, he goes even further in his analysis. It is not just that the experience of meaningful differences is lost; we even lose touch with certain aspects of *being* itself.

> Therefore when writing was withdrawn from the origin of its essence, i.e., from the hand, and was transferred to the machine, a transformation occurred in the relation of Being to man ... The typewriter veils the essence of writing and of the script. It withdraws from man the essence of writing and of the script ... without man's experiencing this withdrawal appropriately and recognizing that it has transformed the relation of Being to his essence.
>
> (Ibid., p. 85)

The computer keyboard is the new, even more efficient, mechanization of the word. The word read and the word typed is in a degraded, but more efficient, state, i.e., mere communication of textual information. It is in effect to "*reduce* the world to a language-like-being." Phenomenologist Don Ihde (2001) explains that the textually mitigated world "is something of an inversion from the 'world of the text' into the 'text as world'" (p. 78). John is attracted to the paired-down state of textual exchange because it makes his learning more efficient. Because he comes to the experience driven to reduce or eliminate redundancy (since he is having to retake many of the courses), John is sensitized to drawing out and expressing this aspect of non-face-to-face learning. Learning primarily through the typed word makes it easier for him to achieve his educational goals.

Wasted Time and the Cost of Learning

Mary expressed an attitude similar to the one brought out by John. In one exchange during our conversations, she reveals her experience with the expected purpose of a non-face-to-face class:

MARY: I felt that most of my other classes in-person were engaging and had good content and I feel like my online classes were very generic classes I had to take as just a prerequisite for my major. So it was easier. Kind of like one of those throw away classes that they just make you take.
STEVE: What do you mean by "throw away"?
MARY: I just feel like they scam you out of money to be honest. [laughs]
STEVE: They charge you the same amount of tuition?
MARY: Yeah, but I already know how to write a research paper but they made me take a class on how to do it. Because it was a prerequisite for my major. You just have to play the game.
STEVE: So in that experience you are feeling a little bit scammed?
MARY: Yes. I just felt, scammed and it was a waste of my time and I wasn't learning. I mean I was learning a few things; it was not a complete waste. I knew a lot of the content. It was redundant so therefore they are easy classes. They are kind of unchallenging but it's hard because you think it is a very easy class and you will get an easy 'A' but then it creates all this stress, scheduling, making sure you got everything done and just working with other students, the projects and things like that. It is just very unnecessary.

Mary feels scammed, like she is wasting her time by being required to do and pay for something she already knows how to do. For her, it's not a learning experience. The gains in efficiency are so great that the course, with regards to her sense of what learning is, has become a waste of time.

A similar situation is occurring nationally across all higher education. The costs remain the same for students, the amount of money they are paying for their learning, but the experience has been radically altered. During the COVID-19 outbreak, most undergraduates continued paying full tuition while being implicitly told that taking their classes at home was equivalent. Of course, it is an incredible advantage that advanced computer technology allows education to continue even during the outbreak of a disease. However, something is lost when students are educated "remotely" even if synchronously on video. Many students learning at home during this situation probably feel that though they are paying for and expecting a full education (i.e., the full "college experience"), they are not getting it. And yet they may still appreciate aspects of efficiency that are offered by the face-less learning. Time will tell whether this difference in experience makes these graduates less prepared for higher education's intended goal. At least as far as future employment is concerned, there exists an economic argument that as long as students can *signal* they have learned what is expected as undergraduates by possessing a diploma, the difference in the learning experience will not matter (Caplan, 2018).

The issue of how much the online courses cost is something other participants mentioned as well. Students have the impression that it is obviously a strategic maneuver by institutions to make classes non-face-to-face. They are not wrong. In their article "Dwelling in the Classroom: A Phenomenology of Distance Learning," the authors explain that "The current growth trend of distance learning … is the result … above all [of] the corporatization of the university which brings pressure to bear on schools to reduce their rising costs while increasing their enrollments" (Koukal et al., 2002, p. 20; see also Whitford & Schifrin, 2022). My participants understand that it is a big money saver to move classes online. What they don't, or can't, realize is that to do online teaching well, it takes at least the equivalent amount of time and often even more effort on the part of teachers (Hislop & Ellis, 2004). Online classes also require administrative oversight as well as the right infrastructure and necessary support staff.

In the end, Mary's point is not about the economies of scale that online classes offer, their ability to be multiplied and filled with more students easier. Rather, for her the money issue is about requiring a course that she did not need because she could already do what it was meant to help students learn. She could have tested out of it but there was no such option. Her school could create low-cost online classes, and because it was low-cost, it could make it a requirement, even for students who could already fulfill the requirement. Mary didn't think she would have been required to take such a "redundant" course if it had been more costly for the school. There may be a huge misperception if online courses are created by schools because they think students want them offered in the format. It also seems like an obvious outcome that if online courses were cheaper most students would probably opt to take them. However, they might realize, like Travis, that they were missing something from the college experience, but the savings might be easily justified if their diploma was still just as valuable.

Hollowness: "No there there"

At another point in our conversation, I asked Mary if she felt anything was missing from her online classes. She said, "I felt like the only thing I was missing was maybe the interaction with people, myself and the professor and myself and other students. But that's the point of an online class." The point of the online class is to "miss" the friction of the human interactions. The texture of individual differences is what makes our interactions with others potentially memorable, sometimes difficult and opens the possibility for joint meaningfulness. Turkle (2017) in *Alone Together* says that online technology facilitates "friction free" relationships (p. 13). The whole way that online classes become efficient is to remove the most in-efficient part of them. The defining characteristics of a non-face-to-face class become its goal. The purpose is to remove what is not directly involved in the learning of the content. As expressed by Mary and also in John's account, there is an explicit understanding by some students that the purpose of online classes is specifically to remove the component of learning that is related to human interactions. By removing the face-to-face contact, the class becomes more efficient, and for some of my students, this is what makes it easier to complete.

John's thought experiment from Chapter 2 showed that a certain kind of *hollowness* seems to be a feature of the experience. It is as if, similar to what Gertrude Stein (1937) says, "there is no there there" (p. 289). Stein meant there was no operative focus from which to orient in order to find significance. Online classes have a kind of emptiness. To a certain degree, they do not have a special character or identity. Unlike a face-to-face class that *can* develop an individual character due to the personalities of the individuals involved and made apparent through their interactions, the online class is like something that is hollow, a ball or an old tree, both having a definite form but nothing substantial on the inside. The online class is something which presents as solid but isn't. It's substantiality an illusion. There really is nothing there that you expect to be there. Thus, with online classes you see the form or shape of a class, but really it isn't; it's something else, since it does not bring about the challenges that regularly are associated with learning. It does not seem like a class at all. It has some features in common, e.g. cost, standardized evaluations and authoritative structure. Moreover, these comparative associations with traditional classroom learning will always exist for undergraduates as long as primary schooling is necessarily in-person.

In his sensitive article "The Call of Pedagogy as the Call of Contact," Max van Manen (2012) shows that a hollowness or void can result when contact is lost:

> The pedagogical contact between teacher and student tends to be seen as "close and personal." This may be especially the case for very young children and their teachers as well as, perhaps, for graduate students and their professors. But for many school and college students that regretfully may not be the case. One may even question whether personal contact is still possible between teacher and his or her many students.
>
> (p. 25)

Interestingly, the loss of contact is not just possible in non-face-to-face learning; it is also possible in face-to-face classes. But whereas contact seems to be possible for van Manen in traditional classes, it is hard to see how we could even talk about the same kind of thing happening in an online class, especially when he says: "Responsive contact means seeing the [student's] otherness, mystery and 'face.' Responsive contact is a relation that sparks responsibility. The [student] experiences his or her uniqueness – being a 'who' (not a 'what')" (p. 28). The face of the other must be seen. Their special difference as someone distinct from others cannot be reduced, as we will see, for example, to something that the Internet can efficiently support, i.e., text. And it can't be flattened, shrunk and framed by a computer screen.

References

Aristotle. (1999). *Nicomachean ethics* (2nd ed.). New York, NY: Hackett.
Caplan, B. (2018). *The case against education: Why the education system is a waste of time and money*. Princeton, NJ: Princeton University Press.
Friesen, N. (2016). Is there a body in this class? In V. M. Manen (Ed.), *Writing in the dark* (pp. 223–235). New York, NY: Routledge.
Heidegger, M. (1976). *What is called thinking* (J. Glenn Gray, Trans.). New York, NY: HarperCollins. (Original work published 1954).
Heidegger, M. (1998). *Parmenides* (A. Shuwer & R. Rojcewicz, Trans.). Bloomington, IN: Indiana University Press. (Original work published 1982).
Heidegger, M. (2000). *Elucidations of Hölderlin's poetry* (K. Hoeller, Trans.). Amherst, NY: Humanity Books. (Original work published 1981).
Hislop, G. W., & Ellis, H. J. C. (2004). A study of faculty effort in online teaching. *The Internet and Higher Education, 7*, 15–31.
Ihde, D. (2001). *Bodies in technology*. Minneapolis, MN: University of Minnesota Press.
Koukal, D. R., Blume, L. B., & Blume, T. W. (2002). Dwelling in the classroom: A phenomenology of distance learning. *Journal of Teaching in Marriage and Family* 2(1), 19–40.
Olt, P. A. (2018). Virtually there: Distance freshmen blended in classes through synchronous online education. *Innovative Higher Education, 43*, 381–395.
Stein, G. (1937). *Everybody's autobiography*. New York, NY: Cooper Square.
Turkle, S. (2015). *Reclaiming conversation: The power of talk in a digital age*. London, UK: Penguin Press.
Turkle, S. (2017). *Alone together: Why we expect more from technology and less from each other*. New York, NY: Basic Books.
Van Manen, M. (2012). The call of pedagogy as the call of contact. *Phenomenology & Practice, 6*(2), 8–34.
Whitford, E., & Schifrin, M. (2022 June). How a little-known California school earned top marks on Forbes' 2022 college financial grades. *Forbes*, 110–115.

10 The Game of Facelessness

The Face and the Screen

John O'Donohue connects his notion of face not just with the immediate reflection of complex inner states but also as a canvas on which the totality of the human being is also revealed. "There is a strange symmetry in the way the soul writes the story of its life in the contours of the face" (1997, p. 44). For O'Donohue, the face is the painting of our lives. The face of the individual shows us the person that they are, based on all that they have experienced, thought and been. Oscar Wilde's incredible and disturbing novel, *A Portrait of Dorian Gray*, fantasized this common idea of how our life experience sculpts the visage of individuals. The story presents the idea that all that we are is shown to others in the face that they see. Max Picard explains this phenomenon in his book *The Human Face*:

> Experiences are not just written down on the face one after the other in the order of their occurrence … the various experiences are united with the soul and merge into a unit, and it is that unit that is stamped upon the face.
>
> (1930, p. 201)

Who we are, the composite of our actions and experiences, cannot really be hidden unless we give up our face. O'Donohue explains what Wilde showed in his novel:

> The face is the mirror of the mind … The human face is an artistic achievement. On such a small surface an incredible variety and intensity of presence can be expressed. This breadth of presence overflows the limitation of the physical form … Each face is a particular intensity of human presence … The human face is the subtle yet visual autobiography of each person … The face always reveals the soul; it is where the divinity of the inner life finds an echo and image. When you behold someone's face, you are gazing deeply into that person's life.
>
> (1997, pp. 38–39)

DOI: 10.4324/9781003349051-10

The face as a face also does not reveal everything. "A world lies hidden behind each human face" (Ibid., p. 41). O'Donohue says that "the human face carries mystery and is the exposure point of the mystery of the individual's life. It is where the private inner would of a person protrudes into the anonymous world" (Ibid., p. 42). When we engage with another person face-to-face, part of the thrill and the possibility for learning (being changed) is the risk of misunderstanding, the reality that not everything is known, that something is hidden and can be discovered. The directness and thus intimacy of the face-to-face encounter creates conditions for learning. When we are face-to-face in real time, uncertainty and adventure are possible. "Real conversation has an unpredictability, danger, and resonance; it can take a turn anywhere and constantly borders on the unexpected and on the unknown" (Ibid., p. 111). Real conversation is made possible by the face. And though it reveals so much about the real-time inner state of the interlocutor and also presents itself as an image of the inner life of the individual, it is simultaneously opaque. The face does not reveal everything even when it seems to show everything.

In his discussion of face, O'Donohue makes a shared connection with Heidegger, the relation of revealing and concealing. The meaning of the face comes both from the magnitude of what it reveals but also in what it hides. The face is not complete access. Indeed, it is only capable of revealing because it also conceals. Heidegger (1977) repeatedly reminds us of the etymology of the word "truth" and tries to draw our attention back to the ancient Greek sense of *Aletheia*. *Aletheia* is unconcealment or disclosure, i.e., what is revealed when something else is pulled back or covered. Heidegger is showing that "truth" for the ancient Greeks was a kind of shining forth of something new, some new way of understanding or the showing up of something that had been obscured and covered. However, each new shining or revealing inevitably also obscures. Just as for Heidegger's account of truth, so too with O'Donohue's tender probing of the meaning of the human face, it reveals and conceals. In contrast to the potential ambiguity and thus attendant rich meaningfulness of the face is the stark clarity of screens or at least the expectation that everything that is relevant and important is laid bare and given.

It used to be that we probably first encountered screens during the experience of watching television. Today it is probably more likely that people first see smartphones or computers. Screens are ubiquitous. In their article, "On the Meaning of Screens: Toward a Phenomenological Account of Screenness," Lucas Introna and Fernando Ilharco (2006) explain, "Whether at work, at home, traveling, or immersed in some form of entertainment, most of us find ourselves increasingly in front of screens" (p. 57). Because of the ubiquity of screens and our constant use of them, they become our window into reality. Like Jimmy Stewart's character in *Rear Window*, we are oriented toward a voyeuristic attitude of the world. Introna and Ilharco's phenomenological account explains that it is not that screens show us what we then take to be reality; it is that we already take what the screen offers to be reality. "The content in front of us is not just presumed relevant, but is *already presumed* relevant" (p. 64). If it is on the screen, it must be important, it must be given attention. Drawing on Heidegger's phenomenological ontology, the phenomenologists explain, "Things are revealed or disclosed as that which they already are within a referential whole in which other things already refer to them and also draw upon the whole to be what they already are taken to be" (p. 60). Thus, the more we use the screens, the more we come to understand everything in a way that conforms to screen-ness. This is a manifestation of the technological attitude. We even come to expect one of the most peculiar entities, human being, to conform to the leveling power of the screen.

Many undergraduates become most familiar with screens because of video games. One of the earliest uses of computers, once they were connected to screens, was to create simple games (Egenfeldt-Nielsen, Smith & Tosca, 2008). The experience of playing games can be foundational for future work done on computers, i.e., it contributes to creating the necessary intuitions that web designers rely on when constructing online learning platforms. Whereas the experience of watching television is a passive relationship to the screen, playing a game requires interaction and manipulation of what is happening on the screen. Being connected by interaction to what is displayed on the screen in non-face-to-face learning implicitly relies on the skillful comportment developed while playing games (Ibid.)

As Wittgenstein (2009) notes, games are hard to define. In a way they are, like many things, impossible to grasp with complete conceptual clarity without the notion of something like "family resemblance." All games tend to have some things but not everything in common. For example, chess is a game but so is Duck Duck Goose. All games have rules. The rules tend to be fixed and, in general, known beforehand. The rules of a game can seem arbitrary, especially to those who play for the first time. Only after experience do the rules start to make sense and seem coherent and necessary. Games can be played for their own sake, i.e., because of the fun that results during game play. However, the allure of games can become tied up with an excessive focus or desire to win. If this happens, then the game is not done for its own sake, for fun, but instead fun is only experienced if the player wins. Those who play certain games only to win can quickly find themselves without playmates.

Classes, like games, can be pursued for their own sake or for their ends. They can be thought of as *intrinsically* valuable or merely as *instrumentally* important. There can, of course, be a mixed attitude as well, but it is probably never a 50-50 split, so one attitude will predominate. However, just like there are many different types of games, not all classes, online or face-to-face, are the same. However, the distinction remains possible between those classes that seem most approachable in terms of their purpose, their final outcome and those that are about the *means* to that end. What is lost in remote learning is a primary focus on the means. What is lost creates a tendency to regard online classes as only important and successful if the final expected goal was achieved according to the student's desires.

Non-Face-to-Face Learning and the Language of Games

Students pursue diplomas. They sometimes seem to play at hunting them down (Caplan, 2018). With a desire to satisfy degree requirements, they, as Mary says, "play the game" of non-face-to-face classes to complete their undergraduate education. Danna calls it "checking a box," and other participants frequently refer to it as "jumping through hoops." John tells me, "If they could make all subjects an online class like a video game that would make me the best learner in the world!" There is an awareness of the "gamification" of education that reflects the way my participants talk about learning. One of my other participants, Nathan, similar in age to Lane and Evan (i.e., a bit older than the normal student), spends his summers in Las Vegas playing professional poker.

Nathan tells me that he really wants to learn, to improve and to get the most out of his classes even if they are online. He wants to become a better writer and develop his capacities. As a student, Nathan knows the text-heavy nature of non-face-to-face classes has the potential to provide him with ample opportunities to practice and amplify his writing talent. For him, this depends a lot on the professor.

> My first [non-face-to-face] class was last summer actually, political science. [John Smith], he is terrible, I feel passionately about this. So yah, not like the best jump start to online courses but it was necessary because it was the only PolySci class available in the summer. I want a lot of feedback, that is one of the most important things for me, for just getting, or figuring out how I am doing, for progress – even if I get a perfect score, I want feedback. If I get a 100/100 and I get a "good job" that's not good enough for me. I want to know what I could have done better. What was good and what was bad. Even if it was just the most minor thing. And I could tell that this professor was very generic, copy and pasting, you could tell, just like "great job on this assignment you fulfilled the following requirements." And you could tell it was very rubric like. And he probably lifted and copy pasted this for anybody with similar scores, so nothing specific to my work.

As a professional game player, Nathan doesn't want his education to be a game. Notions of triviality and fun attach themselves to things that are characterized as "games." Nathan wants to be transformed. If education is defined as the most efficient transfer or at least dissemination of information, then online classes are wonderfully good. However, they are not good for deepening social bonds, creating wisdom and providing individualized learning experience (Gray, 1968/2017). Of course, as he well knows, games can do this too. But the point is, for Nathan, he does not have a lot of patience for how the technological attitude of efficiency levels down his experience of learning, i.e., how his work is not treated as a special product of his personal efforts, even if it earns all the points. He can't learn what he *specifically* needs to learn, if the feedback he is given is generic. The comments, however applicable, need to reflect the distinctiveness of his work in the same way that verbal feedback on a presentation or a paper might. Studies have been done which show that students in online classes crave the missing conversations that they would have in a classroom about their work. They desire the more nuanced and ample "global" feedback that can be communicated verbally (Cavanaugh & Song, 2014).

Rubric Like: The Rules of Online Classes

In characterizing the leveled nature of his experience, Nathan calls it "rubric like." In the book *Rubric Nation: Critical Inquiries on the impact of Rubrics in Education* (2015), rubrics are described as "Typically assign[ing] a score or rating, a rank, or a descriptor that represents the gradation of quality in a particular category based on values for that category that are generally determined prior to performance" (Tenam-Zemach & Flynn, 2015, p. xviii). Rubrics are meant to diminish ambiguity. The word "rubric" derives from the bright red lettering of the directions in medieval religious services. Rubrics for assignments are designed to make the learning explicit, at least the portion that is up for evaluation. Since rubrics make all salient requirements explicit, they can limit possibilities.

> Learning and performance are messy, complex processes, but the assignment of a single score is a move of efficiency that oftentimes disregards, masks, or attempts to reduce that messiness, not because it is pedagogically justifiable but because it is administratively expedient.
>
> (Ibid., p. xix)

The incentives the student may feel to go above and beyond what is required may be diminished since the rubrics are so clear and the incentives for doing extra are not. Moreover, the students who do go beyond, those like Nathan, are probably the ones who would anyway. But they want the professor to take the time to acknowledge and engage with what they have done in such a way that they can get something out of the experience. For Nathan, he wants to be shown; he does not appreciate the kind of learning experience that Danna calls "fact and recall." He, like her, can't get anything out of that. He wants more than just familiarity with new facts.

> I just love constantly working on a piece and constantly honing something. And all my writing was done outside of academia so I want an actual professional, or people who have put in a lot more work in this world, to give me feedback on my writing. It's not like "give me good feedback" it's not like that either. It's got to be critical! I want to get better. If there is one thing I am really self-critical about it's my writing feeling robotic. I want to feel more creative with my writing. And I don't feel like I can get better without trying to do something different. So that PolySci professor was never very good at helping me get out of that autopilot mode. I've taken three online courses total and that was the first, and his was atrocious, that was so bad.

For Nathan, it is about the process. He wants a good outcome, a high grade, for sure, but more importantly is that he feels like he learns. As he describes it, learning requires that he be changed in some way. He wants this change to happen during the class. The transformation he desires does not seem to rely on just completing a course; it requires that the class do something to him.

References

Caplan, B. (2018). *The case against education: Why the education system is a waste of time and money*. Princeton, NJ: Princeton University Press.

Cavanaugh, A. J., & Song, L. (2014). Audio feedback versus written feedback: Instructors' and students' perspectives. *Journal of Online Learning and Teaching*, 10(1), 122–138.

Egenfeldt-Nielsen, S., Smith, J. H., & Tosca, S. P. (2008). *Understanding video games: The essential introduction*. New York, NY: Routledge.

Gray, J. G. (2017). *The promise of wisdom*. Middletown, CT: Wesleyan University Press. (Original work published 1968).

Heidegger, M. (1977). *The question concerning technology, and other essays* (W. Levitt, Trans.). New York, NY: HarperCollins. (Original works published 1962, 1952 & 1954).

Introna, L., & Ilharco, F. M. (2006). On the meaning of screens: Towards a phenomenological account of screenness. *Human Studies*, 29, 57–76.

O'Donohue, J. (1997). *Anam cara*. New York, NY: Cliff Street Books.

Picard, M. (1930). *The human face* (G. Endore, Trans.). New York, NY: Farrar & Rinehart Inc.

Tenam-Zemach, M., & Flynn, J. E. (2015). *Rubric nation: Critical inquiries on the impact of rubrics in education*. Charlotte, NC: Information Age Publishing Inc.

Wittgenstein, L. (2009). *Philosophical investigations* (G. E. M. Anscombe, P. M. S. Hacker, & J. Schulte, Trans.). West Sussex, UK: Wiley-Blackwell.

11 Response-Ability

Responsibility is, as Bauman (1993) puts it, "The first reality of the self" (p. 13). It is the moment the self becomes a self through its possibility of self-awareness. Responsibility is co-determined with selfhood and is when we recognize ourselves as "non-interchangable" (Levinas, 1985, p. 101). Our self-awareness is manifest when we feel some degree of ownership or possession over our own actions. We sense that what has happened is due to our own operations in the world. And though the philosopher Holger Zaborowski, following Levinas, says, "The face of the Other is the most concrete way to experience responsibility" (2005, p. 56), there are other forms of responsibility. My participants seem to focus on the sense of responding to what they are able to do in their classes for themselves. Their sense of responsibility is not for others but for themselves. The non-face-to-face class calls on them to respond to what they are able to do.

Similar to the students I spoke with in my preliminary investigation of non-face-to-face learning, several of my nine participants bring up the direct connection they experience with their learning. They feel like it is on them to determine the role they play in the process of learning. It is not mitigated by anyone else. They contrast the level of weight or burden that the online classes put on them as compared with traditional classes. For John, being able to have more control is ideal. He can determine how much of the work he wants to get done and when. Another participant, Travis, is only able to take advantage of military support for his education through the non-face-to-face options. Students in online classes have greater control over their schedule. For Travis, being in control means he can also determine where he is when he is learning for college credit. As he points out, some of his friends were even in war zones doing "homework" assignments. For John, this means he does not typically have to rely on others, the teacher in particular, like he normally would:

> Online teaching is taking the power of learning away from the teachers and to the students. Because teachers have limited access to their students, they cannot impact their studies in traditional ways. I have

DOI: 10.4324/9781003349051-11

never spoken with one of my online teachers, and only email them if I am submitting an assignment late or another complication comes up. Teachers are so unnecessary in this format that most of the classes I have taken use proctors instead of teachers. They give the "teachers" the lesson plan, have them update and monitor canvas or blackboard, and grade. That's it. I would never think to ask an online teacher something like "hey, what do you think about this paragraph here, is it too strong?" I like it. It gives me a control over my grades that I haven't ever had, and it makes me work harder for them. I'm a person who likes to do things on my own without any hindrance or guidance. I like figuring things out on my own. Self-motivation is the only requirement to succeed in online classes. You have all the resources you need from day one. You could realistically spend the first 2 weeks of an online class to complete everything well ahead of the deadlines. That's the level of control you have.

(John)

Taking from the Teachers and Giving to the Students

John relishes the ability to take control, figure it out for himself and work at his own pace. He doesn't want guidance. Students in online classes can feel that if it is to be, it is up to them to get it done. There seems to be a sense of liberation in how they express this experience, as if, finally, all of the things that typically get in the way of achieving what they want from their classes are removed in an online class. But this control and freedom come at a cost, it is because of the loss of something else.

Nathan explains:

> As I go through this online class there is certainly a lot of work. You have to make up for time lost in-person. Right? No classes, you have to make up for that. It requires a level of responsibility that is different than going to a regular class on site. Ok maybe going to class that is a level of responsibility in itself.

Nathan seems to be emphasizing that for the tasks required to complete a course someone has to be responsible. It could be the teacher or the student, but either way someone is on the hook. However, when it is on the teacher to fill up class time or organize the schedule of when work needs to be done,

> That is easier than completely having to be responsible for the work yourself. Because once you attend the class you can just kind of sit there or maybe coast a little bit. Or maybe you can depend on your peers a little bit more.

Nathan's characterization of face-to-face classes is that they provide a kind of safety net. If you forget something, being in class will remind you or help you in some way. The teacher might say something or a fellow student will help you to keep in mind what is needed to get things done well. However, in an online class he does not experience that same kind of aid or backup to his own efforts. The pressure is on him to make a schedule and do the work. And yet it is all spelled out ahead of time. The explicit requirements dictate what must be done and when.

Some students, like John, prefer the control that allows them to create their own schedule. But this is his responsibility. Mary pointed out that she had to make a schedule to keep up with the requirements to post comments and reply to other students. Likewise, Lane's experience was that he had to keep as diligent a schedule as possible. He was tied to the alerts that he had set up on his phone which were his way of reminding himself to keep up with posting comments and replying to others. Travis also pointed out that if he didn't take the time to find an Internet connection while he was in Germany, he would not have been able to do his classes, i.e., nobody figured out the logistics for him. Ultimately, non-face-to-face classes become as schedule dependent as face-to-face classes, except the responsibility for making and maintaining the schedule is shifted to the students. The shift can help students to feel empowered. They can have a greater sense of ownership as well as preoccupation with their non-face-to-face classes. Similar to what Carl expressed as an overall greater burden by his online classes, the absence of in-person contact with others means more mental load regarding the requirements. Nothing, or at least very little, can be outsourced to others for reminders on what needs to be done and when, and how exactly to do an assignment. John helps to reveal this facet of the experience:

> Online you have to create your own schedule and you have to have your own way of doing things. Whenever a new week would start, I would look at what needs to be done. And I would sort of see how much work is required and I would see what time that week I would need – how much time I would need to dedicate that week and what days I would have free. Sometimes it happened to be the last day possible because I'm a procrastinator and I always have some time on Sundays to always finish it. Or sometimes if it was a little more work I would do it on a free day like a Thursday or a Friday which I usually have free and I would get it done then. So that part was always a little bit cleaner then at school when you are actually going in because you have dedicated days that you have to do things – so that way in planning your own schedule that's so much easier, at least for me and I found being able to control that was a lot better.

Several students highlighted in our conversations how remote classes put the onus of scheduling on them. Carl remarked that it kept online classes perpetually on his mind. What is lost from learning when it is made non-face-to-face allows it to be mastered. There is a certain cleanness born of the increasing control afforded by the efficiency of online learning.

Adult-ing

At the beginning of our second conversation, Mary characterizes her experience in non-face-to-face classes with three words (her idea). She says, "When I was taking the class I felt [1] *stressed*, sometimes, [2] *not challenged* enough and [3] like an *adult*." Under the conditions, Mary describes, instruction and the role of others were invisible. It was not an important part of the experience. My participants gave the impression of solitary workers. The solitude had advantages and disadvantages; being mostly cut off from others was expected and so generally not experienced as a problem.

Mary characterized the responsibility that was put on her in her first online undergraduate class as a verb, i.e., "to adult."

> I felt adulting because of the time management skills that were required. And that was the first time instead of getting my physical body to a place and somebody else, like the professor, being responsible for facilitating everything and assigning everything. Ok you do it this week and not that week and you didn't really know what was coming. The online classes give it to you all at once all of that information, so it definitely felt, I felt more grown-up-ish, because then I had to plan out my time.

Having to figure out what the requirements were, getting the materials together and keeping up with the need to post comments and replies exacted a level of involvement that seemed to Mary to be something that adults did; she said, "the first adulting time of its 'on your time' and 'up to you.'" The online class provided a plane of experience where Mary was treated like someone who could do those things; it was in her capacity to do them. The responsibility made her feel mature, like she was stepping up and doing something that was potentially important. She emphasized many times that she did not feel like she learned in the class and was not challenged, but she certainly felt like she had an experience of being responsible for her learning or at least the outcome of the course. However, she did not feel challenged by the course material. Instead, the challenge was for herself to "grow up" and take responsibility.

The Connected Face of Ownership: Others and Assignments

Besides the implicit responsibility of creating a schedule, non-face-to-face classes also have explicit responsibilities similar to face-to-face classes.

The burden of reaching out to other students and establishing working relationships with those who are members of group projects is one such area. In a regular class, the professor might allocate some time for students to meet or at least tell them that they need to email and respond to each other to set up a time to meet. In the online group projects, my participants recounted just getting the email addresses of the other members and then figuring everything out from there. One of my participants, Carl, took responsibility for getting the whole project done.

> The group did choose the topic but then they did not do the work. So yeah, I did a 15-page paper alone. One guy did come through about halfway through with his bullet point ideas that he was supposed to do.

Problems with group projects are similar in traditional classes, but online it is all on the students. For Carl, there was no recourse: "This is why I hate group projects online because I would email the professor and she would say, 'you have to figure it out.'" In his case, the teacher may have been on a cruise.

Another area of responsibility is how certain assignments are engaged with. Again, this is similar to face-to-face classes but without the direct contact and back-and-forth conversation with a professor in front of a class explaining in real time. In completing an assignment that requires watching a film, Lane says that the professor

> has already kind of given an outline of the movie and he has given us an idea of where we kind of need to go and in what direction, but it is our responsibility to take these questions and present them to everybody.

In non-face-to-face classes, there is a sense that if it can be turned over to the students, it will be whether explicitly or implicitly. As John and others pointed out, the sense is often that the students are on their own and they do not have or need a professor to learn in an online class. As educational phenomenologist Max van Manen would say, they have lost contact:

> Educators rarely reflect on the fact that meaningful learning is always infected with the relational and situational particulars of the moment in which the learning takes place. Whatever we learn is always affected by the contextual details of the living situation and relation in which the learning occurs ... From a pedagogical point of view, learning is not like storing information on a digital storage device, learning means that whatever is learned becomes part of the personal being of the student.
>
> (2012, p. 31)

When some aspects of the learning in a class become the responsibility of the students (e.g., scheduling), it seems like it is easier to make them responsible for more. This pressure on the students to do what they might have traditionally expected from the professor highlights an aspect of their interaction. Several of my participants, in one way or another, alluded to a sort of tacit contract between themselves and their teachers in online classes. The contract, which leads to what some researchers of face-to-face classes have called "surrogate learning" (Sedlak et al., 1986, p. 183), goes something like this. In order to reach a kind of truce that achieves their desired outcome, the student says, "I will not require you to teach." In reply to being alleviated from the need to do the hard work of teaching, giving detailed and individualized feedback for each student for example, the teachers say, "I will not require you to learn." In this way, students get what they want, the grade, and another step toward completing their degree, and the teachers' jobs are made easier. "As long as the test are passed, credits are accumulated, and credentials are awarded what occurs in most classrooms is allowed to pass for education" (Ibid.) However, in online classes the contract is worked out a bit differently, even a bit more expansively. Professors seem to implicitly condone the superficiality of the online discussion board posts because to do otherwise would require that they put more time and effort into the course than is probably possible in the online format. One solution would be to monitor professor feedback. However, it would probably be a managerial and ethical quagmire to have administrators do quality control of professor's online feedback. Instructors thus shift most of the responsibility for the kind of learning that could happen from meaningful conversations with each other to the students. Online discussion boards could be pedagogically powerful if the instructor engaged with the students. However, the time that this would take might make non-face-to-face classes less efficient than traditional courses (Hislop & Ellis, 2004).

References

Bauman, Z. (1993). *Postmodern ethics*. Oxford: Wiley-Blackwell.
Hislop, G. W., & Ellis, H. J. C. (2004). A study of faculty effort in online teaching. *The Internet and Higher Education*, 7, 15–31.
Levinas, E. (1985). *Ethics and infinity. Conversations with Philippe Nemo*. Pittsburgh, PA: Duquesne University Press.
Sedlak, M. W., Wheeler, C. W., Pullin, D. C., & Cusick, P. A. (1986). *Selling students short: Classroom bargains and academic reform in the American high school*. New Your, NY: Teachers College Press.
Van Manen, M. (2012). The call of pedagogy as the call of contact. *Phenomenology & Practice*, 6(2), 8–34.
Zaborowski, H. (2005). On freedom and responsibility: Remarks on Sartre, Levinas and Derrida. *The Heythrop Journal*, 41(1), 47–65.

12 Facing the Void
Body and Soul

From the facets offered by my participants of the phenomenon of non-face-to-face learning, I am presented with different versions and perspectives of what is lost. What is being contrasted in their descriptions are the significance of what is lost in what they hoped to gain from their explicit efforts to learn. Though my participants are for the most part solitary in their learning, they are not fully alone either. The faces of other students are lost but they are not completely gone; vestigial aspects remain. The experiences students convey to me are like the apt title of Sherry Turkle's book; my participants find themselves *Alone Together*. The pedagogical implications for online as compared to traditional classes are profound but go mostly unnoticed by my participants. They do not offer many direct comments about pedagogy in describing their experience. Perhaps many undergraduates would not do so for in-person classes either. And yet our conversations are about the pedagogical contrast between the faceless format and the face-to-face; they talk about what is lost.

One of the biggest contrasts is the physicality of in-person classes and the ephemeral or immaterial nature of contact that is mitigated by advanced computer technology. The online class is a *virtual* connection, not a real encounter. It is true that the two formats might complement each other, be better for different students at different times and certain circumstances. It is hard to say if those gains in efficiency should change the explicit *purpose* of a course and whether it should or can be changed because of its format. However, based on the descriptions I gathered for this book, the goal of a class may be inherently altered and the expectations for it irrevocably changed by making it non-face-to-face.

The Faceless Soul and the Hypothetically Disrespected Body

One of my participants, Scott, took a Russian History class online. He loved it. The class was small. All of the students were very interested in the subject since they were all history majors. He said his professor treated him with respect, like he was a real historian and his ideas had real merit. It seemed like Scott's experience was different than, for

DOI: 10.4324/9781003349051-12

example, Mary's (and others), who characterized their classes as a scam, redundant or annoying (e.g., Danna). His was not an experience with a lower-level remedial class; instead, it was for majors, and because of its small size, he received copious personalized feedback, something Nathan would have loved. Scott also spent lots of time engaging with his fellow classmates, reading and replying to papers and comments. However, Scott came away from his online class feeling deeply disturbed.

He encountered the technological attitude of efficiency in a subtle but profound way. Scott felt and then struggled to articulate how "Our modern scientific and intellectual traditions have reshaped the world – its objects and events – into a 'faceless' collection of beings of mere matter in motion" (Mazis, 2016, p. 77). Scott sensed that the format of non-face-to-face learning was compelling him to accept a kind of dualism about his classmates. The dualist perspective led to a certain sense of doubt about his experience of others. He felt that though he interacted with the other students, he didn't *really* know them, even though he did feel like he knew them. Scott had Cartesian-type doubts as to the reality and tangibility of those he interacted with online. His doubt centered on whether their identities were stable or not. Without full contact with them, Scott was disturbed to realize that if he met any of them in person, he would have no idea who they were, and he would not be able to treat them with the respect he felt for them:

> I don't know how to put that into words but it was disconcerting that the people – because I respected them – I read a bunch of their essays and so it was really good, so I had some respect for these people even though I didn't know who they were – it's weird – even if I didn't know who they were or who I was respecting. It was weird that I would interact with these people online with a certain level of respect but then I could be meeting them in person and not hold that same level of respect for the individual. So let's say Bob deserves "level 8" respect but I meet Bob in person and I give him "level 1" respect because this guy hasn't earned my respect yet, but like, *he had*.

Scott was adamant that this aspect of his interpersonal relationship with the other students haunted his experience. "It felt really upsetting, disconcerting, just dehumanizing. It felt really dehumanizing that I'd be interacting with the same person in two separate ways." It wasn't that he actually did interact in two separate ways; it was only the idea that he could if he happened to meet any of the students in person. The experience of non-face-to-face learning created the possibility for a hypothetical that he found deeply unsettling. To feel like he knew someone and then not to know the same person if he encountered her in-person made him wonder if he knew her at all. However, the more he reflected on what he was getting to know about the other students, the more his epistemological uncertainty seemed to swell.

Scott went so far as to call the online persona, the aspect of the person he knew, their "soul." He felt some kind of connection, and his characterization of coming to that contact as touching the soul relates to phenomenological description, "The experience of contact is that moment when, in a manner of speaking, a soul touches a soul" (van Manen, 2012, p. 24). At the same time, Scott imagined the hypothetical, where he happens to encounter the same person on campus, coming into contact with what he refers to as their "body." What he got to know about his classmates through textual exchanges, e.g., reading emails, discussion board posts and essays, gave him a sense of what he thought he might get from their face. If we follow O'Donohue's (1997) Celtic wisdom insight that "The face always reveals the soul," then we can see why for Scott getting to know the other students through their writing made him feel like he was in touch with "Where the divinity of the inner life finds an echo and image. When you behold someone's face, you are gazing deeply into that person's life" (p. 39). Scott had a sense of connecting to the other students' souls even when he did not ever see their faces. He did not find an image, but he did feel like he was gazing deeply into the lives of others. But without the image to ground what he was coming to know about others he was left in some doubt.

Dis-concerting Ambiguity

In the same class, Scott describes how for a portion of the class they did not know who the teacher was. The confusion began for the students because when they were getting familiarized with the course online, where it indicated who the "course designer" was, there were two names. For a while, based on the email interactions, the students could not tell who was teaching the class. Because there were two names and only one email address, it was ambiguous as to who was actually the teacher. It caused Scott to hesitate and waver and be in doubt about the identity and importance of his textual interactions with the teacher. An educational researcher who focuses on the interactions of so called distance students with faculty noticed in his article "Virtually There," "The core ambiguity of immersion in … online education manifests itself in several ways: in a state of ambiguity regarding group membership, regarding place, and regarding functionality" (Olt, 2018, p. 386). These students who are at a "distance" are sometimes unsure of how they belong. The ambiguity can also impact the teacher's perception of the students.

There is a strong sense that the whole of reality is grounded in ambiguity, i.e., the fact that there are many ways of understanding an experience. Hermeneutic Phenomenology is based on this assumption. As Nietzsche says, "Above all, one should not wish to divest existence of its *rich ambiguity*" (1974/1887, p. 335). Therefore, it is an innate feature of remote learning that the experience is shot through with ambiguity.

Technological innovations can increase or decrease the range of our experiences. Technology can make our experience more superficial; it can also deepen our experience. Don Ihde explains in *Bodies in Technology* (2001) that the possible uses of technology "are always ambiguous and multistable" (p. 131). Though we may live perpetually immersed in ambiguity, uncertainty is not always at the forefront of how we interpret our lived experience. For Scott, the ambiguity came to the fore in a disconcerting way because it related directly to his interactions with others. And for him, having the email address did not help to clarify. Again, it was disconcerting to be in a class, enjoying it and appreciating the feedback and guidance of the teacher but not actually knowing who the teacher was. Their identity was only partial. Because it was only partially clear, it was hard for Scott to know if he knew anything for sure about the instructor.

Similar identity ambiguity plagued the group project in Scott's class. This was set up, like the ambiguity of who Scott's professor actually was, because in a non-face-to-face class, "Others appear as links, email account names, or text generated within listservs, threaded discussions ... Others are ... encountered as complexes of faceless textual signifiers made up of alphanumeric characters" (Koukal, Blume, & Blume, 2002, p. 31). During the project Scott exchanged emails with the other students in his group. However, he didn't know that he was getting emails from different people because he only knew them by their email addresses. In a long string of email exchanges, he got lost and began to be uncertain with whom he was communicating. And the longer he left his uncertainty unresolved, the harder it became to reveal his ignorance. He even doubted how many students he was emailing, whether it was one person or two. As Koukal et al. explain, "To the extent that Others are inevitably imbedded in the textuality of the Internet, it tends to blur identities" (p. 35). Not knowing who you are communicating with can be disconcerting and confusing. It becomes hard to know the significance of what is being expressed if you don't know who it is who wants you to know something.

The scant markers of another human presence, the various letters that come before the '@' symbol of an email address, acted almost like a pseudonym. These few symbols were easily confused, even though they are precise on close inspection. It was hard to distinguish these vestigial indicators of another human presence when they are so uniform and leveled down. A few alphanumeric symbols were insufficient to maintain the necessary continuity of human identity over time. Scott could remember what was being communicated but he was not sure who was saying it. He could not connect the emails to what else he thought he knew about his fellow group participants and the things he knew about them from reading their essays and discussion board posts.

Despite Scott's positive experience in his non-face-to-face class, the void created by the absence of the faces of his professor and classmates tainted the experience. Again, O'Dononhue's Celtic wisdom can be of some guidance here.

> When you gaze into someone's face, a pathway opens, resonant with his or her life and memory. You glimpse what life has made or unmade, woven or unraveled in that life. Each face fronts a different world… The openness of the face shows that we participate in the lives of others.
>
> (1997, p. 60)

All of the insight provided by the face is lost in a remote class.

For Scott, the world O'Donohue refers to, though hospitably opened up, is still in a fundamental sense cut off because he never encountered the faces of those in his online class. In our conversation, the more he thought about his epistemological doubt with regards to others, the more it seems to have clouded his experience. He seemed to be getting at a sense that he felt he could not really get to know anyone in the class. However, he also felt that he knew something; he thought he knew enough to know the "souls" of the other students, which led him to have great respect for them. However, this was not enough for him. It did not assuage his worries. It was still upsetting to him. He felt that if he could not get to know others in the class he could not learn.

What Is Absent

There is an emptiness that can open up in non-face-to-face classes. There is a kind of void that becomes part of the experience, a certain absence that makes itself known because students expect something to be there. Depending on their expectations, the absence can manifest itself in different, sometimes startling ways, as it did for Scott. For other participants, the void in non-face-to-face learning is not about others. Carl told me, "I have never felt like I learned anything in online classes." Learning, the name of the thing students might expect most from a class, was not there. For Carl, the void left where learning was expected was primarily due to online classes never teaching him *how* to learn.

> It's really good when education teaches you how to think. Online teaches you what to think. It does not teach you how to think. It teaches you that this is what you have to do to get this grade and as long as you do that you are ok.

For Carl, online classes have very little way for providing an example of *how* to think as compared to the comparatively more straightforward work of presenting *what* to think. He seems to imply that learning how to think is more likely in a face-to-face class, i.e., for him that is one of the reasons it is better.

Carl's comment also seems to show that online classes reveal the learning experience to be just a matter of getting exposed to the right content. Mastering content, again and again, seems to be what students in online classes are incentivized to do. It is that aspect of their learning experience that is reinforced, e.g. as Danna said, "fact and recall." Since Socrates such learning has been suspect. For Socrates, as it seemed to be for Plato as well, merely *telling* someone the truth and expecting them to recall it in the appropriate context was no way to get them to the truth. Just as important to getting them to the truth was preparing them for it in a way that would cause them to accept it, i.e., be changed by it. Socrates' insight was that learning was a joint process where the teacher did what Heidegger (1976/1954) calls, "letting learn." Presenting information and requiring it elsewhere can familiarize students with vital information. They can be taught *what* to think efficiently in an online class. However, my participants experienced the loss of learning how to think when they were in remote classes. In order for them to know *how* to think, they need something else.

Community and an Implicit Contract

Another aspect of the void encountered in non-face-to-face learning is felt with regards to the sense of community. Evan explained it this way, using the posting of text assignments as an example:

> You spent a decent amount of time posting something about an article you read or an experience you had or a journal entry that you had on to a message board. And then coming back later and writing responses to other people's posts so that was kind of the attempt to form some kind of online community because that is something that's clearly part of the rubric that I think the professors have as well as the students. That you know we want to do something to simulate the classroom experience.

In the design of non-face-to-face classes, there is a clear imperative that the courses must not merely be correspondence courses. The courses try to create a sense of community. Evan's use of the word "attempt" seems to show that community is not likely to be encountered in an online class. Like Nathan, Evan uses the word "rubric" to characterize the constrained nature of the design or the way that online classes seem to be following a kind of externally imposed imperative when it comes to their structure. The courses are designed to have an interactive component that seeks to simulate an in-person class or at least allow for vestigial remnants of the traditional learning experience to remain. There is an attempt, an acknowledgment, that community is part of learning.

Some students seek to be a part of something larger than themselves in their education. They can get a sense of community, feeling like they belong or that they matter, in many ways. For Travis, he felt that he should have been able to find meaningful connection through his classes. "There was at no point, in either of these two courses, I would have called what I was enrolled in a community, which is largely the opposite of what I've experienced since I've started taking normal courses." The way Travis describes this void, it is possible he didn't really know that he was missing a sense of community till he experienced face-to-face classes. However, the absence was something he noticed, so he must have felt like something was missing when he was taking his online classes.

Part of the experience was of a lack, of not being given what should have been offered. Part of this was due to feeling like even if it were offered it could not be fully received through the non-face-to-face medium. I was surprised that Travis had brought up the issue of community in our conversation since he was taking his online classes for pragmatic reasons. As an active-duty member of the military, he had access to a certain amount of funds for his education whether he spent it or not. He started taking classes with this money and hoped they would transfer.

> As much as I appreciate poetry, I don't exactly try to find it in many things. And so, when I take classes, especially like for instance the online ones that I don't necessarily feel too involved in or I feel as though it's more transactional than I'd want a class to be, I don't really observe or feel anything. It's not a journey of self-experience that I feel as though is monumental or significant to me.

The fact that Travis felt like there was an absence of community didn't seem like that would be something that would have mattered enough for him to mention. Like others, his experience was more about the grade, the practical value of learning *what* to think in order to jump through the hoops of higher education, i.e., playing the game. It was about the ability to navigate the process and be able to put the right information where needed. For Travis it did not seem like his online classes were the place to really learn *how* to think. It almost seemed like a kind of joke to him to expect such classes to be able to transform him through opening up the possibility of wisdom (Gray, 1968/2017).

A school that was almost completely non-face-to-face provided Travis' online undergraduate classes. He said that it was likely that the professors never taught traditional classes. Travis said that for active-duty military online classes were ideal. He explained that it was possible that his fellow students were deployed, fighting in wars and were also – shockingly – potentially preoccupied about assignments for their online classes. The professors at Travis' school knew this and took the conditions of their students into account in how they operated the class. There was a more detached formality in how they treated students, no deep interest or attempt to get to know them. Travis said, "In those two classes I saw the professors interact with students in a semi-clinical way, in that they might have been seeing the same deficiencies I was, but from the other side of things." The way the teachers interacted with students was removed and dispassionate.

Travis had a sense that the professors were sensing the same superficiality he felt as a student. He could see that the technological attitude of efficiency shaped how they interacted with students online. They acted more, as what other participants named, as facilitators, not teachers. Travis perceived that the diminished role of the teachers was normal. He explained that it might have been because the professors could also see, what he had observed, that the posts and responses made by students were forced and shallow, but they were done because they were required. Teachers in this more leveled-down capacity did not stand out as special or distinct. Travis didn't see any reason why they should try to be more than just a facilitator or even that doing so was required.

> They would post the prompts and questions to the assignment section and discussion boards, let us give our responses and two responses to each other, and then be on to the next task. Rarely was there ever interaction outside the minimum requirements, like a professor asking why a student saw things that way, or if they had things that would supplement what they had included further. And to be fair, it looked like students, myself included, weren't pushing back on that behavior at all either.

The online behavior of the students and teachers demonstrates that the same implicit pedagogical contract (or truce) was in the atmosphere of Travis' experience. As introduced earlier, this is the attitude that is also possible in traditional classroom learning but seems more endemic in non-face-to-face classes. The pact goes roughly like, "I'll accept that this is a demonstration of you learning if you accept that what I am doing is teaching." Ultimately, it seems to be an agreement to accept mediocrity and settling for learning what to think and not how. The absence of a real incentive to hold each other accountable, whether to actually learn or actually teach, may have contributed to creating the void where community should have been. If a student can't expect to be taught, and can see where those opportunities for teacher are but are left undone, they might feel like they are not expected to do their part. Community is delicate. It is undermined by the vicious cycle of those who are together not doing what is expected. It is also undone by not holding others up to what is expected of them. From Travis' description, it seems that the undoing of community comes from both teachers and students and is based on the essence of what is lost in remote learning.

References

Gray, J. G. (2017). *The promise of wisdom*. Middletown, CT: Wesleyan University Press. (Original work published 1968).

Heidegger, M. (1976). *What is called thinking* (J. Glenn Gray, Trans.). New York, NY: HarperCollins. (Original work published 1954).

Ihde, D. (2001). *Bodies in technology*. Minneapolis, MN: University of Minnesota Press.

Koukal, D. R., Blume, L. B., & Blume, T. W. (2002). Dwelling in the classroom: A phenomenology of distance learning. *Journal of Teaching in Marriage and Family*, 2(1), 19–40.

Mazis, G. (2016). *Merleau-Ponty and the face of the world: Silence, ethics, imagination, and poetic ontology*. Albany: State University of New York Press.

Nietzsche, F. (1974). *The gay science: With a prelude in rhymes and an appendix of songs* (W. Kaufmann, Trans.). New York, NY: Random House. (Original work published 1887).

O'Donohue, J. (1997). *Anam cara*. New York, NY: Cliff Street Books.

Olt, P. A. (2018). Virtually there: Distance freshmen blended in classes through synchronous online education. *Innovative Higher Education*, 43, 381–395.

Turkle, S. (2017). *Alone together: Why we expect more from technology and less from each other*. New York, NY: Basic Books.

Van Manen, M. (2012). The call of pedagogy as the call of contact. *Phenomenology & Practice*, 6(2), 8–34.

13 Facing Some Parts of Learning Online Post-COVID-19

Transition to Insights and Implications

My participants have shown me different things. Their facets have shimmered toward meaning as they encountered each other in my phenomenological joining. What they have shown comes together in unpredictable ways. My participant's expressions meet my thoughts, experiences and interpretive efforts and become something – meaning shines.

There is a sense that our mind, or what used to be called soul (*psyche* or *Geist*), is somehow separate from our body. The soul seems to experience time differently, to almost be able to transcend it: the way happy times pass as opposed to the way anguish or boredom lingers. Moreover, the thinking mind seems not to be constrained by space. With such experiences of the soul, we might seek to unify what is already inseparable. It is our body that gives us the soul or mind that we are capable of. However that may be, we still linger with the doubts of modernity. Descartes may have been completely wrong, but just like the geocentric model of the universe, he was basing his dualism off of what seemed like an obvious experience. Just as we see the sun going around the earth and assume that the earth is the center, in the same way we feel that our thoughts are separate from our bodies. What experience could be clearer? By maintaining this view, we open up, as with so many things in modernity, the troubles of non-face-to-face learning. We create the conditions for loss. Instead, we should be open to considering how to find the place where we can live and dwell and where our thoughts, souls, faces and bodies can meet undivided.

In this chapter, I turn to some insights related to the themes developed in the previous chapters about what is lost for undergraduates when they learn remotely. The hermeneutic work continues here as I seek to present an interpretation of the essence(s) of non-face-to-face learning for undergraduates. That is, I hope to show the meaning of this experience by, again, articulating its context. There is no one intended answer given here. By that I mean the inquiry into the meaning of online classes does not end. As Heidegger aptly explains, "Commonly, an inquiry aims

DOI: 10.4324/9781003349051-13

straight for the answer. It rightly looks for the answer alone, and sees to it that the answer is obtained. The answer disposes of the question. By the answer, we rid ourselves of the question" (1976/1954, p. 158). The question that guides this book as to the meaning of what is lost in remote learning is not disposed of here.

There are no results in a hermeneutic phenomenological study *as there are* in other qualitative and quantitative research methods. As Heidegger explains, "There are 'results' only where there is reckoning and calculation" (1961/1984, p. 48). Moreover, going along with Nietzsche, who says, "An interpretation that permits counting, calculating, weighing, seeing, and touching, and nothing more – that is crudity and naiveté" (1974, p. 335). The sense of the meaning of non-face-to-face learning for undergraduates has to come forth for each reader. It is personal and subjective. The persuasive power and uses of this work will vary. Hopefully they open paths to further concern and inquiry.

It is a deeply philosophical endeavor to render the essence(s) of a phenomenon. Heidegger (2009) says that questions that focus on the essence of something are called "fore-questions [*Vorefrage*]." He explains that this type of question is different than what we normally think of when we use the word "question." "The fore-question, as distinguished from that which we commonly call question, is fundamentally never settled, then the decline and the boundless misinterpretation have already begun" (2009, p. 17). *The* essence (or essences) of what is lost in remote learning is (are) never settled. We approach it and dwell with it poetically.

> Every question, and the question of the essence in a particular sense, arises in the face of what appears strange to us. The strangeness, however, is not removed through the questioning. We let that which is strange come over us in the questioning, but not to come over us so that we are swallowed up in it. We face up to the strange.
> (Ibid., p. 31)

To encounter the essence(s), we must be preoccupied in an active and open way.

Heidegger notes that in asking about thinking, we may never come to anything like what we typically expect of an answer, such as we would from asking, for example, "What is called riding a bike?" "Genuine, that is, essential questioning is sustained by that dark bidding, from which a question arises, over which the individual who poses the question for the first time has no control" (Ibid., p. 15). Endless inquiry can only be of value for its own sake; it cannot produce some instrumental value as the technological attitude would demand. A hermeneutic phenomenological study can open up a way to a free relationship with technology. It does this by questioning. "It would violate the meaning of interpretation generally if we cherished the view that there can be an interpretation which is non-relative" (Heidegger, 1976/1954, p. 177). The results of this book therefore are not definitive or independent of subjective interpretation.

I now look a bit more at the pieces of the face of online learning and what can be shown. This chapter and those that follow continue to explore the experience of online learning. I continue to ask, "What could be lost when learning is altered by the removal of the face-to-face encounter? What possibilities might exist for face-to-face learning so that it can be 'seen' and experienced differently?" Now, in this transition, I ask what has the meaning making process of this phenomenological inquiry done with me? How have I been changed? What will I do? What could others believe or do?

It is also at this juncture that I more fully bring in my experience becoming a teacher, for the first time, of non-face-to-face classes. By doing this, I am following Heidegger's admonition that "The teacher, the one who teaches and speaks, dare not be forgotten" (1984/1961, p. 49). However, the emphasis is still on how students experience learning in online classes. The following chapters continue the work of showing some of the parts of non-face-to-face learning and how they relate to the whole experience. Some of the insights that I seek to open up are poetical. They are delicate and ambiguous. I turn to several poems to heighten our awareness of what a free relationship to technology can be even when it presents as a totalizing necessity. I also develop some recommendations of possible future study that could be done based on my phenomenological interpretation, particularly what this study points to regarding teaching.

COVID-19 Lockdown: Exploring Remoteness

Technology writer Nicholas Carr has sensitively written about the implications of the results of COVID-19 policies and technological solutions:

> What happens when the [COVID-19] pandemic subsides? We almost certainly will rejoice in our return to the human life-world — the world of embodiment, presence, action. We'll celebrate our release from remoteness ... As the research of Sherry Turkle and others has shown, one of the attractions of virtualization has always been the sense of safety it provides. Even without a new virus on the prowl, the embodied world, the world of people and things, presents threats, not just physical but also social and psychological. *Presence is also exposure.* When we socialize through a screen, we feel protected from many of those threats — less fearful, more in control — even if we also feel more isolated and constrained and adrift. If, in the wake of the pandemic, we end up feeling more vulnerable to the risks inherent in being physically in the world, we may, despite our immediate relief, continue to seek refuge in our new habits of remoteness. We won't feel liberated, but at least we'll feel protected.
>
> (Carr, 2020)

Carr is doing the work of a philosopher. He is keeping alive our sense of the milieu in which we find ourselves. He is working to help us learn by remembering, *anamnesis*, by guiding us to draw out from our own experience what is significant so we can construct meaning. He wants us to pay attention to the strange and uncanny, *unheimlichkeit*, "home-less-ness" of our current world when enforced remoteness can happen, i.e., lockdown. He wants us to see that in our protected state we have lost something. Carr wants to remind us to keep alive that which makes us human: our connection with others. Only in these encounters where our vulnerability is possible, the chance to be embarrassed, to say the wrong thing and to be silent with others can we become what we are.

> We receive many gifts, of many kinds. But the highest and really most lasting gift given to us is always our essential nature, with which we are gifted in such a way that we are what we are only through it.
> (Heidegger, 1976/1954, p. 142)

Vital to that nature is being with others.

Since my preliminary years of research, conversations with my participants and creating a text to work hermeneutically, all undergraduate education has to some degree or other or for some period of time become non-face-to-face. With this cataclysmic shock to the normal way of being together and the subsequent tidal wave of technologically mitigated solutions, I wonder what will happen to face-to-face learning now. Do my insights appear moot when non-face-to-face learning is no longer just about optimization in terms of costs and time, but is now done because it is perceived to be a condition for survival, i.e., an unquestionable imperative? That is, many may think, "Who cares if something is lost when undergraduates learn non-face-to-face so long as they are saf*er*." Yes, who can argue against being *more* safe. As long as there is risk, there can be degrees of safety. It is hard to say who should determine what degree should be the standard. As Albert Borgmann (2003) notes, "Safety is a component of availability; in pursing the latter, technology procures the former" (p. 19). With ready technological innovations at hand, how can we keep from using them when it feels like we must?

Online classes are more available due to their frictionless dis-embodied format. As such, non-face-to-face learning is almost by definition "safer." Why ever go back to traditional classroom learning? Really. What is the reason for it? If traditional learning can still be advocated for now, then can't it also be advocated for always, whenever non-face-to-face learning is pushed (relentlessly)? I was drawn to this phenomenon due to a protective urge. I wanted to hunker over something precious, something focal, and safeguard it. Now I do not know if my efforts matter. Why? Because there will always be risks to being together. There will always be something, whether it is a potential health threat or another sort of threat.

What if we always have to wear masks in classrooms? To a certain degree, the concern with non-face-to-face learning in this book can be read as referring to the loss of face-to-face contact due to mask mandates and not just the remoteness of online education. Are there thematic overlaps with online classes in how undergraduates learn when they are in a classroom where everyone is behind a mask? Moreover, do some of my insights also apply when masks come between us in a classroom?

I wonder if university life will ever be able to return to the traditional modes of education now that the standard for safety has been set so high. For example, in the fall of 2020 I was allowed to teach one class face-to-face as long as everyone was six feet apart and wore masks when they moved. I had about 25 students, but the room had around 120 seats. However, at many schools *if* classes did meet in person, masks were required at all times. The faces were covered even when together. Well, at that point why not just "move" to remote instruction on Zoom? The difference between the precautions at my school and others could be due to how updated the ventilation systems in the classrooms were or other technical factors, but ultimately different standards for safety were established at different schools for different reasons. The next semester, spring of 2021, even after vaccines had been developed and more effective therapeutics and hospital treatments were being implemented, all face-to-face classes were canceled (except for a few labs or art classes).

I had to advocate for teaching face-to-face in the Fall of 2020, even engage in some pleading. Most classes had moved to some non-face-to-face form. Of the four different classes I teach, Logic was the one I just could not imagine doing virtually. Fortunately, my administrators were able to make at least my one Logic class in-person. It felt like a triumph. I was exuberant the first day. I felt like I and my students were the brave ones that would show that there was a light at the end of the tunnel, and we could all hope that soon we could be back together. I learned that some of the students had fervently sought out *any* face-to-face class because they had been unable to find the motivation to learn online. In the Spring of 2020, all face-to-face instructions had been canceled. Some students found that they were not getting what they expected from their education. They were grateful to take even my Logic class, because at least then they could meet in-person and not on Zoom.

Understanding

How do we understand the conditions that make any understanding possible? We live life forward but only understand it retrospectively (Kierkegaard, 2019/1843). The technological reaction to COVID-19 has made many aspects of non-face-to-face learning self-evident. But the self-evident is not obvious. "In everything well known something worthy of thought still lurks" (Heidegger, 1991/1961, p. xi). It's hard to think about the common and normal. That which is closest to us conceptually is the hardest thing to understand.

In Heidegger's work, he repeatedly makes the point that the most ubiquitous is the most obscure, sometimes called the "law of proximity," where the closest is the farthest. "To experience the closest is the most difficult. In the course of our dealings and occupations it is passed over precisely as the easiest. Because the closest is the most familiar, it needs no special appropriation" (1982/1998, p. 135) Heidegger continues by explaining that the result is this: "We do not think about [what is closest]. So it remains what is least worthy of thought. The closest appears therefore as if it were nothing" (Ibid.). Before Heidegger, Nietzsche had the same insight, "What is familiar is what we are used to; and what we are used to is most difficult to 'know' – that is, to see as a problem: that is, to see as strange, as distant, as 'outside us'" (1974, p. 301). Not only does this show the strong influence Nietzsche's thinking had on Heidegger, it also gets at the intriguing idea, offered by Heidegger himself, that all great thinkers think the same thought (Heidegger, 1985).

We increasingly live with others via screen mitigated interactions, e.g., Zoom and WebEx. The use of videoconferencing is no longer a novelty. We are getting used to it. Zoom is no longer distant. We are grateful for these technological fixes. However, as they become our most proximal experience, they can fade from thought and scrutiny. On the other hand, there is something about technology; when its influence becomes overweening, it also becomes most noticeable. Even as Zoom becomes normal, we also become aware of what is lost in face-to-face conversations (Turkle, 2017). For example, when I began this project, there were some curious raised eyebrows and not much recognition. Now, in the time of Zoom, when I explain this book, people immediately see the relevance and need.

References

Borgmann, A. (2003). *Power failure: Christianity in the culture of technology*. Grand Rapids, MI: Brazos Press.

Carr, N. (2020, December 31). Not being there: From virtuality to remoteness. *Rough Type*. Retrieved January 10, 2020, from http://www.roughtype.com/?p=8824

Heidegger, M. (1976). *What is called thinking* (J. Glenn Gray, Trans.). New York, NY: HarperCollins. (Original work published 1954).

Heidegger, M. (1984). *Nietzsche volume two: The eternal recurrence of the same* (D. F. Krell, Trans.). New York, NY: HarperCollins. (Original work published 1961).

Heidegger, M. (1985). *Schelling's treatise on the essence of human freedom* (J. Stambaugh, Trans.). Athens, OH: Ohio University Press.

Heidegger, M. (1991). *Nietzsche volumes one: The will to power as art* (D. F. Krell, Trans.). New York, NY: HarperCollins. (Original work published 1961).

Heidegger, M. (1998). *Parmenides* (A. Shuwer & R. Rojcewicz, Trans.). Bloomington, IN: Indiana University Press. (Original work published 1982).

Heidegger, M. (2009). *Logic as the question concerning the essence of language* (W. T. Gregory & Y. Unna, Trans.). Albany, NY: State University of New York Press.

Kierkegaard, S. (2019). *Kierkegaard's journals and notebooks volume 11: Part 1 loose papers 1830-1843*. Princeton, NJ: Princeton University Press. (Original work published 1843).

Nietzsche, F. (1974). *The gay science: With a prelude in rhymes and an appendix of songs* (W. Kaufmann, Trans.). New York, NY: Random House. (Original work published 1887).

Turkle, S. (2017). *Alone together: Why we expect more from technology and less from each other*. New York, NY: Basic Books.

14 The Post-COVID-19 Lacuna in Higher Education

Fiction as a Way to Perceive Unintended Consequences

Science fiction is the interesting genre that understands, explains and entertains the hypothetical. It often focuses on the future like *Star Trek* or to another kind of parallel reality altogether like *Star Wars*. Science fiction can allow us to understand and see ourselves in a way that non-fiction cannot. For example, fantastic exaggerations can elucidate the real risks of existing technology. We can be made aware of certain potential predicaments that technological developments may lead us to. Indeed, many episodes of the *Twilight Zone* pointed out the dangers of television, consumerism and mass society. The show *Black Mirror* (a play on the idea of the television screen itself, and Plato's allegory of the cave) is a science fiction show that continues the tradition of technological moralizing. *Black Mirror* is like a self-appointed prophet, similar to the mythical Cassandra, who is not only cursed to utter true prophecies but also never believed; we are also entertained by the predictions. Perhaps it is a good thing it is that way. "The bulk of *Black Mirror* deals with the consequences our world faces in the aftermath of technology gone wrong" (Robinson, 2020). Except now, in the aftermath of 2020, even the creators of the show are concerned that fiction has caught up with reality. When speaking about a delayed sixth season, the show's creator Charlie Brooker says, "At the moment, I don't know what stomach there would be for stories about societies falling apart" (Ibid.). If some of our popular current fiction is too concerned about the present to make us think about the unintended consequences of technological seduction, the insights still exist.

With the stunning prescience of a great artist, the novelist E.M. Forster (1909) captured distinct aspects of our contemporary technological condition. In his short story, *The Machine Stops*, Forster shows what he imagines would be the consequences of a world where everyone is connected to others by electronic devices. It is a dystopian world. The only hope in Forster's story is the hope that "the machine" will stop. According to this vision, when nobody ever has to be face-to-face, humanity is

DOI: 10.4324/9781003349051-14

reduced to being a pointless insect. The main protagonist of *The Machine Stops* inhabits, like every human, in "a small room, hexagonal in shape, like the cell of a bee" (p. 2). She is a teacher who gives lectures and listens to lectures. Through the story, we are made aware of some of what technological facelessness can do. First, there is a growing and pervasive sense of irritation. As the world becomes perfectly mitigated by technology (i.e., completely frictionless), people are left with no patience. Second, there is only one place. Instead of people being brought to things or events, stuff that is needed and certain types of experiences are brought to people. There is no need for motion, travel and the experience of different or special places. And third, there is a terror of direct experience. The anxieties of dealing with another person directly or being required to physically solve a problem are overwhelming efforts that are never learned.

Before 2020, we used to talk of virtual learning. To some extent, we of course still do, but there has been a noticeable shift in our use in language with regard to online learning since all learning had to be *moved there*. We now tend not to talk so much about virtual learning. Instead, the focus is on how all learning has become non-face-to-face but is still synchronous and "remote" (Carr, 2020). What is this remote-ness? Where have we all been moved to? The "there" where classes are "moved" to online is not an actual place. Indeed, being forced to "move" everything online has caused a reckoning. Educators across the world wonder if learning is happening as they stare at students framed in small boxes on their screens. They wonder if learning is happening because if it is, then what was the point of all the fuss about getting together in the first place? If it is not happening, then what is this thing that is passing itself off now as learning? Perhaps it is sufficient. Maybe it does not make a difference if undergraduates learn remotely (Caplan, 2018). In general, it has not reduced the cost of tuition. Some might, like me, be haunted by what is lost, what is left out of non-face-to-face learning.

Zoom, Zoom, Zooming

The word "zoom" relates to not only aviation but also cameras. It captures the sense of changing proximity (airplane) or perspective (telephoto lens) quickly. In 2014, "to zoom" was entered into the *Oxford English Dictionary* as, "To communicate with (a person or group of people) over the internet, typically by video-chatting, using the Zoom application." Don't we know it. The creators of Zoom knew that their innovation, though not unprecedented, was designed to quickly bring people together. In a snap, distance could be illuminated and work that was usually done by in-person groups could be completed as long as everyone had a computer and access to the Internet.

Zoom is efficient. It solves the problem of how to continue education etc. without exposing anyone to a dangerous virus. However, like all technology, the gains in efficiency and safety come at a cost. There is a trade-off. As many have noted, the initial necessity that has now turned into the new normal is *surprisingly* exhausting (Jackson-Wright, 2020). Even though we are spared the efforts of commuting and physically preparing to be with others, Zoom has its own ways of wearing us down (Ibid.). Its ease and conveyances produce different burdens we are less prepared to deal with. It reminds me of the idea that humans might be ill suited for utopia (which an ironic interpretation of Plato's *Republic* supports). This is the insight that all our ideas of a perfect world end up being dystopias when the details are thoroughly worked out and the unintended consequences become manifest, as in *The Machine Stops*.

Here is one touching scene between the main character Vashti and her son Kuno (we should remember Forster wrote this in 1909):

Vashti uses a glowing "round plate" to connect to her son Kuno "on the other side of the earth." According to Forster's description of the then fictional technology, they both appear to each other just like we see others on FaceTime or Zoom. As they communicate, Kuno explains that he wants his mother to come and "see" him. She says that through the machine she can see him and asks what more he could want.

> "I want to see you not through the Machine. I want to speak to you not through the wearisome Machine."
>
> Vashti says, "You mustn't say anything against the Machine."
>
> Kuno replies: "The Machine is much, but it is not everything. I see something like you in this plate, but I do not see you. I hear something like you through this telephone, but I do not hear you. That is why I want you to come. Pay me a visit, so that we can meet face to face, and talk about the hopes that are in my mind."
>
> (Forster, 1909, pp. 1–2)

Kuno even goes so far to as to accuse his mother of misplaced piety. His criticism of her that maybe she will even worship or pray to the machine is the same concern Abse (1991) raises in his poem about the doctor's instrument, the stethoscope, "Should I pray therefore? … Should I kneel before it, chant an apophthegm from a small text?" The wonders of technology seduce us into forgetting that they are our own creations. However wonderful they may be, they were created by finite mortal minds; they are not divine.

Even with all of the technological wizardry to make her life efficient, everything is brought to her; Vashti is usually busy when her son calls. Greater ease and convenience afforded by technology alters our perception of the world. For instance, we can see this when we consider our relationship with time. Where does all the time go that we save by being more efficient? How do we fill "saved" time? Why does it seem like we can never stop being busy? Being unoccupied or relieved of pressure can even be a fearful state that we late-moderns, those in the technological epoch of being, assiduously avoid (Thomson, 2011). Part of the conundrum is, as Robert Levine (1997) puts it in his book *A Geography of Time*, "Almost every technical advance seems to be accompanied by a rise in expectations" (p. 12). As our expectations increase due to the power leveraged by technological devices, the gains to efficiency can quickly become forgotten as we move on to expecting more from our time and our devices. We do not even realize how rich with time and leisured we could be since we, like Kuno, put so much demand on our time.

Kuno wants to meet his mother face-to-face. He cannot bear the technologically mitigated encounter any longer. We, unlike Forster's original audience, *know* why Kuno names the video call "wearisome." We can also perhaps, from our own experience, relate to his mother's reaction: "You mustn't say anything against the Machine." We have heard this type of reaction when criticism has been leveled at synchronous online learning platforms like Zoom. Since face-to-face interaction was halted, criticism of the videoconferencing alternative *doesn't matter*. There is nothing else to do, so why complain? And so, some may feel that they are in effect being told not to say anything against the machine. They are silenced perhaps because their frustrations are not constructive, and pointing out the flaws in Zoom does little to change its basic mode of orienting us toward each other.

Enframed by Zoom

In Zoom, we are exactly, as Heidegger (1977) says, enframed. We are set off as distinct and separate objects, i.e., leveled. A phenomenological study of advanced computer technology explains it in this way with relation to the etymology of the word "frame":

> Digital media always has some framed structure for viewing something through, or to surround to bring in to focus or enhance. An early use of *frame* is rooted in the Old English idea of profiting, making helpful or joining together, as in framing a house. Old English suggests that *frame* means to promote or to benefit, move forward, make progress, promote or influence. Old Saxon use of frame notes performance, composition, design or fashion, and the Old Icelandic word means advancement or a plan.
>
> (Irwin, 2016, pp. 54–55)

The depths of the word "frame" connect to the attitude of technology that seeks to maximize efficiency. When we are enframed, as objective units in our Zoom boxes, (I also hear them referred to as "tiles" – another building connection), we are homogenized. It is helpful to organize us in this way because it is more efficient. Perhaps a certain increased kind of progress can be made when students present themselves through frames. To show up in the same way as everyone else is to become frictionless. To take up the same space as everyone else, and to manifest personal presence only by way of an animated framed picture, removes texture.

On the Zoom screen, we are pixelated and peeled away from our actual topology (Malpas, 2008). When the visual manifestation of our self is reduced to pixels, our image can be inserted onto the *screen*. A rectangular boundary portions off a bit of our body for others to see. Usually only our head and shoulders appear. We can come to wonder about the rest of the body of those we look at that is *concealed*. I remember when one student stood up and walked across his room and out the door. I noticed how he practically filled the height of the doorway. Though he had a "babyface," he was actually much taller than me. I wondered if I would have engaged with him differently if I had been with him in full embodied presence.

Our pixelated self is the image we present to others. The word "pixel," according to the *Oxford English Dictionary*, comes from two etymological pieces, "pix" and "-el." "Pix" (alternatively "pic") is just a colloquial word for picture. The other part comes from "element," a word that means "a first principle" (Skeat, 1882, p. 187). "Pixel" is an element of a picture. For people to be pixelated, as they are when their image appears on Zoom, is in a sense then to have their first principle become a picture of themselves. To appear on Zoom, a person must leave much behind. When I had to meet with one of my colleagues on Zoom, at the end of our call I told him that I missed him. Though seeing him on Zoom was gratifying and satisfied some longing to experience his wit and insight, Zoom did not fully alleviate the loss of his personality that I experience when I am in his presence. I still felt a longing to be with him. There was something absent in his virtual presence. I was facing a void, the flat, framed video image did not allow for the full sense of vulnerability and inherent connection.

Reflections on Zoom teaching and learning tethers my insights in the following final chapters to the themes presented in the rest of the book. For example, similar to other non-face-to-face formats, Zoom stifles conversation. The ability to control if others even see you on the screen creates an urge to remain anonymous. The itch to remain hidden can become a permanent fixture for those on Zoom, unless it is actively worked against through persistent prompting to be visible. By switching off the cameras, just our name appears in a box. We feel like we are hidden, but everyone knows we could be there listening and observing. With the video cameras off, we become the unhidden voyeur. Those who hide in this way might also actually be absent. The camera is turned off to provide a kind of camouflage while we physically leave the meeting to do something else. With my students in every Zoom class, I must remind them to make themselves visible. Knowing that some feel embarrassed about their appearance or their physical surroundings, I say in a joking tone, "Please turn your cameras on. We are all ugly." All of my students are beautiful. I try to meet them where they might be feeling in order to put them at ease. Most comply with my self-deprecating request, but not all, and at the beginning of the next class I have to make the same plea for the vestigial presence of the merely visually synchronous portrait of my students.

If we cannot see the others in a Zoom class, it becomes a Zoom call. However, to make these remote encounters possible we must all mostly remain muted. The various interactions of ambient sounds from 20 to 30 different microphones would be a distracting cacophony. However, the muted cannot be heard. Unmuting to begin talking can be barrier to engagement. I have noticed that for some students that extra step required to begin contributing to a conversation can be insurmountable. For one thing, unmuting takes time. In many instances I have waited for students to fumble around as they sought to unmute themselves. They seem quite unprepared for the expectation to contribute to the learning by speaking, as if it is not something that is needed in any of their other Zoom classes. These pauses can lengthen out surprisingly fast and are so common that they can be punitive; they can lead to the domination of the Zoom class by just a few voices, usually one, the teacher's. These technological intrusions disrupt the conditions of conversation.

We Need to Be Together

Philosopher Roger Scruton describes the potential devastation that the vulnerability of human interaction can create. He explains that the desire to be safe and avoid vulnerability is exceedingly strong. "Life in the actual world is difficult and embarrassing. Most of all it is difficult and embarrassing in our confrontation with other people who, by their very existence as subjects, rearrange things in defiance to our will" (1999, p. 138). Scruton seeks to engage the question of why – if the risks are so great – we bother to face other embodied persons at all? He argues that only a similarly powerful force could ever overcome our desire to avoid vulnerability. "It requires a great force, such as the force of sexual desire" (Ibid.). With this force we are impelled to overcoming the tendency to avoid the vulnerability of being present face-to-face with others. However, in our sexual desire we are even more exposed, yet many accept such risk. Why? A scientific tale of genetic impulse to propagate is not irrelevant, but it does not capture the phenomenon of lived human experience. We *need* each other. So, in one way or another, whether sexual or not, we are compelled to be with each other. In being with others, we are able to become what we are (Withy, 2015).

Despite the risk of COVID-19, many students are clamoring for a return to normal classes. Some of the students in my Logic class had decided that if they could not take courses in the traditional manner, they would not pursue an undergraduate degree. The face-to-face experience seems to increase the sense of satisfaction for many students. "There is no sign that this appetite for online learning diminishes the interest in studying on campus" (Roth, 2020). Even students highly immersed in the virtual world of advanced digital technology still have a fundamental expectation that undergraduate learning requires face-to-face interactions. They know that what is missing from a class on Zoom is vital to what they need to learn. Evidence shows that having classes face-to-face increases completion rates (Ibid.). This was apparent in the first analysis of MOOCs and continues to be true even as online learning becomes more prevalent.

Deception and Enchantment

Simulation is a central issue or theme when interpreting the late-modern (often called "postmodern") world of significations we inhabit (Thomson, 2011). Online classes attempt to mimic, copy or simulate in-person classes. However, it is in the very effort of copying that they so often fail. It might be that it is the simulation that grates on students, e.g. the discussion board assignments. The non-face-to-face copied versions of what should be done in-person are what they might find most undermine their expectations for learning. A copy can be a kind of deception. In contemplating the experience of my nine participants and thinking about my work with undergraduates for 16 years, I get the sense that they often feel deceived by the simulation of learning in online classes, especially when their expectations are not met.

I first became sensitized to this sense of deception when I was a teaching assistant as an undergraduate. I was a TA for an online Introduction to Philosophy class for one of my favorite professors. I had the responsibility to do some grading and respond to emails from the class. Early on, a small group in the class contacted me to know if they could meet in person. They expressed concern that they were not able to talk out the issues and have them thoroughly explained. They wanted to be able to ask more questions. I heartily agreed with their concerns, but I also wondered why they had taken a philosophy class online in the first place. Then the students asked if I would be willing to meet with them weekly to discuss the readings. They wanted to get more out of the class. They did not feel like they were learning from the online format. To enroll in a class to learn and to then not fully learn was experienced as a basic deception, i.e., a bait and switch. Moreover, it's like the idea that Plato (1997) expressed, how everything that deceives may be said to enchant. If we can be tricked, then there must also be something to the trick; in it lies a precious kind of cunning. And as such, we can become enamored with the power of that which deceives.

References

Abse, D. (1991). *White coat, purple coat: Collected poems.* New York, NY: Persea Books.

Caplan, B. (2018). *The case against education: Why the education system is a waste of time and money.* Princeton, NJ: Princeton University Press.

Carr, N. (2020, December 31). Not being there: From virtuality to remoteness. *Rough Type.* Retrieved February 12, 2020, from http://www.roughtype.com/?p=8824

Forster, E. M. (1909). *The machine stops.* Oxford, UK: Oxford and Cambridge Review. Retrieved March 11, 2021, from https://www.cs.ucdavis.edu/~koehl/Teaching/ECS188/PDF_files/Machine_stops.pdf

Heidegger, M. (1977). *The question concerning technology, and other essays* (W. Levitt, Trans.). New York, NY: HarperCollins. (Original works published 1962, 1952 & 1954).

Irwin, S. O. (2016). *Digital media: Human-technology connection.* London, UK: Lexington Books.

Jackson-Wright, Q. (2020, October 14). How to beat Zoom fatigue and set healthy boundaries. *Wired.* Retrieved March 11, 2021, from https://www.wired.com/story/how-to-fight-zoom-fatigue/

Levine, R. (1997). *A geography of time: The temporal misadventures of a social psychologist, or how every culture keeps time just a little bit differently.* New York, NY: Basic Books.

Malpas, J. (2008). *Heidegger's topology: Being, place, world.* Cambridge, MA: The MIT Press.

Oxford English Dictionary. (n.d.). Retrieved July 11, 2022, from https://www.oed.com/dictionary

Plato. (1997). *Complete works* (J. Cooper, Ed.). Cambridge, UK: Hackett Publishing Company.

Robinson, B. (2020, May 6). *Black Mirror* season 6 on hold because the world is too bleak right now. *Screen Rant.* Retrieved March 11, 2021, from https://screenrant.com/black-mirror-season-6-on-hold-charlie-brooker/

Roth, M. S. (2020, July 18). Will the pandemic blow up college in America? *Politico Magazine.* Retrieved March 11, 2021, from https://www.politico.com/amp/news/magazine/2020/07/18/will-the-pandemic-blow-up-college-in-america-368067?__twitter_impression=true

Scruton, R. (1999). *An intelligent person's guide to philosophy.* New York, NY: Penguin Books.

Skeat, W. W. (1882). *An etymological dictionary of the English language.* Oxford, UK: Clarendon Press.

Thomson, I. (2011). *Heidegger, art and postmodernity.* Cambridge, UK: Cambridge University Press.

Withy, K. (2015). *Heidegger on being uncanny.* Cambridge, MA: Harvard University Press.

15 Interlude
Engaging Poetically with Insights and Implications

Better than Nothing Becomes Better than Anything

The attempts to simulate traditional undergraduate learning with videoconferencing on Zoom are, however, often better than nothing. Even if online classes deceive some students into simulating learning, not doing anything clearly seems like a loss. It might be better to have an online degree than none. With technology, it often seems the case that if something is deemed better than nothing, it then advances to a further stage. It is in the second stage where the problem arises, as Sherry Turkle (2017) points out, when our technological innovations, which were once just better than nothing, become better than *anything*. It is the necessitation phase of technological development that makes us forget that every technological advance is a Faustian bargain (Postman, 1992). When technology becomes necessary, it is allowed to remove what was once precious without our noticing. In this regard, I am reminded of these lines from *Paradise Lost*:

> And with necessity,
> The tyrant's plea,
> excus'd his devilish deeds
>   (Milton, 2003/1667, p. 96)

Just like how politicians could vehemently advocate for their particular policies based on necessity, technology too can have a tyrannical bent. The drive to make everything as efficient as possible becomes a total necessity. And the devilish outcome is the unrealized trade-offs that are demanded to realize the necessity.

Nicolas Carr is someone who has not failed to stop thinking about technology, even as it becomes ubiquitous. Like Heidegger, he wants to show that we can learn to be sensitive to what is lost from technological innovations like Zoom. That is, if we are willing to think about what is hardest to think about, we can still have a free relationship to technology. With careful insight, Carr gives this description:

But the pandemic has also given us a lesson, a painful one, in the limits of remoteness. In promising to eliminate distance, virtuality also promised to erase the difference between presence and absence … Being remote is a drag. The state of absence, a physical state but also a psychic one, is a state of loneliness and frustration, angst and ennui. What the pandemic has revealed is that when taken to an extreme — the extreme Silicon Valley saw as an approaching paradise — virtuality does not engender a sense of liberation and exultation. It engenders a sense of confinement and despair. Absence will never be presence. A body in isolation is a self in isolation.

(Carr, 2020)

As my participants described, we all now find in our experience of technologically mitigated remoteness a diminished sense of vulnerability. Just as they said in our conversations, there is absence even in the presence of non-face-to-face connection. In these conditions of remoteness, it is difficult for us to feel connected to others. Indeed, our sense of dependency remains but without the ability to satisfy its deeper, even sometimes inarticulate, longing to be with others.

The Effect of Panopticonism and Reciprocal Voyeurism

In Michel Foucault's book *Discipline and Punish: The Birth of the Prison*, he engages with Jeremy Bentham's (1748–1832) proposal for a new kind of prison, the "panopticon." The idea was to design a way of incarceration that was as efficient as possible. Bentham (1962/1843) sought to maximize the utilitarian imperative of the greatest good for the greatest number. To bring about the greatest efficiency in the prison, he wanted a layout that would require as few guards as possible and as much compliancy by the inmates as possible. The result was to make it possible for few guards to *potentially* be watching any prisoner at any time. However, the prisoners would know that only a few guards would be available to watch. The inmates would know that they could not all be watched simultaneously. The prisoners could never be sure whether the guards were watching them or not. Thus, their conformity depended on the chance that they were always open to observation. It was a kind of disciplinary voyeurism; the prisoners knew they *could* be observed at any time, and so they would avoid breaking the rules. Foucault's analysis culminates in this point:

> He who is subjected to a field of visibility, and who knows it, assumes responsibility for the constraints of power; he makes them play spontaneously upon himself; he inscribes in himself the power relation in which he simultaneously plays both roles; he becomes the principle of his own subjection.
>
> (1995/1975, pp. 202–203)

Under Bentham's scheme of the panopticon, prisoners become their own wardens. A subtle but powerful cycle develops. The watched are motivated to scrutinize their own actions. Habituated to this tendency, they become the enforcers of own constraints.

Now we find ourselves remote from each other, more than ever before. We interact via reciprocal cameras. Echoing in our own time Foucault's insights about the panopticonic cycle, Carr presents its new manifestation:

> Think about the cramped little cells in which we appear when we're on Zoom. It's hard to imagine a better metaphor for our situation. The architecture of Zoom is the architecture of the Panopticon, but it comes with a twist that Jeremy Bentham never anticipated. On Zoom, each of us gets to play the roles of both jailer and jailed. We are the watcher and the watched, simultaneously. Each role is an exercise in remoteness, and each is demeaning. Each makes us feel small.
>
> (Carr, 2020)

As watchers and watched, we swim in the pool of reciprocal voyeurism. We never know how much we are being watched but we know at any moment we could be being watched. And so, when students have their cameras on during a remote class, they know that they have to behave in a certain way. They narrow their actions and constrain their behavior. The disembodied nature of online interaction is one of the conditions necessary for reciprocal voyeurism.

We need our bodies to become what we are. Non-face-to-face learning is primarily a move to take away our bodily engagement with learning, especially the encounter of other bodies, fellow students and teachers. Just as in a parallel way, reading a book takes the learner away from the immediate presence of others:

> Writing and reading are solitary activities that throw the psyche back on itself. A teacher speaking to a class which he feels and which feels itself as a close-knit group, finds that if the class is asked to pick up its textbooks and read a given passage, the unity of the group vanishes as each person enters into his or her private lifeworld.
>
> (Ong, 1982, p. 69)

What is lost from remote classes is the sense of unity; the sense of shared purpose is diminished.

As wonderful and precious as solitary learning is, the self-development, discipline and discovery that come from dedicated private study are not the whole of learning. Most usually, they seem to take this as self-evident for early K-12 learning. Feeling connected to others by virtue of the shared intimacy of directly experiencing the embodiment of others creates conditions for other kinds of learning beyond those familiar to the autodidact.

The attitude expressed by the essence of modern technology helps to perpetuate Cartesian dualism. Indeed, that may be one of its *essential* consequences. Thus, we might think we are a mind or a soul in a body, and we might have not just experiential but also technological justifications for our dualistic tendency, but an appropriately sensitive phenomenology shows embodiment as fundamental. When we consider non-face-to-face learning, we should not think of being in two "places," e.g. a physical world and a virtual world. One of the things that is lost in a remote class is a real sense of place. It is contradictory for students, course designers, administrators and teachers to assume that an online class can provide anything but the ineffectual vestigial remnants of place.

Does non-face-to-face learning result in a kind of atrophy of the self, a diminished capacity for being human? Repeatedly being conditioned by interactions that excise an aspect of being a person, direct human embodiment, we may begin to lose something without even noticing. If it becomes dire enough, our plight may be revealed by the depths of our peril (Heidegger, 1998). For example, it could be that the perpetual absence of the face helps us to re-call what is precious when we encounter each other in our full embodiment. We can dwell as disembodied beings, and such existence might be meaningful if there is something at stake. The movie *Ready Player One* (2018) shows this kind of disembodiment, and what could be risked, similar to many who live online in the world of games and artificial reality. But ultimately, no matter how incredible the virtual world, the message of that movie is its final line, "Only reality is real." On the other hand, as shown in *Ready Player One* and in the thoughts of futurists like Ray Kurzwiel, there are possibilities created by the non-face-to-face encounter. The question then becomes how compensatory are these experiences, i.e., are they worth the tradeoff? That is, will this way of being allow a flourishing to burst forth? Perhaps non-face-to-face learning is allowing more people to be exposed to more information for learning than ever before and will lead to a neo-renaissance.

Poetically Facing Non-Face-to-Face Learning

To find further insights into the meaning of what is lost in online learning, I use poems as my guide in following final chapters. Turning to poetry is fitting for a philosophical inquiry. As Heidegger says, "All great philosophy is inherently thoughtful-poetic" (1984, p. 73). Over the years of my work on non-face-to-face learning for undergraduates, several poems have preoccupied my mind. They are not about online classes. Thus, their inclusion here could cause some apprehension. Moreover, as technology writer Nicholas Carr says, "We rarely look to poetry for instruction anymore" (2015, p. 213). The relevance of these poems does not come from any explicit connection to non-face-to-face learning. Even so, they are helpful for doing the interpretive rendering of a hermeneutic phenomenological study.

These poems seem to lift and open up what can be shown about the meaning of non-face-to-face learning for undergraduates. As Carr says, "A poet's scrutiny of the world can be more subtle and discerning than a scientist's" (2015, p. 213). I hope that with presenting them here and engaging with them in a way that relates to online undergraduate learning, I can open up my interpretation. I hope that these poems help to show the meaning of non-face-to-face learning. In this effort, I seek to follow the guidance of Heidegger and Nietzsche, both philosophers who leaned heavily on poetry, even publishing some themselves. I seek to follow their example of thinking through and with poems to enrich my interpretation. Though the poems are not about technology per se, they elucidate relevant aspects of online learning. To make this jump to the more poetical, I trust that these poems may lift the thinking of my interpretation and what can be revealed to my readers. I do this because, "What is stated poetically, and what is stated in thought, are never identical; but there are times when they are the same ... This can occur when poesy is lofty, and thinking profound" (Heidegger, 1976/1954, p. 20). I am sure these poems are lofty. They are rich in beauty, ambiguity and desire. I am not as confident about the profundity of my thinking.

In poems we are able to see how we should let go. Our thoughts are directed but let free. We engage with language in a primordial sense in the poem. It can *take* us. The experience is hard to put into words since it is our words that themselves can become at issue in a profound poem. Plato explains, "As long as a human being has his intellect in his possession he will always lack the power to make poetry or sing prophecy" (1997, p. 1172). We must let go a bit in the poem. The release is ever more requisite when we, as I am trying to do here, use poems to help interpret a phenomenon.

Hermeneutic phenomenology is philosophical. It is a philosophical way of revealing. My interpretive work seeks to do what Heidegger says philosophy does: "Philosophy searches for a knowing that, at the same time, is before all science and goes beyond all science; it searches for a knowing that is not necessarily bound to the sciences" (2009, p. 13). Moreover, he explains that "All great philosophy is inherently thoughtful-poetic" (Heidegger, 1984/1961, p. 73). The poems can be relevant. They can help to make my work poetic. And hopefully they can unite the whole of my work and help readers to make connections far beyond it. "Poesy is the water that at times flows backward toward the source, toward thinking as a thinking back, a recollection" (Heidegger, 1976/1954, p. 11). A full interpretation of the meaning of what is lost in remote learning requires such thought, i.e., thinking that transcends this book.

In his book *Things Merely Are: Philosophy in the Poetry of Wallace Stevens* (2005), philosopher Simon Critchley presents a view of poetry that tries to show how it can expand our experience of life. "Poetry is ambiguous. This is what appalls some philosophers and appeals to others" (2005, p. 17). Critchley says that it is because of this ambiguity that poetry can "get at the evasiveness of poetry's matter" (Ibid., p. 18). And what is the "matter" of poetry? Why *reality*, of course. By that view, Critchley is affirming the ambiguous nature of reality itself, which is why poetry is so well suited a medium for helping to interpret our experience. Critchley shows that the impressions that can be gathered by poems cover a wide radius. Poems have a force of articulation and awareness of the linguistically mitigated world of human relational thought that can surpass most other forms of expression.

References

Bentham, J. (1962). *The works of Jeremy Bentham* (J. Bowring, Ed.). New York: NY: Russel & Russel Inc. (Original work published 1838–1843).
Carr, N. (2015). *The glass cage: How computers are changing us*. New York, NY: W.W. Norton & Company.
Carr, N. (2020, December 31). Not being there: From virtuality to remoteness. *Rough Type*. Retrieved March 10, 2020, from http://www.roughtype.com/?p=8824
Critchley, S. (2005). *Things merely are: Philosophy in the poetry of Wallace Stevens*. New York, NY: Routledge.
Foucault, M. (1995). *Discipline and punish: The birth of the prison* (A. Sheridan, Trans.). New York, NY: Vintage Books. (Original work published 1975).
Heidegger, M. (1976). *What is called thinking* (J. Glenn Gray, Trans.). New York, NY: HarperCollins. (Original work published 1954).
Heidegger, M. (1984). *Nietzsche volume two: The eternal recurrence of the same* (D. F. Krell, Trans.). New York, NY: HarperCollins. (Original work published 1961).
Heidegger, M. (1998). *Parmenides* (A. Shuwer & R. Rojcewicz, Trans.). Bloomington, IN: Indiana University Press. (Original work published 1982).
Heidegger, M. (2009). *Logic as the question concerning the essence of language* (W. T. Gregory & Y. Unna, Trans.). Albany, NY: State University of New York Press.
Milton, J. (2003). *Paradise lost*. Indianapolis, IN: Hackett Publishing Company. (Original work published in 1667).
Ong, W. J. (1982). *Orality and literacy: The technologizing of the word*. New York, NY: Methuen & Co. Ltd.
Plato. (1997). *Complete works* (J. Cooper, Ed.). Cambridge, UK: Hackett Publishing Company.
Postman, N. (1992). *Technopoly: The surrender of culture to technology*. New York, NY: Alfred A. Knopf Inc.
Turkle, S. (2017). *Alone together: Why we expect more from technology and less from each other*. New York, NY: Basic Books.

16 Works and Days

A Response to the Void in Higher Education after COVID-19

Hesiod is one of the first that we know of to give us the gods. There were of course many others before him and the oral tradition he is credited with writing down extends back into the eons of time. However, it is not his *Theogony* that I want to introduce here. I want to make a connection to his poem *Works and Days* – sometimes referred to as a kind of ancient Greek agricultural almanac (Lamberton, 1988). I want to focus on aspects of this ancient poetical revealing to bring to light the focal aspects of learning face-to-face.

Works and Days is written in the first person. It is a poem that is meant to teach, almost like a distillation of ancient traditional wisdom. It is Hesiod's advice to his lazy and conniving brother Perses. One keen commentator, Robert Lamberton, explains the poems context and meanings:

> What [Hesiod] has to say is vast, infinitely removed from the muddled sphere of our misdirected strivings against each other and against a reluctant and impoverished world. The content is global, in touch with the principle of Justice itself, with the gods and the relations of gods and men, in touch, finally, with a vision of a society ruled by justice, of what the world *could* be.
>
> (Lamberton, 1988, p. 106)

The range of topics is so wide, it is as if the poem casts a linguistic net over our world. It shows how the practical is connected to everything, other people, animals, seasons, stars, the divine (that which is outside or beyond human control) and humanity.

Works and Days recounts several mythological scenes, fables and advice about practical matters relating to farming, social interactions and sailing. For example, Hesiod seeks to educate his brother by telling him, "Whatever your lot, work is best, if you can manage to turn your witless mind from other men's goods back to your work, and, as I tell you, care for your living" (Hesiod, 2009, p. 81). The advice dispensed is also

DOI: 10.4324/9781003349051-16

directed to the reader so that we may not suffer needlessly. As Lamberton interprets it, "Experience is the worst source of knowledge" (1988, p. 125). The "experience" referred to is not in the phenomenological sense of "lived experience." Here it means something more like the events of life, i.e., what happens to us. Things just happening to us is a way to learn. It is the kind of learning we may lament in a youth who does not heed the advice of those who are wiser for having been through the same situation. Sometimes this kind of experience is the only way to learn; no matter how good the advice, we may just have to go through on our own. However, Hesiod's point is that when we can give our attention to someone who knows, a different kind of experience can be cultivated. We will still "go through" with whatever is going to happen to us, but we can have a better outcome by heeding a teacher. We should listen to the expert, when appropriate, so that the experience we do have can make us live more by becoming more skillfully engaged in the world.

The potential for shame is one reason we may avoid being with others. There is the risk that we will say or do something wrong. We know that we may have good reason to regret what we will do with or in the presence of others. The possibility of shame is part of our embodied vulnerability. Vulnerability can be a barrier, but it also makes possible deep connection, which leads to fully becoming what we are. "Shame is no good at looking after a man who is needy, shame is a great harm to men, and a great benefit too – shame leads to no great prosperity; boldness goes with wealth" (Hesiod, 2009, p. 82). Shame is not valuable in and of itself. We do not seek it. But to avoid shame is to cower and not receive benefits. In a sense, boldness is required. We must have courage and encounter others, all the while acknowledging that shame is a possibility. We grow, learn and become prosperous by exerting ourselves. We have to get out of our comfort zones. This has to become a habit that is learned explicitly or implicitly in our interactions with others. As Hesiod says, "For every small thing, when piled on a small thing, done often, grows large" (Ibid., p. 83). Gradually, one of the great things that is learned with others is how to act without shame.

The homeostatic womb of a screen-mitigated existence, like the one in *The Machine Stops*, is too com-*fort*-able. To be fortified is to be separated off, protected and safe. Ensconced in our informational lair of televisions, computers, smartphones and appliances we experience what it is to be cut off from reality. Indeed, screens are the literalized physical manifestation of the false (from a phenomenological perspective) Cartesian ontological divide between a subject who knows and an objective world. Descartes' ontology and epistemological implications bring forth the familiarity with which we regard screens. On the screens, reality is represented just as Descartes has caused us to imagine that reality is represented in our minds and not experienced directly. Heidegger explains this view by saying, "Representation and the one who is representing are *co*-represented in human representing" (1961/1984, p. 108). As with Descartes' philosophy with screens, we are still able to experience the world, but it is so arranged as to blunt, dilute and dissipate the way things merely are, because "Representation gives only the semblance of reality" (Ibid., p. 131). For instance, there in front of their screens it is too easy for students to shy away from being challenged bodily with others. It is too easy to imagine them gone, as mere representations. Online with a screen, it is too simple to ignore the imperative of risk to allow for the chance of growth. An online class is not conducive to drawing us out at our best as we engage with others in something that matters.

Thinking Requires Embodiment

It is not just having a brain that allows us to think. It is not just being able to speak so others will hear us that allows us to communicate. Our whole body is involved. Moreover, "All ways of thinking, more or less perceptibly, lead through language in a manner that is extraordinary" (Heidegger, 1977, p. 3). It is fascinating. How is it that language, something that seems arbitrary and contingent, should be the means by which we encounter what seems most fundamental to our being, i.e., our conscious life manifest in thought? Language *is* our world. "Only where there is language, is there world, that is, the constantly changing cycle of decision and work, of action and responsibility, but also of arbitrariness and turmoil, decay and confusion" (Heidegger, 2000, p. 56). Language is a social and historical phenomenon that binds us all together. The trillions of cognitive handshakes that constitute language are the basis for our ability to act outside of the causal order of nature (Tallis, 2016).

Bound by our common usage of language and our embodiment, thinking requires that we *see* each other. It requires that we be with each other. Hesiod crystalizes this fact beautifully, "Looks and thoughts should keep company" (Hesiod, 2009, p. 95). To really learn requires face-to-face contact because that is how we confront and perceive. "Man is the animal that confronts face-to-face. A mere animal, such as a dog, never confronts anything, it can never confront anything *to its face*; to do so, the animal would have to perceive *itself*. It cannot say 'I,' it cannot talk at all" (Heidegger, 1976/1954, p. 61). Animals are bereft of language. They have no linguistic thoughts to keep company with their looks. Animal training is not the same as our learning.

Humans learn most basically from each other because human beings are with others. Just because undergraduate education has in general come to be an economic imperative does not mean that the potential for other areas of growth and being should be neglected. There are ambiguous kinds of growth that can happen when we are with people. They can be calculated and related to certain skills and methods, but there is always the potential for more. We learn from our earliest days face-to-face. That *is* learning. If *anthropos* is the being who has a human face, then learning to be what we are and do what we are able to do means that learning too must have a face, a human face. It is the face of the teacher and fellow learners together in close physical proximity. It is how we learn everything, to be face-to-face with it. "What becomes of the face-to-face, the meeting, the seeing, the forming of the idea, in which the tree presents itself and man comes to stand face-to-face with the tree?" (Heidegger, 1976/1954, p. 42). To learn ever more about being human, we must be face-to-face with others as consistently as possible and not in front of a screen.

Being Educated Means Being-With Others

In many places in the *Works and Days*, we are reminded of how to be with others when we are together. "A sparing tongue is a treasure among men; to speak in measure the greatest grace. Those who speak evil very quickly hear evil, and more evil, of themselves" (Hesiod, 2009, p. 95). In knowing our own vulnerability and the potential for shame, we also then understand what others face. When we engage, we should be sparing, in the sense that we hold back what we know could be cutting. In doing so, we help to create the learning environment. As others join us in the place of learning, they can come with trepidation and excitement. We know that the others we encounter are vulnerable, and it is our responsibility to comport ourselves to them in a sheltering way so that they can be with us and be welcome. We know that we need them and therefore we know that they need us.

Hesiod gives us a view of the educated person. It has little to do with *how* one becomes educated – though we can make inferences. Instead, Hesiod shows what the outcome of learning should be, i.e., its purpose. "That man is best, altogether, who thinks things through for himself" (2009, p. 81). Hesiod's ideal is a person with independence of mind. Someone who has learned the tools of thinking, perhaps by some experience with trial and error but primarily by being able to give heed to guidance. The theme of "response-ability" as expressed by my participants relates to this point as well as the frequent distinction they made about real learning, e.g., when Carl talked about learning how to think as opposed to what to think. As exemplified by the Socratic method discussed in earlier chapters, learning that is thought through for oneself has a tendency to be powerful. If we are able to learn how to approach conclusions on our own, they are often the most convincing. This level of learning is not that of a novice. What Hesiod describes is more like the master who is able to create. That level of learning is not reached in isolation or without face-to-face guidance (Dreyfus, 2008).

Hesiod continues by indicating what is the distinctive attribute of the educated person. He says the educated person is someone "who figures what will be best later on and finally" (2009, p. 81). It is the kind of person who is attuned to the Law of Unintended Consequences. That is, they know that what might *seem* best now, might not be overall, or in the long term. They know that solutions are necessary, but despite our best efforts, all of our solutions will create new problems. The new problems will hopefully be more manageable. Their ability to "figure" is the mark of practical wisdom, knowing how to act well, not perfectly. Hesiod's view of the educated person is of a person who is not dogmatic, because such persons work things out for themselves. However, they are also the type of person who can establish goals and objectives in order to get things done that matter. They are practical, capable of action and minimizing suffering.

The description of the ideally educated person is rounded out by an explicit connection to other people. The theme expressed by my participants of how others are largely absent in the experience of non-face-to-face learning means that ideal education, the kind that has the power to change the student, is elusive online. Hesiod says, "Someone who can listen is good too; he hears when someone speaks well. But a man who won't listen and knows nothing himself, who takes nothing to heart, he is useless" (2009, p. 81). To be able to listen is to have the ability to pause and be humble. It is the disposition to recognize both when guidance is needed and when it should be heeded. Hesiod's fully educated individual takes things to heart because of the impact that the full presence of others has. As well as being able to "think things through," educated individuals show a deep connection to what is learned and the process of learning.

Learning in Our Hearts: Finding Meaning

What does it mean, as Hesiod says, to take something into our hearts? The ancient apostle Paul wrote in a similar visceral way about the gospel of Christianity, that it be, "written not with ink, but with the Spirit of the living God; not in tables of stone, but in fleshy tables of the heart" (*King James Bible*, 2013, 2Cor. 3:3). Paul was many things, but he was also a Roman citizen who wrote and spoke Ancient Greek. His education probably included learning Hesiod's poems. Paul was writing to Greeks who were all probably familiar with *Works and Days*. To have something in your heart was probably a fairly common metaphor then, as it is now. However, the word "fleshy" really blurs the line with metaphor. As if what is learned is tattooed or carved into the flesh. But that is the idea that Hesiod is expressing. To take something into your heart is for it to manifestly become part of how you feel and act. It is part of your character and deepest intentions. Educated people are transformed when they listen to others. As they are willing to be guided, what they learn changes their deepest dispositions and motivations.

Ultimately, the *Works and Days* emphasizes an anti-utopianism realism that cuts against euphoric technological hopes. In this world, with the days we are given there will *always* be work. We can make this world better by working and seeking justice for ourselves and toward others. To do that, learning is necessary. Mastery born of quasi-apprenticeship – that cannot be done alone – is required (Dreyfus, 2008). There is no way out of the efforts and costs to our existence. The days will keep coming. The burdens that are lightened by a technological innovation, like the scythe for mowing, do not change the realities of this world. Technology increases our capacities but it cannot fundamentally alter our world. It is like what Heidegger says:

> The men of this earth are provoked by the absolute domination of the essence of modern technology, together with technology itself [devices, algorithms, and systems] into developing a final world-formula which would once and for all secure the totality of the world as a uniform sameness, and thus make it available to us as a calculable resource. The provocation to such making-available orders everything into a single design, the making of which levels the harmony of the infinite design.
>
> (2000/1981, p. 122)

The flight into ease or the restless urge for a totalizing synoptic view of everything is not a real avenue of escape. The panopticonism of the all-seeing eye that tries to capture everything together at once is the same tendency that abhors the infinite, i.e., that which cannot be controlled. The technological attitude is a drive to efficiency, but it is also an inexorable urge to perpetually simplify human existence. The simplification diminishes ambiguity and thus the potential for meaning.

Meaning, in the sense of feeling like one's own life has significance and therefore matters, seems to be related to taking responsibility (Peterson, 2018). If this is at least somewhat relevant to finding meaning, and if there is nothing distinct (i.e., perceived to be concrete) to differentiate all that lies before us and constitutes our options for choice, we may be unable to find meaning because we will not know how to take responsibility. In such an existence, our human world of experience would *be* a machine, utterly dumb and pointless. As the great wrestler of meaninglessness himself saw, "An essentially mechanical world would be an essentially *meaningless* world" (Nietzsche, 1974, p. 335). Our conscious minds are not machines. And though it can cause great agony, we continually seek to find ways to understand how things matter, particularly ourselves, in a bewildering cosmos.

With every innovation, there are trade-offs. Often the exchange is worth it. Usually the advantages of technology are what we become familiar with first. They probably would not have come to our attention if they did not have some novel utility. However, if one does not pay rapt attention to the tendency to create unintended consequences, no matter how noble our intentions, the innovation, in the end, may not be worth it. Benefits may be there but they are not distributed equally (Postman, 1992). The gains may exist but only in the short term. Our ability to live meaningful lives may be threatened. A glaring example is the devastating consequences of social media, i.e., Facebook, Twitter, and Instagram (Haidt & Lukianoff, 2019). Even in the cases where the technology is a net gain, there is still something that is lost. This is what I take to be the inexorable rule of technological innovation, whether recognized or not. And if what is lost is most precious and essential to our goals, we should be like Hesiod's educated individuals and eschew such technology.

Alienation

The Marxian concept of "alienation" that comes into the English language through translations of Hegel's philosophy addresses the concept of a separation between what ought to be unified (Leopold, 2018). Alienation as originally propounded by Marx and Hegel relied on an essential human nature (Ibid.).

> To be alienated is to be separated from one's own essence or nature; it is to be forced to lead a life in which that nature has no opportunity to be fulfilled or actualized. In this way, the experience of 'alienation' involves a sense of a lack of self-worth and an absence of meaning in one's life. Alienation in this sense is not fundamentally a matter of whether your conscious desires are satisfied, or how you experience your life, but instead of whether your life objectively actualizes your nature, especially (for both Marx and Hegel) your life with others as a social being.
>
> (Wood, 2005, p. 21)

The philosophical arguments of Marx and Hegel are aimed at explaining that certain activities, systems, governments, etc., could bring about a division within human *being* (what Heidegger would call *Dasein*) that was not just inappropriate but also bad. For example, one application of alienation to education would depend on maintaining that education has a certain purpose due to essential human nature, i.e., what all humans need (Rorty, 1999). Therefore, education should have the purpose of bringing about, for example, full human self-realization (Leopold, 2018). If education has some other end, such as one dictated by dogmatic ideology, it would cease to be education and become instead indoctrination. The results of such one-sided or manipulative pedagogical programs might result in alienation because such blinkered perspectives and purposes do not fully accord with essential human nature. Moreover, education that is so strictly focused by the demands of efficiency imposed by the technological understanding of beings, can make the thriving of essential human nature difficult (Wendling, 2009). Thus, one of my insights about the meaning of what is lost in remote learning is that it can be alienating. Students can sometimes sense that they should be directly connected face-to-face with those they are learning with and their teachers. My participants did not always express this sense so clearly, but in the themes elaborated in earlier chapters related to absence, they articulated a sense of how online learning was alienating. The theme of absence in non-face-to-face learning can be felt as alienation for students and also teachers.

References

Dreyfus, H. L. (2008). *On the internet (thinking in action)*. London, UK: Routledge.
Haidt, J., & Lukianoff, G. (2019). *The coddling of the American mind: How good intentions and bad ideas are setting up a generation for failure*. New York, NY: Penguin Books.
Heidegger, M. (1976). *What is called thinking* (J. Glenn Gray, Trans.). New York, NY: HarperCollins. (Original work published 1954).
Heidegger, M. (1977). *The question concerning technology, and other essays* (W. Levitt, Trans.). New York, NY: HarperCollins. (Original works published 1962, 1952 & 1954).
Heidegger, M. (1984). *Nietzsche volume two: The eternal recurrence of the same* (D. F. Krell, Trans.). New York, NY: HarperCollins. (Original work published 1961).
Heidegger, M. (2000). *Elucidations of Hölderlin's poetry* (K. Hoeller, Trans.). Amherst, NY: Humanity Books. (Original work published 1981).
Hesiod. (2009). *Theogony & Works and days* (S. Nelson, Trans.). Newburyport, MA: Focus Publishing.
King James Version Bible. (2013). KJV Online. Retrieved April 16, 2020, from https://www.kingjamesbibleonline.org/
Lamberton, R. (1988). *Hesiod*. New Haven, CN: Yale University Press.
Leopold, D. (2018). Alienation. In *The Stanford Encyclopedia of Philosophy*. Retrieved February 22, 2020, from https://plato.stanford.edu/archives/fall2018/entries/alienation/
Nietzsche, F. (1974). *The gay science: With a prelude in rhymes and an appendix of songs*. (W. Kaufmann, Trans.). New York, NY: Random House. (Original work published 1887).
Peterson, J. (2018). *12 rules for life: An antidote to chaos*. Toronto, CA: Penguin Random House.
Postman, N. (1992). *Technopoly: The surrender of culture to technology*. New York, NY: Alfred A. Knopf Inc.
Rorty, R. (1999). *Philosophy and social hope*. New York, NY: Penguin Books.
Tallis, R. (2016). *Aping mankind*. New York, NY: Routledge Classics.
Wendling, E. A. (2009). *Karl Marx on technology and alienation*. London, UK: Palgrave Macmillan.
Wood, A. (2005). Alienation. In Ted Honderich (Ed.), *The Oxford guide to Philosophy* (p. 21). Oxford, UK: Oxford University Press.

17 Face-to-Face Learning Is a Focal Practice

Robert Frost's *Mowing*

Hesiod refers to a moment in the farmer's season "when the iron [or sickle] for mowing is first sharpened" (2009, p. 84). He is talking about the scythe that is used to cut the stalks of grain, probably one of the most vital tools for an Ancient Greek farmer. Once the scythe had cut the stalks, they could be gathered and the harvesting process completed. One of Robert Frost's (1874–1963) early poems, "Mowing," published in his book, *A Boy's Will* (1915), is related to the idea of harvesting work, the process of accruing and laying up in store. In "Mowing," the emphasis is decidedly focused on the present, the current moment of the mower doing the work and listening to the sound of his scythe.

Frost writes about the sound he heard as he labored on a farm as a young man with a small family. For Frost, it is whispering something. What I image is the swishing sound of the swinging scythe that seems to speak in a soft language of its own. The poem follows a path of thought as to what the tool, in its use, may be trying to express. Every time I read the poem different words stand out to me. The poem is saturated with ambiguity. I cannot get a hold of it completely. It seems too great. However, on every reading two words stand out, "truth" and "fact."

Besides the idea of hard labor (the effort required to learn) and the use of a tool – a technological innovation – the connection of this poem to remote learning may seem obscure. What seems to draw me to it most in this context is the notion of there being certain facts necessary for any interpretation. These facts just are the way of the world, in a sense immutable. Similar to Hesiod's sense of the divine, they are outside of human control. Like with *Works and Days*, the realization of the poet is that something can be denied but that does not change the fact. One fact is expressed in Hesiod's ideal of the educated person and the successful consequence of the Socratic teaching method; the student is wise who most comes to know what they do not know. One who has learned at a high level attains wisdom when they know their limitations. This is a fact.

DOI: 10.4324/9781003349051-17

What does "fact" mean? It directly conjures notions of the correspondence theory of truth, a verificationist project to validate propositions about the world. We assume that the "facts of the matter" will settle the case, but this does not always happen. Although somewhat the gold standard of truth in the sciences, the correspondence theory is deeply flawed. So where does that leave the fact? Are there no facts? To paraphrase Nietzsche, is it that there are no facts only interpretations? But what then are the interpretations based on if not some notion of factual content? For example, how the content of my conversations with my participants are the facts on which I base may interpretation. Heidegger says, "'Fact' is a beautiful and beguiling word" (1976/1954, p. 161). This statement is practically a poem itself. It is given with almost no commentary and is ambiguous. That the idea of facts certainly seems beautiful, it posits an objectivity upon which consensus might be reached and to which our free subjectivity might be beholden. Moreover, the fact can provide consensus which can motivate cooperative action. However, in many matters, especially those that are most important, it is hardly ever so straightforward. And so I consider, what are the facts about non-face-to-face learning? At this point, I hope I have shown some of them. The fact that occupies me the most is that which is lost; without face-to-face contact, undergraduate education can be lost.

Fact versus Artifact

One distinction that seems illuminating in this context is the difference between a fact and an artifact. However much the facts may be disputed about something, they are still in some sense more real than artifacts, i.e., "an object made or modified by human workmanship, as opposed to one formed by natural processes" (Oxford English Dictionary, n.d.). The scythe is an artifact. Indeed, so is, in a related sense, the planting and tending that culminates in mowing. An "artifact" includes "art" and relates to crafts and skills. It is a kind of contrivance. The word connotes a sense of being a copy or unoriginal.

In the context of archeology, "artifact" would mean a kind of object that is a clue and indicator, because it is evidence of craftsmanship. It, therefore, allows for understanding but not direct access. The artifacts of the Egyptians do not really establish what the Egyptians were. The artifact in that sense can be seen to not be the real thing, as in its scientific use of "artifact," "a spurious result, effect, or finding in a[n] … experiment or investigation, especially one created by the experiment technique or procedure itself" (Ibid.) In this sense, "artifact" is similar to the origin and use of "factoid." For example, "Norman Mailer introduced the word *factoid* in his 1973 book *Marilyn*. He invented it by combining the word *fact* with – *oid*, a scientific suffix that means 'resembling but not identical to.'" In other words, it's something that looks like a fact, but isn't. Factoids are built from rumors and used by irresponsible journalists to create a story when none exists (Lennox, 2003, p. 141). Moreover, "artifact" is related to "artificial" and "artificer." The artifact can be a kind of imposter. It can present itself as the fact because it too is something real, i.e., it has a certain ontology. However, it can also be "a non-material human construct" (Ibid.). It is with that connotation that non-face-to-face learning is a kind of artifact of education. It happens. It is real, but it is only a kind of vestigial remnant, a going through the motions in order to mostly signal learning and bring about measurable completion (Caplan, 2018). It is most often an imitation of the real thing.

"Fact" certainly is a beguiling word, and not just in Heidegger's German. The *Oxford English Dictionary* entry is several pages and has nine different definitions and several senses for each. The overall meaning has to do with truth and reality in its usage. And like the truth, the real deep down of how things are or what something is, we can be pulled to the facts as expressed in "Mowing" because they are the most precious products of our work (Frost, 1915, p. 36). Our focused efforts are strivings to make or find facts. What can be the *fact* of learning? What is the real aspect uncreated but still within this human activity, which is itself a sort of artifact?

One commentator, Benjamin Voigt (2016), suggests that Frost, like Shakespeare and other great artists, incorporates a commentary on his own medium into some of his poems. There is a sense that Frost is saying the meaning of poems though ambiguous is not fantasy; it is fact. There are many facts to be found in a poem. There are many meanings to be discovered in a phenomenon like what is lost from remote learning. It is labor that brings forth those facts. I take this to mean the directed energy that must be expended to approach the real. Of course, labor can be expended in online learning, when we read and study alone, but the effort I want to emphasize is the work lost in the pursuit of efficiency, when we streamline human interactions to make them frictionless. This is easily accomplished by making learning non-face-to-face. Some of my participants referred to these desirable gains in efficiency as explicitly related to the absence of others.

The constant push to render scarce resources more efficient at the costs of tradition and lofty ideals, i.e., the result of a liberal education, can become tiresome or irksome as my participants noted. As Heideggerian philosopher of technology, Albert Borgmann says, "There is at least a drowsy and perhaps even a dawning sense in the contemporary culture that the paradigmatic blessings of technology are vacuous" (2003, p. 21). Even though we hear that there might be dramatic improvements in enrollment, retention and GPAs because of non-face-to-face learning, I sense that it is a house of cards. That is a criticism which can also be leveled at many traditional aspects of undergraduate education (Caplan, 2018). However, with face-to-face learning it is a fact that more is still possible than *could* happen in an online class.

Borgmann's Philosophy of Focal Practices

The simple task of mowing grain rendered in profound poetic depth by Frost has shown a connection to how I see the thing I feel called to foster and protect, face-to-face learning. In this study, I have researched remote learning, but here I turn squarely to what it replaces. The expectations of those who take online classes is shaped by their previous experience. If they have had online classes before, they typically seem to have low expectations for learning but are glad for the efficiency. For those who want more than the credits and a boost to their GPA, who really want to learn and have never taken an online class, they are usually disappointed. Their expectations are not met. But the thing they feel is lost is unclear, though the fact of its existence is apparent.

Borgmann explains a way by which we can understand how the facts of learning can be obscured by technology. "Does anything of philosophical moment turn on the fact that in some cases a traditional, contextual thing has been replaced by an article that is opaque and more available?" (Borgmann, 2003, p. 16). He is illuminating the point that our advanced microtechnology is inherently obscure but also ubiquitous. We do not understand it even though it is readily available. A student showing up at an undergraduate classroom and learning with others is understandable. What is happening is generally self-evident and meaningful because it takes place in the context of tradition, but it is a kind of laborious ritual requiring vast coordination of schedules, space and resources. The mechanics of an online class seem to be like a face-to-face class, but the fact is, much is mystery when learning becomes highly mitigated by technology. Borgmann's point is that we do not understand how the devices which facilitate such an interaction work or the details of how we remain connected when we are remote. We do not understand these things like we can understand a scythe or an old motorcycle. Like the stethoscope, and Hesiod's view of the divine, technological innovations can start to seem magical or holy because they are certainly mysterious. However, artifacts seem to be beyond human control. "In fact, thoughtful reflections on technology are typically haunted by ambiguity and ambivalence" (Ibid., p. 17). We cannot generally fathom how any one person could fully understand something like a computer and its connectivity, the power grid or systems of international travel and trade, though we have a strong faith that certainly there are such individuals.

In relation to the fact of in-person learning and the artifact of online classes is Borgmann's thoughtful philosophical response. In his book *Technology and the Character of Contemporary Life* (1987), he carefully works to describe a way toward Heidegger's (1977) idea of a "free relationship" to technology. In his book, Borgmann is setting out to show a way to be with technology. He is trying to answer the question "What should our relationship to technology be?" The question is important because no matter what we must relate to technology. The path of total rejection, like the Luddite, is still a chosen way of relating to technology. Borgmann's relationship to technology depends on what he describes as focal things and practices. "Focal [things and practices] on their part live in hiding and at the margins of the official technological culture" (Borgmann, 2003, p. 23).

Borgmann builds on Heidegger's (1971) definition of "the thing" to explain what he means by focal things and activities. "The orienting force of simple things will come to the fore only as the rule of technology is raised from its anonymity, is disclosed as the orthodoxy that heretofore has been taken for granted and allowed to remain invisible" (Borgmann, 1987, p. 199). This is the saving power to which Heidegger (1977) refers. As the technological attitude becomes so pervasive, it will become obvious and it will draw attention to itself in such a way that human beings will seek to preserve that which should not be technologized.

Borgmann explains:

> Once we have learned tentatively to recognize the instances of focal things and practices in our midst, we must acknowledge their scattered and inconspicuous character too. Their hidden splendor comes to light when we consider Heidegger's reflections on simple and eminent things.
>
> (1987, p. 196)

The entities that Heidegger (1971) used as examples of "things" were simple and everyday (jug and bench, footbridge and plow, tree and pond, brook and hill, heron and deer, horse and bull, mirror and clasp, book and picture, crown and cross). In the same way, Borgmann explains that the power of focal things is found in their simplicity and their ability to be in constant contact with our experience. These focal things can be noticed in their triviality and in their non-enframing essence, i.e., the sense in which they resist being made efficient. They are resistant to efficiency because to make them efficient is to destroy them; they just would not be what they are anymore. Once focal things are noticed, they require certain practices in order to thrive (Ibid.). Borgmann focuses on two focal practices to make his point: running and the large community road races with a festive atmosphere and the culture of the table, i.e., communal eating (Ibid.). However, these are only examples, presented as templates to elucidate what a focal practice is so that we can recognize them in our own lives.

Borgmann highlights the contrast between how cars have made travel more efficient and the focal activity of running. He says that in running the "split between means and ends, labor and leisure is healed" (Ibid., p. 202). In running there is no standing reserve of petrochemical production, maintenance facilities and highways as there is in the efficient travel by car. Instead, we just run (or walk or hike) and are put in motion and contact with the ground and our surroundings. Through the practice of running, "The unity of ends and means, of minds and body, and of body and world is one and the same" (Ibid., 203). Thus, the example of running as a focal activity shows that it must be something that connects us to our surrounding physical environment and brings together the means and ends of what the practice is pointed at. That is, the motion of running cannot be stored up or recorded. When we are running, we are simultaneously producing and experiencing the results of our physical motion.

The culture of the table and the environment surrounding the feast meal is Borgmann's second example employed to define focal practices.

> Human eating is the union of the primal and the cosmic. In the simplicity of bread and wine, of meat and vegetable, the world is gathered ... We can begin with the simplicity of a meal that has a beginning, a middle, and an end and that breaks through the superficiality of convenience food in the simple steps of beginning with raw ingredients, preparing and transforming them, and bringing them to the table.
>
> (Ibid., p. 204)

From this description of the focal activity of the feast, Borgmann agrees with Heidegger (1971) that a world can be gathered or truth can happen in the things that we do. That is, there is a union made possible by focal practices. This opens up a realm of significance in which we can connect to things not simply as resources. We can recognize them for their individuality similar to the way certain words express profound difference and fundamental relationships, e.g., mortals, divinities, sky and earth (Heidegger calls these, in many places, "the fourfold").

Face-to-Face Learning Is a Focal Practice

The focal activities of running and the culture of the table are presented by Borgmann as counteracting contrasts to the essence of technology. This means the more we engage in cooking in celebratory thanksgiving or running in a sense of communal festivity, the more we inculcate in ourselves a sense for other ways of understanding beings besides that of standing reserves. Focal practices are all around us. We need only attune ourselves to them. "Once we have learned tentatively to recognize the instances of focal things and practices in our midst, we must acknowledge their scattered and inconspicuous character too" (Borgmann, 1987, p. 196). From Borgmann's two examples, we learn how we can recognize a focal practice. The most obvious feature is how human beings are present with each other. It is the interaction of a group of people. It cannot be done alone. They must be gathered together around something that is important to them. And what draws them together, the activity, must require some degree of skill in order for it to really be happening. The result of a focal practice, if it is really operating in its counteractive manner to the technological attitude, is to bring the people involved out at their best in their personal distinctiveness.

Every focal practice is centered on a "communal devotion to a focal thing" (Borgmann, 2003, p. 22). In relation to remote classes, my emphasis is on the resulting practice, teaching and learning in-person. However, the focal thing is still important, the text, or method of thinking that the class is focused on for that day. The focal things of a classroom filled with undergraduates are not like other things. They have a kind of inexhaustibility. These things are needed, like anything that can lead to wisdom, but they cannot be used up. Teaching, as a focal practice, settles on these types of things. In so doing, the practice stands out as different than other ways of comporting toward entities.

There is another sense in which focal practices push back against technological ways of revealing. "Focal things and practices are the crucial counterforces to technology. They contrast with technology without denying it, and they provide a standpoint for a principled and fruitful reform of technology" (Borgmann, 2003, p. 22). My phrase "push back" is not quite right because it is not exactly a displacement. Instead, it is a transformation of how we understand what is already there. Borgmann says focal practices, "Gather our world and radiate significance" (Ibid.). Focal practices create a space like "the clearing" that Heidegger often refers to throughout his later work. The ontological and relational space opened by focal practices allows us to see things in their own significance with their own essence(s). Engaging in focal practices around focal things, e.g., the dialogues of Plato, allows us to comport ourselves toward the world as something other than just resources. Another way of thinking of resources is with the name "commodity," e.g., grain, electricity and money. Commodities are also often needed by everyone but not for the same reasons as focal things. Moreover, commodities can be used up or exhausted, not so with focal things.

Borgmann explains that part of the powerful seduction of technology is its ability to increase what is available for consumption. However, this should not persuade us into thinking that the boons of technology are universal. He argues that technology *is* fundamentally and permanently limited. "There is an essential, as opposed to a merely extensive, limit to technology, the latter understood as the procurement and consumption of commodities" (Borgmann, 2003, p. 22). The essential limit of technology is not then in a halt to consumerism, e.g. the ability to create diversions and flood our world with sensual necessities. The essential limit has to do with something besides the bounty that technology can produce.

Face-to-face classes can be a focal practice. The activity of learning face-to-face and the care that is required does not stand in reserve to be expended. When students learn with a teacher face-to-face, they have the chance to be more united in a common project. The fruits of the teacher's labors can be reflected back. Students can engage with the teacher fully. Similar to running, learning in-person cannot be stored up like a commodity. Learning face-to-face cannot be recorded. What happens in real time cannot be captured. Plato, too, emphasized this great lesson from his master Socrates, i.e., learning happens in the moment of conversational exchange. It cannot be written down. In face-to-face learning, we communally gather in devotion to the focal thing, a tradition or set of texts, knowledge, the pursuit of wisdom, understanding, mastery and a greater sense of how to become more fully what we are together. The free relationship comes when we communally acknowledge the preciousness of our focal things. Then we gather in vulnerability to practice our devotion to focal things. The means of learning are as important as the ends, if it is understood as a focal practice, i.e., something that frees us from the technological attitude.

One of my great concerns has been with how non-face-to-face learning divides the means from the ends. It also seems to add greater confusion to the already-muddled purpose of undergraduate education in the contemporary world. Thus, Borgmann's philosophy of focal practices is helpful in reestablishing the significance of the means of learning. It renders them on the same plane as the ends. Understanding face-to-face learning as a focal practice heals the division and provides a way of understanding what should be protected. How do we foster face-to-face learning as a focal practice? We let it be. It will not always succeed. We accept the risk. Just like the big festive meal is not always a success and running does not always bring people together at their best. But in these activities we can get a sense of how to have a free relationship to technology. We do not reject technology in the classroom, but we know when to use it and when it should be put away. We acknowledge the efficiency of online classes but use them only when needed, when they are better than nothing, and never allow them to creep into the sphere of better than anything (Turkle, 2017).

References

Borgmann, A. (1987). *Technology and the character of contemporary life: A philosophical inquiry*. Chicago, IL: The University of Chicago Press.
Borgmann, A. (2003). *Power failure: Christianity in the culture of technology*. Grand Rapids, MI: Brazos Press.
Caplan, B. (2018). *The case against education: Why the education system is a waste of time and money*. Princeton, NJ: Princeton University Press.
Frost, R. (1915). *A boy's will*. New York, NY: Henry Holt and Company.
Heidegger, M. (1971). *Poetry, language, thought*. New York, NY: HarperCollins.
Heidegger, M. (1976). *What is called thinking* (J. Glenn Gray, Trans.). New York, NY: HarperCollins. (Original work published 1954).

Heidegger, M. (1977). *The question concerning technology, and other essays* (W. Levitt, Trans.). New York, NY: HarperCollins. (Original works published 1962, 1952 & 1954).

Hesiod. (2009). *Theogony & Works and days* (S. Nelson, Trans.). Newburyport, MA: Focus Publishing.

Lennox, D. (2003). *The little book of answers: The how, where, and why of stuff you thought you knew*. New York, NY: MJF Books.

Oxford English Dictionary. (n.d.). Retrieved July 11, 2022, from https://www.oed.com/dictionary

Turkle, S. (2017). *Alone together: Why we expect more from technology and less from each other*. New York, NY: Basic Books.

Voigt, B. (2016, January 19). Robert Frost 101: His poems can be read many different ways. *Poetry Foundation*. Retrieved March 15, 2021, from https://www.poetryfoundation.org/articles/70308/robert-frost-101

18 Death in the Desert
Finding the Soul of Undergraduate Learning

The work of swinging a scythe to harvest grain is something I have never done. It does remind me of a repetitive manual task of my youth, chopping wood. In rural Iowa, we had to cut down dead oak trees, chainsaw them into logs and then haul the logs home to be split into pieces that could fit into the stove. I spent many hours wielding a heavy splitting maul. Like the scythe, you cannot do much else when you are doing such work. You have to pay attention and be present. If you are not careful, the work will take longer and you might get hurt. During the hours of effort, the mind can resign itself to the rhythm of the task. The mind seeks to explore but remains constrained by the task. Thinking cannot neglect the work; it has to remain connected to the task. Ideas come in moments of peace between the focused bursts of concentration. For example, a train of thought can be carried out in the moments when the blade is at rest or as the next log is being positioned. Though there may be many pressing responsibilities, there is a kind of relief when you know not only that one thing needs to be done, but you can only do that thing.

Uniting Means and Ends: Labor for Its Own Sake

There is something tautological when means and ends are united and we do something for its own sake. There are times when I am performing trivial work a kind of peace enters. I sometimes find solace folding the laundry. What is the source of the peace? It seems to come from knowing that the laundry is not going to fold itself, just like the wood will not split itself and the grass will not mow itself. As technology writer Nicholas Carr says:

> When we embark on a task, with our bodies or our minds, on our own or alongside others, we usually have a practical goal in sight. Our eyes are looking ahead to the product of our work … But it's through the work itself that we come to a deeper understanding of ourselves and our situation.
>
> (2015, p. 214)

DOI: 10.4324/9781003349051-18

The centered feeling of being confronted by the work is knowing that the task at hand is the task that needs to be done and nothing else matters because nothing else can matter until you do the chore.

The fact of the work stands independent of however grandiose or dramatic other endeavors may be. Carr also makes the point, with breath catching acuity in relation to non-face-to-face learning, "Labor, whether of the body or the mind, is more than a way of getting things done. It's a form of contemplation, a way of seeing the world *face-to-face*" (2015, p. 213, *emphasis added*). Mathew Crawford (2009) presents a similar insight in his wonderful book, *Shop class as Soulcraft: An Inquiry into the Value of Work*. "Skilled manual labor entails a systematic encounter with the material world … From its earliest practice, craft knowledge has entailed knowledge of the 'ways' of one's materials – that is, knowledge of their nature, acquired through disciplined perception" (p. 21). The embodied toils of life, the works that fill our time, are not intellectual vacuums. The focused work of a teacher is not purely intellectual; it is a craft.

It is always possible to regard anything as a means to some other end. But is that the best way to live? For example, it is unsustainable to constantly be living in a state of perpetual preparation. The idea of preparation can become ingrained through education. If every grade and stage of learning is just preparation for further preparation, how is life given space to happen? John Dewey confronted the instrumental attitude in education in a profound way. He said:

> What, then, is the true meaning of preparation in the educational scheme? In the first place, it means that a person, young or old, gets out of his present experience all that there is in it for him at the time in which he has it. When preparation is made the controlling end, then the potentialities of the present are sacrificed to a suppositious future. When this happens, the actual preparation for the future is missed or distorted. The ideal of using the present simply to get ready for the future contradicts itself. It omits, and even shuts out, the very conditions by which a person can be prepared for his future. *We always live at the time we live and not at some other time*, and only by extracting at each present time the full meaning of each present experience are we prepared for doing the same thing in the future. This is the only preparation which in the long run amounts to anything.
>
> (1938/1997, p. 49, *emphasis added*)

Dewey's description is of how to make manifest the unity of means and ends in education. He shows that they must be united if education is in fact going to do what we expect it to do. The moments in the classroom have to matter for their own sake and not for some "suppositious future." Preparing only works when the activities of preparation are done for their own sake, i.e., they have to be relevant and matter when they are being done and as they are being done.

There is a special kind of peace for the mind when it engages in activities that shield it from interruption. In these means-ends united moments, perhaps a certain kind of mental energy is saved and maybe even focused creatively, e.g. I have heard people say that their best moments of thinking happen when they are bathing. But when we feel that we could be doing more, that our attention should be elsewhere, all tasks might feel a bit more burdensome.

To find the unity of means and ends is to taste the "free relationship" to technology that Heidegger (1977) sets a path toward. To experience something as an end in itself is to be relieved of the constant pressure to always regard everything in an instrumental manner, i.e., as a tool for something else. There are moments, as shown by Borgmann, when focal things and practices unite means and ends. In the focal practice we set aside the burden of merely instrumental ways of thinking and constantly preparing for the next challenge. Focal practices can include technology, for instance, mowing and even, of course, teaching.

An "Ecosystem of Interruption"

Science fiction writer, Cory Doctorow says, "Whenever we turn on our computers, we are plunged into an ecosystem of interruption technologies" (Carr, 2011, p. 91). It is just what computers are. As Carr puts it in his book *The Glass Cage: What Computers are Doing to Us*:

> The computer screen is intensely compelling, not only for the convenience it offers but also for the many diversions it provides. There's always something going on … Yet the screen, for all its enticements and stimulations, is an environment of sparseness – fast moving, efficient, clean, but revealing only a shadow of the world.
>
> (Carr, 2015, p. 219)

An "ecosystem" is used to describe certain complex relationships within an environment. The natural world is a system of interactions between organisms that depend on and relate to a myriad of physical and biological processes. As we observe them, these interactions are all related, i.e., if you change one, you will alter all of the others. Thus, to speak of computers in this way is to say that once we enter into one part of the ecosystem of interruption, we are entering a system or even a cycle of interruption. We may go from one interruption to another, carried along by what we know not, until we decide to break out.

It can be hard to get anything done on a computer or the Internet. For example, some of my most profitable writing time is on the D.C. Metro commuting to school. Why? Well because there is no reliable connectivity.

On the metro, my computer becomes mostly a single function tool, i.e., a word processor. Though even then, there are many other possibilities; there are still other forms of interruption that can intrude. For instance, if I go hunting for a source I think I downloaded and begin scrolling through files and find something else, or am reminded of this or that the computer can again be full of interruptions. It is interesting that new developments like cloud computing and having our documents saved there (i.e., in the cloud) means that they can never be lost no matter what happens to our own computer. Though to reap the benefits of such safety, we have to remain constantly connected.

Dealing with computers is a necessity. But how do we have a free relationship with such a thing? How do we know when to put it away and not use it, especially since it is so efficient? In those times, quite plentiful, when we are getting a lot done with our computer, there seems like there might be a background expenditure of energy that is needed to keep on track and resist the frogs of interruption that can bounce up at any time.

Our devices are engines of distraction. In her chilling book, *Addiction by Design: Machine Gambling in Las Vegas*, Natasha Dow Shüll (2012) shows how the operation algorithms of machines are capable of putting people into a trance like state. The condition is called the "machine zone." Advanced computing technology did not *have* to be this way. Be that as it may, our devices were designed to be profoundly seductive.

It is not typically possible to use or think of a computer as a *single* function tool. Thus, when we expect people (e.g., students) to treat it as such, we are not considering the general connection and experience people have with computers. The device that makes non-face-to-face learning possible is a multipurpose gadget. And its most familiar use for students may not be learning at all. Students occupy themselves at their computers according to the dispositions that they have developed with them. For example, it is obvious that the computer is a medium of communication. One of the most distracting offerings available on the computer is its lines of social cohesion which would be better described as *simulated* cohesion according to some (Haidt & Lukianoff, 2019). Therefore, students in a Zoom class, if not already texting on their phone, are likely to be looking at their screens intently because they are following the thread of a typed conversation and not because they are paying attention to the class. They do not do this all of the time. But it is remarkable to see how often there are clues that this is happening. Think about how often students in synchronous video lectures suddenly have big smiles on their faces or rock back and forth with laughter (muted by their audio of course) when there is no reason for such a reaction in the context of the class. The cause of such behavior has to do with them interacting with computers in their normal way. Speaking of Zoom, the program itself has a built-in chat feature which unless you take the effort to figure out and turn off will be used in relevant or irrelevant ways that are hard to manage or are time consuming if you use it when teaching.

Computers, phones, pads, pods etc. are so distracting because they are very interesting. They are interesting because they offer something of immediate value. Any Internet-connected device is like a sail we can throw up into a blizzard of information. They offer us so much that it seems relevant to our limited attention.

> The distinction between distraction and interest is hard to draw exactly. After all, you cannot be distracted by something without also being interested in it. But the interest stops with the next distraction. The mind does not *keep hold* of the first object of attention, since it is incapable of pursing its interest if the stimulus is not renewed.
> (Scruton, 2018, p. 20)

The computer conditions us to feel like there should always be something more interesting than what is currently holding our interest (Carr, 2011). It is certainly possible that this could be described as an anxious condition, i.e., because of the nature of the Internet we feel constantly pressed and ill at ease with how we are occupying ourselves. We often get the sense that since our time is limited, we should really be perpetually seeking for the best thing to occupy it with.

The energy needed to stay focused on a computer, during an online class, is part of the experience. Students might get distracted, but they could be pulled back to paying full attention if something stands out to them in a certain way. It seems hard to know how to keep everyone's attention all the time. Often I notice that if students start speaking up and making comments, especially back and forth to each other, the visages in the Zoom tiles seem to perk up. That is, I see more students looking up, straight ahead, rather than maybe just listening or multitasking. They want to see who is talking. The live exchange draws their attention back to the discussion. But it can fade again. It's the back-and-forth of full attention to something distracting I wonder about. What cost does attention occilation have for the quality of the overall experience? Many of my students ask where they can find the recordings for our classes together. I explain that I make no such recordings. I tell them that what matters is what happens when we are together in real time. I think, for many of these students who want recordings, they just want to be able to listen and not have to engage at all. They are trying to find a sort of loophole that shows that they were "there" but in fact nothing much was required of them.

A Soul Divided by Simultaneous Tasks

A metaphorical way of approaching the condition of distraction is by saying that one's soul is divided. The sense of this metaphorical language is that the soul is who we are, a kind of seat of our inner intentions or character. For example, Heidegger speaks of the soul in this way, "The soul then pours forth its wealth of images – of visions envisioning the soul itself" (1977/1954, p. 140). The soul is a kind of seat of our inner eye. It is where our ideas and images of thought and reality are encountered. And here in Heidegger there is circularity; the soul is the source of itself, it is the font of the idea of soul. Elsewhere Heidegger says, "To be sure, in the ruling definition, the human being is determined precisely with regard to body, soul, sprit" (2009, p. 59). Whether we accept that there really is such a thing as a soul (typically understood as an immaterial aspect of a person) or not, it is one of the most common metaphors for understanding human beings. As noted in the last chapter, we have a sense, rightly or wrongly, of an immateriality to our being.

There is a particular verse from Robert Browning's (1812–1889) poem, *A Death in the Desert*, that thinks about what a human being is. It works to articulate essential features of that entity which is closest of all to our understanding, ourselves: "How divers persons witness in each man,

> Three souls which make up one soul … What Does, what Knows, what Is; three souls, one man".
>
> (1989, pp. 171–172)

We have an aspect of ourselves, a kind of soul, that is related to the Earth because we are made from the material of the Earth. On the Earth, we toil and in one way or another are worn out (Berry, 1981). The repetitive tasks of survival, renewal and tradition reciprocate and echo through our language, the basic constituent of the human relational world (Wittgenstein, 2009). A thing like that, the entity that we are, with body, mind and soul, as described by this poem, captures the richness and texture of human thought, the iterative quality of ideas and how they constitute us. What captures my attention here is the sense of order but also fragility, how it is possible to disrupt and remake ourselves.

With the idea of soul in mind, we can consider the metaphor of division within the soul. If that thing – the soul – is constantly being switched back and forth between activities, even if according to its own desires (as when one choses to start texting with a friend during class) it is split. The soul experiences a kind of conflict. It is at war with itself. If habituated by this constant experience, the metaphor of the divided soul would say that at any one time someone in that condition might not know what they want or understand fully what they should be doing. They are trying to do many things at once. The technological attitude and its imperative to maximize everything, most especially one's own time, means trying to multiply one's efforts.

Traditionally it seems that one of the goals of learning was concentration. The ability to focus on a task, e.g. reading and solving a problem, were the hoped-for outcomes of education. However, that ideal is now encountered with some skepticism because of computers. It seems that increasing numbers of administrators, teachers and students are persuaded that since the conditions of labor will now always be done on computers, learners should become as familiar with them as possible, as soon as possible, in order to be better at multitasking. That is, the ultimate aim of education should be greater facility with the oxymoronic idea of divided attention. Even in his time, Nietzsche noticed the same tendency.

> We think too fast, even while walking or on the way, or while engaging in other things, no matter how serious the subject. We require little preparation, not even much silence: it is as if we carried in our heads an unstoppable machine that keeps working even under the most unfavorable circumstances.
> (1974, p. 81)

With the wonders of our machine technology, we have invited the machine like way of being to become increasingly our own. Hence, we can increasingly feel there is no time to take time.

The idea of being able to divide attention, and not just achieve the same results but better, has been soundly drubbed by empirical research summarized in many places (Carr, 2011; Haidt & Lukianoff, 2019; Turkle, 2017). Multitasking is based on the false assumption that human attention can be occupied by more than one thing at the same time. The assumption is supported by the flexibility of our attention. We are able to switch among many tasks simultaneously. The constant shift can give us the sense that we are doing many things at the same time. In fact, we are not. Instead, we are using our undividable attention in short spurts in different directions. If we are listening to a lecture and a movie, we do not understand both fully at the same time. Our intellectual capacity can fill in the gaps a bit and again give us the sense that we are doing two things at the same time, but in fact we are just degrading the experience of both in order to have a sense of doing two things at once. However, the pervasive sense continues that (a) multitasking is possible and (b) it is good to multitask. And why wouldn't it? The necessity and goodness of multitasking is what the technological attitude demands.

The Seduced Soul or Face of Learning

It is the technological attitude that shapes the expectations of undergraduate students and teachers. With the sense that the only meaningful distinction is efficiency, precious things can be lost. Engulfed in the destiny of this ontology, it is hard to notice (Heidegger, 1977). And in these conditions, it is like Nietzsche says, "Ideas are worse seductresses than our sense" (1974, p. 333). Ideas are able to shape what we sense. Part of the seduction is to make the technological attitude so close to our understanding that we do not notice it.

The seduction of technology is something we dwell with. As my participants showed, one outcome of the seduction is a sense of the defilement of learning. The word "debauch" means "to seduce." With this connection, we can see that there is a sense that what is seduced is ruined. What my participants brought forth was that often it is the case that there is a sense in the experience of online classes that it is masturbatory. It is not the actual thing; instead, it is a sort of artifact, i.e., a degraded or compromised form of learning. The resulting copy is a kind of perversion of learning. Though it can create a kind of experience of learning, it was primarily experienced as a waste.

Etymologically "to dwell" is related seduction. To "dwell" means to linger, to abide and to stay. To "seduce" means to cause to delay or linger. The seducer causes the seduced to stay where they otherwise would not. They are enticed to dwell where they would not. Not all dwelling need be the result of seduction. In the case of the technological attitude and the soul of learning, we are tied to a place. We orbit around a fixed sort of learning that is simplified and frictionless. It certainly has its appeal. To move on from the place, to be with the face of learning in classrooms, we have to acknowledge the seduction. To carry on and to dwell, we also have to think of what then does this mean for teaching, to which I turn next, as I look to the final insights gained from my study.

References

Berry, W. (1981). *The gift of good land: Further essays cultural and agricultural*. Berkeley, CA: Counterpoint.

Browning, R. (1989). *Robert Browning selected poems*. New York, NY: Penguin Books.

Carr, N. (2011). *The shallows: What the internet is doing to our brains*. New York, NY: Norton and Company.

Carr, N. (2015). *The glass cage: How computers are changing us*. New York, NY: W.W. Norton & Company.

Crawford, M. B. (2009). *Shop class as soulcraft: An inquiry into the value of work*. New York, NY: Penguin Press.

Dewey, J. (1997). *Experience and education*. New York, NY: Simon & Schuster. (Original work published 1938).

Haidt, J., & Lukianoff, G. (2019). *The coddling of the American mind: How good intentions and bad ideas are setting up a generation for failure*. New York, NY: Penguin Books.

Heidegger, M. (1977). *The question concerning technology, and other essays* (W. Levitt, Trans.). New York, NY: HarperCollins. (Original works published 1962, 1952 & 1954).

Heidegger, M. (2009). *Logic as the question concerning the essence of language* (W. T. Gregory & Y. Unna, Trans.). Albany, NY: State University of New York Press.

Nietzsche, F. (1974). *The gay science: With a prelude in rhymes and an appendix of songs* (W. Kaufmann, Trans.). New York, NY: Random House. (Original work published 1887).
Scruton, R. (2018). *Culture counts: Faith and feeling in a world besieged*. New York, NY: Encounter Books.
Shüll, N. D. (2012). *Addiction by design: Machine gambling in Las Vegas*. Princeton, NJ: Princeton University Press.
Turkle, S. (2017). *Alone together: Why we expect more from technology and less from each other*. New York, NY: Basic Books.
Wittgenstein, L. (2009). *Philosophical investigations* (G. E. M. Anscombe, P. M. S. Hacker, & J. Schulte, Trans.). West Sussex, UK: Wiley-Blackwell.

19 Teaching Undergraduates after COVID-19
Harder to Learn to Let Learn than to Learn

In the concluding chapters of this phenomenological work, I gesture toward further paths of inquiry. All the great questions are connected: e.g., What is justice? What is human nature? What is the good life? Like these questions, our world of experience is a relational web. One phenomenon connects to many others. The strongest or at least one of the closest linked phenomenon to the experience of non-face-to-face learning for undergraduates is the experience of online teaching. Since I am a teacher of undergraduates, I have been able to bring in some of what that experience may be like. However, this study is not about what is lost in online teaching. That should occupy a significant portion of phenomenological study now that we have all been deeply thrust into non-face-to-face education. Though teachers interact with learners, their experience of what they do online is profoundly different.

If online classes are created by schools because they think students want them, then that reasoning may not always be true. Often, it seems, the rationale for a course is confirmed by it being filled. The rationale seems to go like this: Step (1): create online course offerings (often in a competitive effort with other institutions who are already offering them); Step (2): measure the enrollment to determine how popular the online classes were; Step (3): if enrollment fills the classes, more are created. What role, if any, are teachers given in this process? If teachers want to teach online, what reasons do they give? What expectations do they go into the teaching experience with that make it seem like online instruction will be satisfying to them, that it will fulfill their view of teaching?

Learning to Let Learn

Some of the participants in my study explicitly mentioned the issue of expense in relation to online learning. Students know online learning is cheaper. It has a scalability that in-person classes cannot match, and it uses less of schools' resources. However, the struggles of conscientious remote teachers remain mostly opaque to the students. They probably do not realize that it takes more time for teachers to *do it well*. Needing

DOI: 10.4324/9781003349051-19

more time means that online education can actually be *more* expensive. Further phenomenological study of non-face-to-face teaching needs to be done.

The conditions created in undergraduate education because of COVID-19 have made many teachers aware of the effort to bring high-quality online instruction to their students. I assume that many, like me, almost immediately learn that they cannot just copy what they did in a classroom. Instead, teachers have to come up with whole new ways of presenting and engaging their students. The work teachers must do to re-learn how to teach, especially when the teacher hopes to have the same effect on students, can be frustrating and overwhelming. It can also be depressing to sense that you are no longer able to "reach" students in the same way as you could in a classroom.

Non-face-to-face classes may supersede the bounds of space and create ways for students to more efficiently use their time, but often that comes at the cost of teachers working even more, especially initially. The effort of the teachers is multiplied. In this context, there is an interesting connection to Heidegger's pedagogical insight, "The teacher is far less assured of his ground than those who learn are of theirs" (Heidegger, 1976/1954, p. 15). The teacher has to always, and in a way ever anew, be learning how students learn. On the other hand, students only have to learn, i.e., it is more stable for them. Making classes remote has added an enormous burden on teachers who strive to keep learning how to "let learn" (Ibid.). They have to balance that effort with what is often an almost completely foreign medium of instruction.

Teachers on Zoom, like other non-face-to-face instructors, have to take time to figure out how to make new lesson plans and assignments that will compensate for more direct engagement that might take place in a classroom. Of course, not all teachers take the effort to do this, and others may have no need. Be that as it may, it was pointed out, for example, at a meeting at my school, that many teachers had to take so much longer to cover the same material on Zoom. There is something about the format that is like wading in concrete. It is difficult to get into topics and get on with things. Course content from one day keeps getting carried over into the next, and it can be hard to ever fully "catch up."

Teachers in certain disciplines really need to "cover" a certain amount of course content. If they want their students to be prepared for the next level of classes in their discipline, they have to make sure the fundamentals are established. Admittedly, this sense could in part be due to the technological attitude. However, in some disciplines the strain of covering the content within the time constraints of online teaching could take years to figure out. If the courses were standardized, these problems would be removed. But so would the teachers. They would be, just as some of my participants saw them, merely course facilitators. Since the courses at many schools are not standardized, teachers try to figure out how to practice their craft, often without training or experience. Many of them may not even want to take the effort to do the training even if it would help. Part of the difficulty for the instructors is the fatigue of not knowing how much to alter in their instructional methods. They do not know how long they will be working remotely. If they knew it was permanent, maybe they could solve the issues. However, again, it takes so much initial effort to revamp a course for remote instruction.

Teleological Redux: Education as a Civic, Economic or Social Resource

In 1997, David Labaree wrote an influential article, "Public Goods, Private Goods: The American Struggle over Educational Goals." In his carefully researched and argued piece, Labaree presented education in the USA in terms of three primary ends: (1) The creation of good democratic citizens, the civic purpose of education; (2) the training of a competent and skilled workforce, the economic purpose of education; (3) providing the opportunity and means of social mobility. The first two were defined by Labaree as public goods, the third as a private good. These goals for education still inform how education at all levels in America proceeds whether in-person or non-face-to-face. This diagnosis of the ails of American education, Labaree argues, results in, "Historical conflict over these competing visions of education" (1997, p. 39). As a result of this strife, our education system produced "a contradictory structure" that has "sharply impaired its effectiveness" (Ibid.). Labaree's description is helpful to consider as it clearly shows how the technological way of revealing influences our thinking about education. As he says, "The social mobility goal has reshaped education into a *commodity*" (Ibid., *emphasis* added).

As soon as education is circumscribed to the domain of "goods," whether public or private, it is still nevertheless, in either case, primarily understood as a *resource*. The very discussion of "goods" in this sense is what Heidegger's fundamental phenomenological ontology of technology seeks to explicate (1977). In Patrick Fitzsimons piece "Enframing Education," his assessment of modern education reflects Labaree's concern but goes to the ontological root of the issue: "When we take education primarily as a technology for national economic development, that 'technology' is focused on some predetermined goal, itself already evaluated as of value. Education so configured does not suggest or ask about education's purpose. The process to the ends is purely to produce the predetermined ends, and the human is part of that structure" (2002, p. 184). Education in the technological age itself becomes enframed as a resource. The resource-oriented nature of Labaree's discussion is especially evident since in either case, education as a private or a public good, the motivation can be to make more money. For example, the civic attitude is imposed from the perspective of the public, which understands all citizens as potentially better or worse resources for advancing and perpetuating some notion of progress as defined by that nation.

I have been teaching undergraduates since 2012. Judging by my conversations with them and the emails and announcements I get from the schools I have work at, administrators see their role and the purpose of the university increasingly as highly political and ideological. Students are often aware of the dominate political ideology that is acceptable in the context of their formal learning. Of course, this might be difficult to notice for those within the ideology, that is one of the definitive marks of an ideology, it becomes invisible to its adherents. For my students and from my own experience it can be difficult to see how the tone or content of these communications and the general political tenor of universities today can be taken as balanced or objective.

Those who disseminate messages with politically laden language and establish the political atmosphere of the college rarely seem to exhibit an understanding, as it were, of what it would be like if the shoe was on the other foot. Like all of our hypocritical biases, they fall into a blind spot. It is clear from what my students have expressed to me that a certain political perspective is dogmatically adhered to by undergraduate institutions. This political aspect of higher education is also manifest in the names of conferences, presentations and article titles. Thus, what else are students to suppose than that the purpose of education is political and that their role in society is to take a certain specific civic role in society? That is, students are treated as resources for gaining and implementing political power. Based on the comments I have heard from students while teaching at four different undergraduate institutions, they are often consciously aware of how they are perceived as political resources. Some of them resent the narrowing effect this has on their educational opportunities. There is no end to the problematic unintended consequences resulting from broad acceptance of the dogmatic politicization of undergraduate education.

The other two modes of thinking about the ends of education, economic and social mobility do not escape enframing either. Each of these can be merely modes of thinking of others or ourselves as resources, i.e., something that can be made maximally efficient as measured by how much money we make in a certain amount of time. We might also measure ourselves as resources in terms of how well we are able to consume resources.

When education is merely a resource (e.g., a credential seeking exercise) and not engaged in for its own sake, its purpose will constantly be at issue (Labaree, 1997). Maybe that is the way it should be. On the other hand, if education is for wisdom, if that is its purpose, then maybe the civic, economic and social mobility goals will come naturally to those who need them the most. That is, perhaps education is like most good things it cannot be sought directly in an explicit manner.[1] To do so would destroy the conditions necessary for its attainment, e.g., "One converses better when one does not say, 'let us convers'" (Lewis, 2014, p. 309). What I mean is that perhaps education is like what Victor Frankl said in *Man's Search for Meaning*, "For success, like happiness, cannot be pursued; it must ensue[2] ... Happiness must happen, and the same holds for success: you have to let it happen by not caring about it ... success will follow you precisely because you have *forgotten* to think of it" (1992, p. 13). In this context, I am reminded of the phrase, "Don't let your education get in the way of your learning." Might it be that for students to learn there in fact cannot be too much concern for their education? If this is true, it can seem frustratingly paradoxical given how vital the issue. There are many good reasons, from the perspective of the technological attitude, for our explicit and controlling attitude toward the ends of education, e.g. we often hear that so much is at stake. However, this attempt to control and circumscribe education to our predetermined ends may contribute in no small part to the stifling of the joyous fruits of learning. If we focus on their attainment too intently, all of the good things that we might aim at (e.g., romance, sleep, health, beauty, peace, happiness and learning) might disappear like a mirage. As Heidegger might say, sometime we have to let things be for them to be at all.

Overlap of Learning and Teaching

There are of course overlapping aspects of the online teaching experience with the online learning experience. For example, even in a synchronous format like Zoom, teachers may also face the seduction of multitasking. It might become very obvious to students if teachers are doing something else besides engaging with the class. However, even within the context of the class there are ways a teacher might be excused for trying to do more than one thing at a time. For example, in Zoom there is a chat function. During class, this is often left on and students are free to post text about whatever they want. Unless a teacher turns off the chat function, it can be complicated or at least time consuming to "manage" the chat while also moving the class along.

I have decided the more opportunities students banished to remoteness by COVID-19 have of connecting with someone else the better. I tell my students that I will not be monitoring the chat because I just cannot do it at the same time. I could, but it would waste class time as I would have to take time to read back through it. Sometimes, things get out of hand in the chat. Even though I do not read the chats, Zoom shows you a number of how many have been added. It can really blow up. At those times I stop and ask the class "what is going on in the chat?" Usually some topic from class or something I have said has led to a tangential discussion (often about dogs, food etc.). It would be good if further phenomenological work on the teacher's experience of online learning explored their relation to distraction and multitasking.

The possibility of distraction is also possible for teachers even in or especially in the synchronous online format. A lot of the potential distraction comes from the different way that students comport themselves on Zoom as compared to how they would be in a classroom. On Zoom, they do not always just sit and stare at the camera dutifully taking notes. As I have said, I have even seen students driving (bless their heart for leaving their cameras on so I could be terrorized by these images). Often, students are getting up to go do something; some even do class while they are at work (with masks on to help prevent the spread of COVID-19). Many students, despite my pleading, are on their phones or other programs during class. This is doubly distracting to teachers because the facial expressions (smiles and laughter) may have nothing to do with what is going on in class. As a teacher I find myself getting distracted by thinking about whether or not I am interpreting the visual feedback from my students correctly. I again start to wonder about the purpose of education.

Notes

1 Here is how C.S. Lewis put the point, "You can't get second things by putting them first; you can get second things only by putting first things first" (2014, p. 310). In this context, the wisdom that may result from education or the full flowering of the inherent dignity of a human being would be the first thing and the three purposes articulated by Labaree would be the second thing.
2 Frankl is here following Aristotle's discussion of *Eudaimonia* ("Happiness") in the *Nicomachean Ethics*. Aristotle argues that happiness is the result of virtuous activity, that is, it is secondary effect of living in the way that happy people live. Happiness is therefore not for Frankl and Arisotle what it is often considered to be, i.e., merely a pleasant psychological state. For them, it has more to do with feeling fulfilled and living a meaningful life.

References

Fitzsimons, P. (2002). Enframing education. In M. A. Peters (Ed.), *Heidegger, education and modernity* (pp. 171–190). Lanham, MD: Rowman & Littlefield Publishers.
Frankl, V. E. (1992). *Man's search for meaning: An introduction to logotherapy* (4th ed.). Boston, MA: Beacon Press.
Heidegger, M. (1976). *What is called thinking* (J. Glenn Gray, Trans.). New York, NY: HarperCollins. (Original work published 1954).
Heidegger, M. (1977). *The question concerning technology, and other essays* (W. Levitt, Trans.). New York, NY: HarperCollins. (Original works published 1962, 1952 & 1954).
Labaree, D. F. (1997). Public goods, private goods: The American struggle over educational goals. *American Education Research Journal, 34*(1), 39–81.
Lewis, C. S. (2014). *God in the dock: Essays on theology and ethics*. Grand Rapids, MI: Eerdmans.

20 What Is the Meaning of What Is Lost in Non-Face-to-Face Teaching?

Simulation Is Not Duplication

Like the students that participated in this study, I understand the necessity of online education. There are times when we need to be remote and use Zoom. The COVID-19 outbreak forced everyone to realize that online instruction could continue the goals of undergraduate education in the face of extreme barriers. However, even before the global disease there were reasons to hail the advantages of remote learning brought about by Internet connectivity.

Non-face-to-face education has the ability to reach people across space and time. If students or teachers cannot travel to class, they can usually find a way to the Internet. If students need greater flexibility to complete their degrees due to work, family or health, the marvels of asynchronous education are now available. Materials can be posted and accessed whenever is convenient, e.g. recorded videos of experts. Due to these moments of necessity and the imperative for convenience, the sense is that non-face-to-face education is a replacement for the traditional classroom experience. Thus, the design and presentation of online undergraduate classes is to make them as much like an in-person class as possible, or at least aim at accomplishing the same thing that is supposed to happen in-person. For example, in the Zoom class the urge is to try and copy and simulate the traditional components of a classroom. Designers, teachers and administrators of online classes do not want the students to miss out. They want the experience to be as much as possible like education has always been.

I hope this book has shown that the face-to-face experience cannot be copied. A technologically mitigated interaction with others is a different kind of experience. Similar to how we may learn by reading a book or in a different way by having a conversation, online learning is a fundamentally altered experience than what undergraduates have had before the Internet. Even in its closest approximation, the synchronous videoconference, the copied experience of a class "on Zoom" has little in common with a traditional classroom. Because Zoom

DOI: 10.4324/9781003349051-20

instruction during COVID-19 throughout 2020 and 2021 has been a necessity, we can, like myself, tell ourselves, that it is *like* the real thing, but it is not. When confronted with the attempt to copy and simulate, concerns about the true nature of our experiences can be destabilizing. If the doubts are deep enough, or if the simulation comes to be accepted as the original real thing, then it can come to seem like nothing matters.

Nihilism and Embodiment

Nihilism is the condition created by what Nietzsche called the "death of god." Two contemporary philosophers explain this pronouncement in the following way, "What [Nietzsche] meant by this is that we in the modern West no longer live in a culture where the basic questions of existence are already answered for us" (Dreyfus & Kelly, 2011, p. 20). The end of all absolutes, that is, any shared or individual criteria of meaning is dissolved in the condition of nihilism. The empty blankness of meaninglessness tends to escape metaphor, but it is like falling. It can also be thought of as the frictionless state of weightlessness (Nietzsche, 1974). Nihilism is an abyss of choice but no reason to make any. It is the sense of absolute freedom but with no purpose. However, even the characterization of "falling" is not adequate because that requires a shared idea of directionality and rules that are followed if certain conditions are met. But in nihilism there is simply nothing, only a deep gnawing malaise of dissatisfaction and homelessness, and even these torturous conditions are a relief compared to the utter emptiness of true meaninglessness. How do we confront this gaping abyss without also becoming the abyss? The abyss seems to yawn open before us as technological advances seem to create ever more possibilities (Borgmann, 1987). When we remove the face from learning, is this a sign of the nihilistic consequence of becoming seduced by technology?

    The dualism of dividing the body from the mind opens up the possibility of nihilism. The split has important ramifications for non-face-to-face learning. The idea that the body could be separated from the soul or mind reinforces the thinking that the life of the mind was one thing and the life of the body is something else. The body is bad, carnal and should be subordinated to, and mastered by, the soul. The solidity of this distinction leads to the self-evident seeming conclusions that though the body may occupy a certain set place in space the mind can be in another place altogether. The distinction supports the notion that it does not really matter where the body is as long as the mind has access to the appropriate stimulation. For example, the body can sit in bed and the mind can learn the information needed to earn a credential. To diminish the importance of where the body is when the mind is at work can lead to the un-grounding condition of nihilism, the state of being where nothing matters.

Nihilism can threaten to extinguish meaning and purpose in human life, but it can also serve as a stimulus to our greatest reaching, our most profound moments of *aporia*. The collective deadening or depression of the Western psyche is caused by the rejection of our human embodiment. Forgetting our bodies, our lived embodiment and disparaging our corporeal existence as finite creatures *is* the death of god. Conceptually departing from our bodies, ceasing to think of ourselves as embodied, and merely as minds, perpetuates the dualism of Descartes and all of the inherent difficulties associated with the subject versus object ontology (Heidegger, 1962/1926). More importantly, ignoring embodiment also leads to the same possibility of nihilism that Nietzsche identified in all transcendental systems. Remote learning embraces the kind of dualism that leads to a disembodied regard for the self and others. Teaching with such conditions can become nothing more than the supposed transfer of information which in the age of Google and YouTube looks increasingly pointless.

Embodiment implies "in a body," i.e., in-body-ment. The persistence of the container metaphor of our bodies, that we are in them, probably has something to do with how our brains are unable to perceive themselves directly, in much the same way that consciousness is always consciousness of something else and not itself (Carr, 2011). But thinking of one thing being contained in another is not accurate and perpetuates an inadequate dualism, e.g., a faulty phenomenology of human being. Even so, the continual persistence of distinguishing between mental experiences on the one hand and actions that we engage in with our bodies on the other is the foundation for online education.

We are not *in* our bodies. We are our bodies. We are embodied in the sense that to be a human is to be a human body. There is nothing *inside* of us, no matter how much we may have come to believe this metaphor. The mind is a metaphor to capture our experience of the staggering complexity of our bodies, the complexity of being embodied and knowing it. Indeed, in our path since the death of god we have come not just to the realization but even the expectation that human beings could exist as human beings without their bodies (Kurzweil, 2000). However, as Hubert Dreyfus (2008) seems to prove in his book, *On the Internet*, there is no sense in which we could still be humans without our bodies.

Overcoming the possible despair and meaninglessness of nihilism that is engulfing the world requires a return to that which is closest to us. In the everyday experience of the world, there is a call for a return to the wonder of our embodiment and the preciousness of the condition in which we find ourselves as conscious beings in a material world, bodies that contain *material* information, a four-letter digital code etched in our DNA, passed down for millions of years (Meyer, 2009). Encoded in our beings is the lessons of genetic ancestors and their vast experience interacting with reality directly and with each other.

What Is Lost in Remote Teaching

Now that I have had the experience of teaching online, I can bring forth some insights. On Zoom, there is a certain barrier to how we normally experience each other in a group. In a face-to-face setting, there is an experiential sedimentation. As people take turns talking to each other, they can also begin to talk over each other. In conversation, there is a need to listen but also participate. Those involved in conversation signal their increasing need to participate in many ways. If their signals are not received, they may start to say bits of words as they begin to interject or even interrupt. Far from always being rude, conversation depends on a back-and-forth that allows the experience to build up, like falling particles at the bottom of the ocean. Just as one person allows themselves to be interrupted, they can then expect, when the time is right, to be able to talk over and silence the other person. A good conversation should allow for this because it is by definition not one sided; all participants are needed.

In a traditional class, there is an overall *layering* of the experiencing. Teaching face-to-face multiple things can be happening at the same time. Each thing that is happening can be contributing to the overall experience. It is like the experience of a good Jazz performance; everything becomes incorporated into the experience. My students ask me why my class is different on Zoom. They ask, because I have told them it is different and that it is much harder for me to do on Zoom what I would like to be doing. I struggle to tell them why it is different even though it is so obviously different to me in every way. I stammer, "Well, it's different because I can't move around, I can't perform, demonstrate and draw on the board like I would with you in a classroom. Everything is slower on Zoom. It is harder to be spontaneous." But that is not adequate. It does not satisfy them. Since they have never experienced *my* class in-person, they do not know what I mean. They are probably also thinking, "Well just do all that on Zoom. Draw, move around be spontaneous." What I try to articulate about the difference does not capture all of the variation, not even close. It's something more. It's about how *they* act in Zoom as compared to the in-person classroom. The way they act changes how I am able to teach. And since there is no layering, the overall experience online is fundamentally different.

Even in the synchronous online class I do not, sense that there is a joint building up by all involved to *make* the overall experience what it is. There can be some simultaneous cooperative effort. However, on Zoom, many students often just tune in and watch and listen a bit. They have been conditioned to regard the screen as a voyeur. They watch but do not interact because it is easy to just sit there. It is hard to know what to do in the face of how we have been conditioned by the screen. Coercive effort to induce and even force participation from students does not respect their free will. It is a kind of violence. If engagement is demanded, it can even be dehumanizing. Moreover, students have been conditioned to seek easy and be less proactive in online class discussions due to the emphasis on efficiency that is already the main selling point of remote learning, e.g. the attitude of "why should I do anything extra, isn't the whole point that I don't have to do as much?"

The halting, jolting nature of real-time interactions on the Internet is probably the most obvious example of how the experience is different and cannot be but a simulation of in-person interactions. It seems like nothing can happen at the same time in Zoom that is also part of the overall experience, i.e., additive and not diminutive. As discussed earlier in this book, in a video format for communication it is hard, or even impossible, to track in the normal way the micro-expressions that people might usually use to indicate a need to comment, interrupt or disagree. It can happen but it is difficult. For instance, on Zoom it is awkward to have a conversation with even one other person it is closer to using a walkie-talkie than a real conversation. With 35 it *is* impossible to have an open and full conversation.

It is hard to tell when to stop talking, and on Zoom you quickly realize how much of conversation depends on not necessarily interruption, but at least signals of the need to interject so as to feel like you are contributing and not being left behind. On Zoom, you can only wait. I make deliberate pauses and ask for input to allow students to speak up. The emphatic pauses and explicit requests are most awkward at first but they always stand out as different because in a normal conversation, when people are involved, you do not have to be so deliberate.

The layering or overall stratification of the in-person experience that I am talking about is different than what happens in multitasking. When we are using our conscious focused attention to jump from one task to the next, while simultaneously trying to keep the activities distinct and also endeavoring to complete them at the same time, it is a different kind of experience. In a classroom, there might be multiple things going on, but they are all part of the same overall event. A student on Zoom can actually be doing several different tasks that are unrelated to class (e.g., as I mentioned before, I have even, unfortunately, seen students *driving*). These other experiences do not need to be part of the class. They might all add up to what the student is doing during the time allotted to class, but they are not additive to *that* experience. They are pulls in other directions.

References

Borgmann, A. (1987). *Technology and the character of contemporary life: A philosophical inquiry*. Chicago, IL: The University of Chicago Press.
Carr, N. (2011). *The shallows: What the internet is doing to our brains*. New York, NY: Norton and Company.

Dreyfus, H. L. (2008). *On the internet (thinking in action)*. London, UK: Routledge.

Dreyfus, H. L., & Kelly, S. D. (2011). *All things shining: Reading the western classics to find meaning in a secular age*. New York, NY: Free Press.

Heidegger, M. (1962). *Being and time* (J. Macquarrie & E. Robinson, Trans.). New York, NY: HarperCollins. (Original work published 1926).

Kurzweil, R. (2000). *The age of spiritual machines: When computers exceed human intelligence*. New York, NY: Penguin.

Meyer, S. (2009). *Signature in the cell: DNA and the evidence for intelligent design*. New York, NY: HarperCollins.

Nietzsche, F. (1974). *The gay science: With a prelude in rhymes and an appendix of songs* (W. Kaufmann, Trans.). New York, NY: Random House. (Original work published 1887).

21 Questioning Is the Piety of Thought
The Wonder of Education

What have I uncovered with the question of this book? In questioning after the meaning of what is lost in remote learning, I have dwelt near questions concerning the true essence of learning. In this book, I have looked at the experience as it has been shown in some of its thematic facets. An interpretation has been offered.

In an online class, the body is removed. Undergraduates are made frictionless and more efficient in large measure by the irrelevance to their embodied engagement with others, the professor and fellow students. Of course, students in non-face-to-face classes still *have* a body, but that does not matter in the way it matters for a traditional class. By disparaging and distancing ourselves from our bodies, by making our embodiment irrelevant to learning, we invite the confusion of the Oruroburos. Mixing up the relation of our bodies and our minds is symbolized in the paradox of the Ouroburos. The snake that eats its tail does not realize the fact that its tail is *part* of its head. Without our bodies in an online class, we are not fully able to be engaged. Embodied learning is lost. It is a subtle kind of presence. It is not like the obvious necessity of our bodies in learning a technical craft like welding or painting. With the sense that our individual body is not relevant to the experience of learning, as is apparent in online classes, a blind spot is created. When we tug on what seems like a small or irrelevant thread, we can potentially unravel everything we strive to sustain.

As a teacher I would never define myself as *essentially* anti-remote learning. To do so would only entrap my pedagogy further in that which I wish to extricate myself. I am drawn to this attitude by what Dewey says, "There is always the danger in a new movement that in rejecting the aims and methods of that which it would supplant, it may develop its principles negatively rather than positively and constructively. Then it takes its clew[1] in practice from that which is rejected instead of from the constructive development of its own philosophy" (1997/1938, p. 20). Likewise, I do not think that an outright conflict or competition with non-face-to-face learning is what will preserve traditional learning, because, "Just as there lies concealed in all hatred the abysmal dependence upon that from which hatred at bottom always desires to make itself independent – but never can, and can all the less the more it hates" (Heidegger, 1976/1954, pp. 103–104). If we adopt the attitude and posture of resistance, then we become defined by and beholden to that which we would oppose. When faced with the question of outright resistance to the technological attitude in order to achieve a free relationship (e.g., a technological rebellion like the Luddites), Heidegger (1977) offers guidance, "Nevertheless, as a mere countermovement it necessarily remains, as does everything 'anti,' held fast in the essence of that over against which it moves" (p. 61). Instead of becoming "anti-," we must resolutely explore the greatest domain of freedom, human imagination. We should delve into the pedagogical possibilities that are before us.

Further Phenomenological Study: Freedom, the Hand and Learning

The possibilities of being human are infinite. Our thought, on matters limitless, seems to connect the infinite to our conceptualization of freedom. Freedom as a sense of a sort of deep openness, leads to the realization that we can, or do, stand distinct among entities (Mele, 2014). The freedom afforded by our consciousness imparts an ability to connect to the branching causal chains of the material world. The result of our freedom is that though we know we are *in* the world, a piece and part in it, we also have a distinct sense that we are not totally *of* the world (Scruton, 2014). We stand partially outside of it, or, as our comprehension seems to dictate, "under" the world, i.e., human self-awareness allows us to *under*stand. Being able to understand the world means that we can act upon it. We can tap into what can be initiated by causes in the present to thereby influence and change the future. Retroactively, our experiences with manipulating the causal chain of events give us memories and a sense, true or not, of the contingency of the past.

What gives us this creative possibility to manipulate our physical world and construct our understanding of it? How is it that we realize ourselves as human, which is to say free, and also recognize that the rest of reality is not so flexible? The ability of language to create an infinite number of sentences is one conduit by which we might understand how we are drawn into the possibilities of freedom. Deeper still than language is what Aristotle called, the tool of tools, the human hand. Like the face and its infinite depth of expression and interpretability, our hands help us to access the infinite and grasp the wisps of freedom. In Raymond Tallis's book *The Hand: A Philosophical Inquiry into Human Being*, he establishes:

> There is simply too much to say about the hand: I realized, soon after deciding on my subject, that its scope was potentially boundless … The many-dimensional and almost limitless versatility of the human

hand is offered as a key to the awakening of the cultured human being out of the natural pre-human animal, opening up the vast distances between human culture and the natural world. Through the hand, human culture waves away animal nature.

(2003, pp. 11–12)

Our hands, like language, and other peculiar human attributes, are part of what makes us transcendent.

Heidegger's influential book *Being and Time* (1962/1926) establishes what could be considered an ontology of the hand. The basic distinction in his exploration of the entity that we are *Dasein*[2] is between the "present-at-hand" and the "ready-to-hand." There are many ways to explore this division of reality for human being. For example, imagine you are skillfully using a hammer. When you are hammering well, there is a sense in which the tool disappears and you almost do not fully realize it is there, so integrated has it become in fulfilling your current project. Now image that as you are using the hammer, it breaks. Suddenly the tool ceases to become invisible and is now instead dramatically explicit. And yet, it is no longer a hammer (the head has flown off or the handle snapped). It is merely an object in front of you, a thing that is present-at-hand but not ready-to-hand as it was when it functioned for your purposes.

The world of physical entities in which we inhabit is full of both the ready-to-hand and the present-at-hand. The former seem to communicate to us. For example, as we approach a door the handle tells us what to do because we can skillfully engage with doors. However, if the handle fell off as we were trying to use it, we would be left holding a fairly mysterious object. What do you do with a broken handle? Moreover, what exactly *is* a non-functioning or door handle? They are merely objects reduced to their material being. Heidegger's deep insight into how we exist as being-in-the-world comes by way neither of the human face, nor language but because of our hands. I wonder how advanced computer technology, the kind that makes non-face-to-face learning possible, alters our relationship to the world through our hands?

I use my hands when I teach. Communicating through gesture, I also use my hands for emphasis when presenting arguments (I admit, my arguments do sometimes depend on what philosophers call "hand waving"). Besides the expressive aspect of the hands themselves, I love to use the chalkboard. There is a sense in which I feel naked without it. I get the dust on my clothes, and my students experience the expressiveness, ambiguity and humanness of my handwriting. I know witnessing the work of my hands does have the potential to enrich the experience for some students. Of course, as with direct real-time face-to-face contact, many might concede the importance of hands for early education. What more can we discover about the role of the hands in the meaning of the experience of teaching and learning at the undergraduate level? For something that is integral to our embodiment and allows us to touch the infinite, it is surely vital to the meaning of the experience of learning at all levels.

To continue the work of this book, a fruitful phenomenological study would examine the hand in online learning and teaching. Moreover, the role of the hand in learning and teaching with computers could also more fully elucidate the meaning of non-face-to-face learning. For example, since hands are so communicative, how does their absence inform the meaning of the experience?

Not a Copy of Face-to-Face Learning but Something Different

Two of my participants, Scott and Lane, were very satisfied with some of their online learning. It met and even sometimes exceeded their expectations for undergraduate learning. Despite significant differences in age, interests and even the schools they went to, there were clear overlaps in what each said. The aspects of their non-face-to-face learning experience that were valuable to them related to what could (or could not) also happen in a traditional classroom.

Both Scott and Lane explained that they *chose* to take their online class. They did not have to take the class online; it was not a requirement. They could have taken a different course to satisfy the same major requirement, i.e., it was an elective that fulfilled a degree requirement. There were in-person courses that would have done what they needed. Instead of opting for a traditional setting, they both, not because they preferred the non-face-to-face format at all (it had nothing to do with their choice), decided to take the class because they were intently interested in its subject matter.

The next similarity was a profoundly transformative aspect as compared to what my other seven participants recounted. In both instances, where Scott and Lane felt like they were really learning in non-face-to-face classes and not just jumping through hoops or frustrated by the lack of presence, it was in an *upper-level course only for majors*. This difference set the online learning experience off from the rest of my participants who usually were in a lower-level course that was required, e.g., sometimes non-face-to-face was their only option.

The major specific upper-level aspect had a clear sorting effect on the students who would be in the class. They were all more advanced in their undergraduate studies. They were potentially more serious and knowledgeable about the subject matter. They could also be more motivated to get more out of their learning experience.

For both Scott and Lane, taking an upper-level class only for majors online had another vitally important outcome for their experience: *the classes were small*. For both, neither of their classes had more than 15 students. This had wide-ranging effects on the overall experience. In the smaller online class, both students could get to know the other members of the class better. They could keep track of the different personalities and how they were shaping the experience. Moreover, another huge impact was the amount of attention the teacher could spend responding individually and grading assignments.

Both Scott and Lane described their professors differently than the other seven participants. Because the class was an upper-level course only for majors, it meant that the level of training and interest of the professor would be high. Both participants explained that it largely precluded the chance that the teacher would be a mere course "facilitator." That such teachers seemingly constitute the majority of online instructors is not encouraging (Whitford & Schifrin, 2022). Instead, the teacher would have to be an expert, and therefore there was a greater chance of their own personal involvement with the material. The class was a personal expression of the teacher's own interests and perspective, i.e., it was not a template course.

Scott and Lane explained that they were highly involved in their courses. Lane formed a relationship with his professor and was even able to teach a class (Lane had started this relationship in a previous face-to-face class). Scott said that he felt like he was respected as a historian in his own right. Even though there was ambiguity about the identity of the professor, Scott was eventually able to feel connected because of the copious individual comments his teacher gave to his written work. His teacher always responded with long emails to any questions that he asked.

The largely positive outcome of the experience for Scott and Lane turned on the fact that their experience was not a copy of an in-person class. Instead, the aspects that they most valued were in areas where the class *could* have been more efficient, but was not. For instance, the courses could have been larger. Because they were small and all the students in the classes really wanted to be there, the entire dynamic changed. The learning was technologically mitigated but the attitude to make it as efficient as possible was held at bay.

It seems like even if non-face-to-face classes are not copies of in-person courses, they can be something different. And the thing that they are can be valuable for certain levels of learning (Dreyfus, 2008). However, this is only possible if the imperative to constantly be making the learning experience as efficient as possible is conscientiously rejected. Space and time have to be left for teachers and students to interact, even if only through asynchronous text, so that they can feel "respected" and be able to contribute in their own personal way to the educational experience.

Technology is part of who we are (Carr, 2015). We can know this because of how technology changes our capacity to experience and engage with the world. As Heidegger elucidates in his profound history of being which explicates the way we are situated in history, "We must experience history as the release of Being into machination" (1961/1984, p. 196). The machine, the calculative, is all around us. Our current world of experience is made of recipes and formulas, i.e., algorithms. However, the opportunity for a free relationship with technology, a way of experiencing the non-calculative, is what we can seek, the ability to pick up or leave our devices, algorithms and systems when we engage in other ways of thinking (Heidegger, 1977).

The free relationship toward technology in undergraduate learning is manifest in the experience of Scott and Lane. In their experience the urge to technologize was curtailed. There was a sensitivity to not just what should or should not be thought of in terms of efficiency but also *when* something should or should not be thought of as maximizable. Students were allowed to show up as special, as were the teachers, and participate together in something that mattered.

Understanding teaching as a focal practice can help show a way toward dwelling with non-face-to-face learning in a way that allows us to be what we are. If we understand that online learning cannot copy face-to-face classes but can be something else, we can follow a path toward the educational goals of individualization that we seek, e.g. helping undergraduates to become who they are.

Heidegger presents a translation where "to know" means "to face what is unconcealed" (1961/1984, p. 94). When we face remote education, both the learning and teaching, we can come to know paths that will not reduce learning to a transaction or students to commodities or teachers to mimes for algorithms. I am hopeful that even online learning and teaching can be fruitful to some degree. Continued phenomenological study of online education can help to make the experience *human*-ly rich and not merely mechanistic, as was, for example, Booker T. Washington's, "The older I grow, the more I am convinced that there is no education which one can get from books and costly apparatus that is equal to that which can be gotten from contact with great men and women" (*Up From Slavery* 1901/2018, p. 38). Online education can be something valued not just because it happens to be a necessity, i.e., "better than nothing," but because it can be understood as something beyond a replacement, something engaged in for its own sake.

Notes

1 "The original spelling of *clue* was C-L-E-W, and its forgotten meaning is a ball of yarn or string. A clew of string was unraveled as a guide out while entering an unfamiliar maze or a cave. If you become lost, all you had to do was follow the string back to the point of origin" (Lennox, 2003, p. 171).
2 Transliterated from the German, *Dasain* could mean "there-being" or "being there." It could also capture the sense that human beings do not just take place but are free to pick a place.

References

Carr, N. (2015). *The glass cage: How computers are changing us*. New York, NY: W.W. Norton & Company.

Dewey, J. (1997). *Experience and education*. New York, NY: Simon & Schuster. (Original work published 1938).

Dreyfus, H. L. (2008). *On the internet (thinking in action)*. London, UK: Routledge.

Heidegger, M. (1962). *Being and time* (J. Macquarrie & E. Robinson, Trans.). New York, NY: HarperCollins. (Original work published 1926).

Heidegger, M. (1976). *What is called thinking* (J. Glenn Gray, Trans.). New York, NY: HarperCollins. (Original work published 1954).

Heidegger, M. (1977). *The question concerning technology, and other essays* (W. Levitt, Trans.). New York, NY: HarperCollins. (Original works published 1962, 1952 & 1954).

Heidegger, M. (1984). *Nietzsche volume two: The eternal recurrence of the same* (D. F. Krell Trans.). New York, NY: HarperCollins. (Original work published 1961).

Lennox, D. (2003). *The little book of answers: The how, where, and why of stuff you thought you knew*. New York, NY: MJF Books.

Mele, A. R. (2014). *Free: Why science hasn't disproved free will*. Oxford, UK: Oxford University Press.

Scruton, R. (2014). *The face of God: The Gifford lectures*. London, UK: Bloomsbury Publishing.

Tallis, R. (2003). *The hand: A philosophical inquiry into human being*. Edinburgh, UK: Edinburgh University Press.

Washington, B. T. (1995). *Up from slavery*. Mineola, NY: Dover Publications. (Original work published in 1901).

Whitford, E., & Schifrin, M. (2022, June). How a little-known California school earned top marks on Forbes' 2022 college financial grades. *Forbes*, 110–115.

Index

Administrators 10, 12, 29, 107, 121, 135, 161, 167, 170
Alienation 144–145
Animal 62, 138, 140, 178
Aporia 2, 25, 172
Asynchronous 3, 29, 50, 55–57, 60, 62, 65, 67, 170, 180
Art 5–6, 25, 147
Aristotle 2, 88, 169, 177

Being and Time 178
Body 3–4, 14, 19, 30–31, 58, 73–74, 76, 78, 84–86, 105, 108, 110, 117, 128, 133, 135, 140, 151, 156, 160, 171–172, 176
Body language 30–31
Borgmann, Albert 7, 120, 148, 149, 150, 151, 152, 153, 157
Browning, Robert 160

Camera 3, 15, 62, 82, 125, 128–129, 134, 169
Carr, Nicholas 7, 8, 64, 119, 120, 132, 134–135, 155–157
Calculative 7, 118, 181
Compartmentalizing 12
COVID-19: digitization of learning x, 3, 10, 12, 15, 170–171; effects of 164–169; masks 121, 169; policies 29–30, 40, 91, 117–122, 124–131

Dialectic 6, 25
Dialogue 6–7, 25, 60
Derrida, Jacques 65
Design 27, 58, 67, 84–85, 89, 99, 113, 125, 127, 133, 143, 158; designers 60–61, 63, 97, 110, 135, 170
Dewey 70, 75, 156, 176

Education as a tool 12, 41, 141, 146, 157, 158, 178
Efficiency 65, 71, 75–77, 91, 105, 132–133, 148–150, 153, 161, 181; as a goal 83–85; as a selling point 174; attitude of 51; in education 4, 10; technological 7, 12–13, 18–19, 99, 109, 115, 125–126, 127, 143–144; maximization of 34–35, 42–44; tedium 47–49
Effective 10, 28, 48–49, 52, 76, 85, 121, 166
Einstein, Albert 2
Embodiment 54, 74, 78, 84–86, 119, 134–135, 140, 171–172, 176, 179
Enframed 23, 127, 150, 166–167
Epistemology 6, 12, 19, 31, 110, 112, 139
Epstein, Robert 78
Eudaimonia 169
Eye contact 15, 16, 17, 18, 21, 29, 62, 155, 158, 159

Face 29, 46, 77, 84, 141; *aletheia* of 74–75; as a window to the soul 110, 112; covered by masks 121; depersonalization 42; facelessness 95–97, 109; meaning of 11; phenomenology of 13–20; responsibility of 102; responsive contact with 94; synchronous 53–56; textual replacement of 62–65; loss of 39–40
Facetime 18, 126
Facial expression 14, 16, 169, 177
Forster, E.M. 124, 126–127
Frankl, Victor 168–169

Free relationship with technology 5, 6, 8, 118–119, 132, 149, 153, 157, 158, 177, 181
Friesen 3, 44, 61, 62, 70, 81, 82, 85, 89
Frost, Robert 146, 148–149

Gadamer, Hans-Georg 25–26
Grades 13, 20, 27, 32, 33, 103

Heidegger, Martin x, 165; *Alethiea* 2, 5, 74, 96; *Being and Time* 178; *Dasein* 41, 144; efficiency 83; *Elucidations of Holderlin's Poetry* 89; enframed 127; focal practice 151–152; history 180–181; law of proximity 122; poetry 136; *Question Concerning Technology* 5, 12, 57; soul 160; technology 44, 149–150, 157, 166, 177; *The Nature of Language* 53; *The Origin of the Work of Art* 2; Phenomenology 97; *Vorefrage* 117–118; *What is Called Thinking* 90

Interpretation x, 7, 10, 21, 23, 36, 40–41, 76, 117–119, 126, 136–137, 146–147, 176

Kant, Immanuel 69
Khan Academy 10, 27, 32, 49

Labaree, David 166–116, 169
Law of unintended consequences 4, 71, 124, 126, 142, 143, 167
Levinas, Emmanuel 13, 14, 15, 62, 102

Man's Search for Meaning 168
Marx, Karl 144
Mask 74
Mastery 43, 143, 153
Mazis, Glen 48
Merleau-Ponty 48, 77, 78
MOOC 4, 10, 12, 14, 19, 21, 130

Nietzsche, Friedrich 9, 18, 64, 110, 118, 122, 136, 147, 161, 171–172

Paradise Lost 132
Plato 2, 6–8, 22, 34, 65, 113, 124, 126, 130, 136, 152, 153
Policies 23, 29, 119, 132
Postman, Neil 7, 77, 78

Rorty, Richard 4, 10
Rubric 98, 99, 113

Science 2, 21, 25, 26, 136, 147
Science fiction 124
Scientism 9
Shakespeare, William 76, 148
Skype 3, 16, 18, 62
Stein, Gertrude 43, 93
Synchronous 3, 15, 29–31, 46–49, 54–56, 60, 76, 82, 91, 125, 127, 129, 158, 168–170, 173

Turkle, Sherry 7–9, 15, 49, 55, 64, 76–77, 88, 93, 108, 119, 132

Video 3, 20, 174; asynchronous lecture 50, 52, 62; synchronous lecture 62, 76, 91, 158; videoconference 15, 29–31, 82, 122, 127–128, 132, 170; video chatting 125; video games 97–98
Van Manen, Max 4, 14, 17, 22, 58, 93, 106, 110

Wittgenstein, Ludwig 23, 78, 97
Webex 3, 122

Zoom 3, 15, 18, 29, 30, 76, 121, 120, 122, 130, 132, 134, 165, 170, 173, 174; chat 158; efficiency of 125–126; enframed by 127–129; eye contact 62; lurking 82; tile 74, 127, 159, 168–169